Pilgrimage in the Hindu Tradition

Salvific space is one of the central ideas in the Hindu traditions of pilgrimage, and concerns the ability of space, especially sites associated with bodies of water such as rivers and lakes, to grant salvific rewards. Focusing on religious, historical and sociological questions about the phenomenon, this book investigates the narratives, rituals, history and structures of salvific space, and looks at how it became a central feature of Hinduism.

Arguing that salvific power of place became a major dimension of Hinduism through a development in several stages, the book analyzes the historical process of how salvific space and pilgrimage in the Hindu tradition developed. It discusses how the traditions of salvific space exemplify the decentered polycentrism that defines Hinduism. The book uses original data from field research, as well as drawing on main textual sources such as Mahābhārata, the Purāṇas, the medieval digests on pilgrimage places (*tīrthas*), and a number of Sthalapurāṇas and Māhātmyas praising the salvific power of the place. By looking at some of the contradictions in and challenges to the tradition of Hindu salvific space in history and in contemporary India, the book is a useful study on Hinduism and South Asian Studies.

Knut A. Jacobsen is Professor in the History of Religions at the University of Bergen, Norway. He has published widely on religions in South Asia and in the South Asian diasporas.

Routledge Hindu Studies Series

Series Editor: Gavin Flood, Oxford Centre for Hindu Studies

Former Series Editor: Francis X. Clooney, SJ, Harvard University

The *Routledge Hindu Studies Series*, in association with the Oxford Centre for Hindu Studies, intends the publication of constructive Hindu theological, philosophical and ethical projects aimed at bringing Hindu traditions into dialogue with contemporary trends in scholarship and contemporary society. The series invites original, high-quality, research-level work on religion, culture and society of Hindus living in India and abroad. Proposals for annotated translations of important primary sources and studies in the history of the Hindu religious traditions will also be considered.

Epistemologies and the Limitations of Philosophical Inquiry
Doctrine in Mādhva Vedānta
Deepak Sarma

A Hindu Critique of Buddhist Epistemology
Kumarila on Perception
The "Determination of Perception" chapter of Kumarilabhatta's
Slokarvarttika translation and commentary
John Taber

Samkara's Advaita Vedanta
A way of teaching
Jacqueline Hirst

Attending Kṛṣṇa's Image
Caitanya Vaiṣṇava Mūrti-sevā as Devotional Truth
Kenneth Russell Valpey

Advaita Vedānta and Vaiṣṇavism
The philosophy of Madhusūdana Sarasvatī
Sanjukta Gupta

Classical Sāṃkhya and Yoga
An Indian metaphysics of experience
Mikel Burley

Self-surrender (prapatti) to God in Śrīvaiṣṇavism
Tamil cats and Sanskrit monkeys
Srilata Raman

The Caitanya Vaiṣṇava Vedānta of Jīva Gosvāṃī
When knowledge meets devotion
Ravi M. Gupta

Gender and Narrative in the Mahābhārata
Edited by Simon Brodbeck and Brian Black

Yoga in the Modern World
Contemporary perspectives
Edited By Mark Singleton and Jean Byrne

Consciousness in Indian Philosophy
The Advaita doctrine of 'awareness only'
Sthaneshwar Timalsina

Desire and Motivation in Indian Philosophy
Christopher G. Framarin

Women in the Hindu Tradition
Rules, roles and exceptions
Mandakranta Bose

Religion, Narrative and Public Imagination in South Asia
Past and place in the Sanskrit Mahābhārata
James Hegarty

Interpreting Devotion
The poetry and legacy of a female Bhakti saint of India
Karen Pechilis

Hindu Perspectives on Evolution
Darwin, dharma, and design
C. Mackenzie Brown

Pilgrimage in the Hindu Tradition
Salvific space
Knut A. Jacobsen

Pilgrimage in the Hindu Tradition

Salvific space

Knut A. Jacobsen

Routledge
Taylor & Francis Group
LONDON AND NEW YORK

First published 2013
by Routledge
2 Park Square, Milton Park, Abingdon, Oxfordshire OX14 4RN

Simultaneously published in the USA and Canada
by Routledge
711 Third Avenue, New York, NY 10017
First issued in paperback 2014

Routledge is an imprint of the Taylor and Francis Group, an informa business

British Library Cataloguing in Publication Data
A catalogue record for this book is available from the British Library

Library of Congress Cataloging in Publication Data
Jacobsen, Knut A., 1956-
Pilgrimage in the Hindu tradition : salvific space / Knut A. Jacobsen.
pages cm. – (Routledge Hindu studies series)
Includes bibliographical references and index.
1. Hindu pilgrims and pilgrimages. 2. Salvation–Hinduism.
3. Space–Religious aspects–Hinduism. 4. Hinduism–History. I. Title.
BL1239.32.J33 2012
294.5'351–dc23
2012006270

ISBN 978-0-415-59038-9 (hbk)
ISBN 978-1-138-84466-7 (pbk)
ISBN 978-0-203-10251-0 (ebk)

Typeset in Times New Roman
By Swales & Willis Ltd, Exeter, Devon

Contents

Preface viii

Introduction 1

1 Concepts and sources 4

2 Salvific space, narratives and space as divinity 19

3 The origin of the Hindu traditions of salvific space 41

4 The growth and omnipresence of the Hindu traditions of salvific space 71

5 Narratives and doctrines of salvific space: the example of sage Kapila 96

6 The structure of Hindu salvific space: a pluralistic pilgrimage tradition or why there is no Mecca of Hinduism 122

7 Contradictions and challenges 146

Notes 171
References 177
Index 187

Preface

First of all, I want to thank the numerous pilgrims at many Hindu places of pilgrimage in India who took time to answer my questions and talk to me about their pilgrimage, and the *paṇḍā*s and *sādhu*s at these places for their guidance and advice. Many other persons have provided ideas and suggestions but I especially want to thank Mark S. G. Dyczkowski, Peter Flügel, Kay Hutchings, Madhu Khanna, Gerald James Larson, Julius Lipner, Sri Narayan Mishra and Rana P. B. Singh. I am most indebted to my partner and co-pilgrim, Hanne Svendsen. I thank the University of Bergen, Norway for numerous grants to visit pilgrimage places in India.

I have used diacritics in the names of *tīrtha*s, but anglicized forms of the modern states of India, i.e. Vārāṇasī, Prayāg, Miśrik and Naimiṣāraṇya, but Uttar Pradesh; Gaṅgāsāgar, Tārakeśvar, but Bengal; and Badrīnāth and Kedārnāth, but Uttarakhand, and so on. The words Brahman and Brahmanical have become part of the English language and are written without diacritics.

Some of the material in Chapter 5 has earlier been published in Knut A. Jacobsen, *Kapila: Founder of Sāṃkhya and Avatāra of Viṣṇu*, New Delhi: Munshiram Manoharlal, 2008.

Introduction

This book is a critical study of Hindu traditions of salvific space. I emphasize the word critical. Some of the writings on Hindu pilgrimage typically just repeat the ideology of the sacred places promoted by the texts that celebrate the place: the *Māhātmya*s and *Purāṇas*. They read like, and may even become, modern *Māhātmya*s and *Purāṇas*. Critical studies, on the other hand, try to understand the processes that create and maintain or terminate salvific space. This book addresses the nature of Hindu salvific space and the questions of how and why salvific space attained the central role in Hinduism. My interest in this topic is as a scholar of religion. I am interested in salvific space as the idea and practice has unfolded in the history of Hinduism, in the tradition attributing salvific or salvational power to space and in the Hindu idea of salvific power of space. Hindu pilgrimage texts are important sources for knowledge about ancient Indian geography and they have, to a large degree, been studied for the purpose of attaining such knowledge. My interest is in salvific space as a particular religious conception and practice that has a historical origin and a history, and the dynamics of Hindu pilgrimage traditions as they have developed over time. I am interested in the ascription of sacredness, divinity and salvific power to places, and in pilgrimage rituals as sources for understanding an aspect of the history of Hinduism. No religion has more elaborate conceptions of sacred space than Hinduism, and in this religion sacred space is also salvific space. Space is, in a number of ways, presented as a source of the attainment of salvational goals.

The study of Hindu pilgrimage is the study of texts and places, their social and cultural organization, the value and meaning attached to places, and of people and their rituals. This study of Hindu pilgrimage is based on the examination of historical textual sources (Sanskrit and Hindi texts), as well as contemporary literature praising the places, the academic texts on the topic and my own field research and studies of living pilgrimage traditions. Some historical questions about the phenomenon are in focus: how did pilgrimage traditions become such an important feature of Hinduism – that is, how did pilgrimage originate and what are the reasons for its immense success? In the Vedic tradition, pilgrimage to sacred places was unimportant or perhaps non-existent. It will be argued that power of place became a main element in Hinduism at different stages through a historical process. Chapter 1 introduces the subject, the concepts and the sources. In

Chapter 2, I describe some significant and unique features of the Hindu traditions of sacred places. In Chapters 3 and 4, I discuss the origin and development of the traditions. Pilgrimage was promoted by Brahman priests and was related to transformations of Vedic religious traditions and the growth of other religious traditions. The association of divinities and salvific power to particular places marks a dramatic change from the Vedic traditions. The emergence of the Śramaṇa traditions reduced the importance of sacrifice and there was a decline of the Vedic sacrificial tradition. The competition with Buddhists and other ascetic movements for ritual gifts was probably an important reason for promoting worship at sacred places. The presence of Buddhist and other Śramaṇa pilgrimage traditions might have contributed to the production of forms of Brahmanical pilgrimage traditions. There is an important economic factor in pilgrimage traditions, and sacred places and their rituals became a new and important source of income for the Brahmans. The origin and the success of the Hindu pilgrimage traditions need to be distinguished. A second phase in the development of Hindu pilgrimage is the immense growth in the number of pilgrimage places. One important factor seems to be the decay of some urban centers in the Gupta (320–550 CE) and post-Gupta periods that led to many Brahmans leaving cities and settling in agricultural and tribal settings, and other Brahmans promoting the cities as *tīrtha*s in order to attract clients for their rituals and to secure economic income. Vedic sacrifice gradually disappeared and ritual gifts received at sacred places replaced sacrifice as income for many priests. The geographical expansion of the tradition of *tīrtha*s led to the integration of large geographical areas into a Hindu religious framework. Many sites on the periphery of the Brahmanical areas that belonged to non-Vedic gods and goddesses were transformed into sacred places of the main gods of Hinduism. This was probably an important method for spreading Brahmanical culture and influence, and also for integrating large areas into a common Hindu religious culture. In Chapter 5, I use as an example the pilgrimage places associated with the ancient sage Kapila to analyze narratives and doctrines of salvific space. In an earlier study, I investigated the pilgrimage places related to the sage Kapila in the Hindu tradition (Jacobsen 2008a). From this, I learned that almost any religious phenomenon in Hinduism is related in some way to sacred sites and pilgrimage. What started as a study of the textual sources related to the plurality of Kapila figures in the Hindu traditions led me to the sacred geography of Kapila in contemporary India. The number of sacred sites associated with sage Kapila amazed me. When I started the research project on Kapila in 1993, I did not know or expect that the sage Kapila was worshipped in India today at a number of places claiming to be associated with his life. Sacred space seemed to relate to most dimensions of Hinduism. In Chapter 6, I analyze various structures and networks of pilgrimage sites and emphasize the plurality and systems of places. There is an element of henotheism in the presentation of the Hindu sacred sites in the *Purāṇas* and the *Māhātmya*s. Each place that is described and paid homage to is celebrated as the best and most powerful of all sacred places and the most important pilgrimage site on earth. Nevertheless, Hindus do not consider all the different pilgrimage places to be equal in status. Some sacred places are obviously considered more important than others and these are often organized in structures and networks of pilgrimage places. Chapter 7 analyzes some contradictions in the pilgrimage texts and some contemporary challenges, such as the contradictions between the salvific power of the *tīrtha*s themselves and the merit of travel and between the divine omnipresence and the power of particular places, the ability of the pilgrimage places to grant the salvific goals to all, no matter what, and the limitations of the rewards to those able to perform self-control.

In the chapters of this book, a number of pilgrimage places are mentioned and some features of them described; their characteristics and their place in the pilgrimage system are analyzed and the rituals of pilgrimage and some contemporary developments are portrayed. Sacred space as a source of salvation is an opportunity, not a duty. A large part of Hinduism is about sacred landscapes, sacred sites and the geography of gods and goddesses. For many Hindus, religion seems to relate more to sacred geography than it does to sacred texts; the landscapes can in many ways be said to be sacred texts. It is noteworthy that the emphasis in many of the Hindu traditions of salvific space, especially in the texts that promotes the individual pilgrimage places, is not on the journey to the pilgrimage place but on the arrival – that is, on performing the rituals and visiting the important sites at the sacred place, or even living or dying at the sacred place. According to these texts, it is often not the journey but the pilgrimage site and the walking pilgrimage at the places themselves, such as performances of circumambulations (*parikrama*), which are the sources of salvific power.

1 Concepts and sources

Pilgrimage (*tīrthayātrā*) and pilgrimage places (*tīrtha, kṣetra*) are some of the most visible aspects of Hinduism. Pilgrimage takes place in public and often involves a large number of people. Many of the places of pilgrimage are sacred complexes with monumental temples, numerous shrines and scores of ritual performers. Several pilgrimage sites are places of natural beauty, situated in striking natural surroundings in or on mountains, next to rivers, lakes or waterfalls, and many of the most beautiful Hindu temples are found at pilgrimage places. Most Hindu pilgrimage sites have temples and sacred structures, but the natural surroundings are nevertheless important parts of the pilgrimage place. The ground itself, the *kṣetra*, is sacred, regardless of any temples built there. In many foundation stories of pilgrimage places, the site itself reveals its sacredness to persons. Sacredness is inherent in the site. Sacred centers such as the city of Vārāṇasī in Uttar Pradesh and Puruṣottama (Purī) in Orissa have grown into huge cities but are still objects of pilgrimage travel. At the pilgrimage places, annual festivals attract a large number of people, and some of these festivals constitute the largest gathering of people on earth for a single purpose. The *kumbhamelā* festivals, of which the largest assemblies are those in Prayāg (Allāhābad) every twelfth year (or actually every 11.86 years, as the festival is regulated by the movement of the planet Jupiter around the sun, so sometimes there are only 11 years between two Prayāg *kumbhamelās*), attract tens of millions of people during the approximately five weeks it takes place, and on the main bathing days of the 2001 Prayāg *kumbhamelā*, perhaps around 20 million people were present. At the next festival, in 2013 (27 January to 25 February), around the same time as the publication of this book the number of pilgrims will probably be even higher. Also, many other pilgrimage festivals attract large crowds, and new and faster methods of transportation over the last century and a half have greatly increased the number of pilgrims.

Some Hindu pilgrimages are procession rituals and involve a large number of people walking together for many days. The Vārkarī pilgrimage in Maharashtra to the shrine of the god Viṭṭhal in Paṇḍharpūr (see Deleury 1960; Karve 1962; Mokashi 1990) is the largest, but there are several others, such as the pilgrimages that take place in spring and mark the opening of the many Himālaya shrines – for example, the cave temple of Śiva and Pārvatī in Amarnāth in Kashmir and the temple of Śiva in Kedārnāth in Uttarakhand. Pilgrimage involves travel and the

Hindu pilgrimage has its background both in the crowded temple festivals and in the lonely wandering of ascetics, who often moved between, or stayed at, sacred places. Monasteries have been established at pilgrimage sites for the ascetics to stay and for ascetic organizations to establish their presence. Many of the most famous Hindu temples are those found at pilgrimage places; some were built on established pilgrimage places, others developed into pilgrimage places after they were built. These temples are frequented not only by the local population, but also by people from the larger locality and the region, and even by visitors from outside the region. Pilgrims travel to most pilgrimage places individually or in smaller groups, or, as has become popular over the last decades, in buses organized by travel agents specializing in pilgrimage tourism for that purpose.[1] However, at the great festivals, a huge number of people are on the move and the trains, which transformed pilgrimage travel in nineteenth-century India, continue to be the main means of pilgrimage travel for a large amount of people.[2]

The most significant places of pilgrimage are associated with important sacred narratives of gods and goddesses. The enormous number of pilgrimage sites in Hinduism reflects the large number of gods, goddesses, gurus and saints, traditions and organizations, and the fact that the sacred narratives about the activities of gods and goddesses took place on earth, thus creating innumerable sacred sites. In addition, pilgrimage places are associated with sacred narratives about ascetics, gurus and saints, such as descriptions of ascetics stopping at certain places to perform ascetic exercises (*tapas*) and therefore endowing the places with salvific or salvational power, and with the narratives and *samādhisthāna*s of the holy figures. Monasteries have often been established at pilgrimage sites, and the presence of ascetics is part of the sacredness of the place and an important element of pilgrimage places. They arrive at festivals in great numbers – one reason being the easy availability of food and alms. Other significant religious factors in generating the large number of pilgrimage places are: the importance of the last stage of life, the *saṃnyāsa āśrama,* in which an ascetic life of wandering from place to place is defined as the proper way to live; the fact that the institution of pilgrimage has provided a livelihood for a great number of pilgrimage priests and others involved in the pilgrimage trade; the vitality and proliferation of the textual genre of the *Purāṇa*s; the view of the Hindu tradition that the divine is present in the world in a number of different ways, also as *arcāvatāra*, the descent (*avatāra*) of god in a statue worshipped by devotees; and the idea of the world as non-different from the divine. In addition, there are a number of social and economic reasons that also will be discussed in this book.

The traditions of sacred geography and the rituals of pilgrimage together constitute such a central dimension of Hinduism that it is perhaps not an overstatement to say that, for a large majority of Hindus, their religious practice is more oriented around sacred space than around sacred books and that the ritual of pilgrimage and visits to temples is of more relevance in their religious life than rituals involving books. For many Hindus, visits to sacred landscapes and places, including their temples, rituals and pilgrimage festivals, are probably considered high points of their religious life. The pilgrimage temples are often the most important of the

Hindu temples, and the pilgrimage festivals the most important and extravagant festivals. The gods, goddesses and sacred figures of Hinduism are connected to sacred sites and, to many Hindus, thinking of these sites and hearing narratives about them is an important dimension of their religious life. Traveling to them represents some of the most significant events of religious life. The Hindu textual tradition is full of praise of the sacred sites. For a lot of Hindus, sacred geography, pilgrimage places and the ritual of pilgrimage confirm the truth of sacred narratives and doctrines. The sacred geography proves that the gods, goddesses and sages were present on earth; the sacred sites where the activities of the divinities were supposed to have taken place verify the truth of the sacred narratives. Being there, at the place where it happened, fills the pilgrim with an embodied experience of truth that often cannot be doubted, then or afterwards.

Conceptions of sacred space are found in many religions, and connecting sacred narratives, rituals, institutions and persons to the sacred sites is probably one of the fundamental ways that religions function. However, not all religions have an idea of *salvific space*, the concept that will be explored in this book. And in no other religion, probably, has the idea of sacred space been developed into a multiplicity of forms and traditions to the degree that it has in Hinduism. There is, in Hinduism, a very close relationship between sites, divinities and sacred persons, and salvific attainments. Divinities have manifested themselves at particular sites, where their power continues to be accessible. Sites are associated with particular powerful manifestations of individual divinities. At many of these places, the divinities and the sites have blended to such a degree that the manifestation of the divinities at the particular sites becomes individualized, with unique iconography, mythology and rituals. Jagannāth is a particular manifestation of Kṛṣṇa in Purī in Orissa, but the ritual of place to Jagannāth in Purī, the chariot procession, *rāthyātrā*, has been reduplicated worldwide, and the iconography of Jagannāth is recognized as the particular form of Kṛṣṇa who "lives" in Purī. Veṅkaṭeśvara in Tirumala/Tirupati in Andhra Pradesh is a particular manifestation of Viṣṇu associated with that place. Temples to Veṅkaṭeśvara are found in many other places, but in these other temples it is the Veṅkaṭeśvara, whose most powerful presence is in Tirumala/Tirupati, that is worshipped. Kāśī Viśvanāth is the powerful manifestation of Śiva in Vārāṇasī and is associated with the salvific power of this city, but temples to this particular form of Śiva are also found in other places. The gods and goddesses have "geographical descents," descents at particular sites, and these manifestations of gods associated with particular places gain individual existence and are thus able to be worshipped at places other than their main location. Some sites have more powerful manifestations of a god or goddess than others. Gods such as Viṣṇu, Śiva, Mahādevī and goddesses such as Lakṣmī and Pārvatī are not the same everywhere; they become individualized as particular manifestations associated with specific sites, and these geographical descents of gods and goddesses at the specific sites are individual powerful presences on earth.

Not only do the manifestations of gods and goddesses at particular places gain individual existence, the individual sites as well can become personified as divinities. According to the narratives about sacred sites, these sites personified as divinities do themselves travel on pilgrimage to take advantage of the salvific power of other sacred sites. The view that sites themselves can be divinities and are personified and the idea that the sites, at least according to the sacred narratives, are thought to go on pilgrimage to other sacred sites are probably unique features of Hinduism, illustrating the extraordinary importance of the traditions of pilgrimage and sacred space in the Hindu religious traditions, as well as the great religious imagination that has been applied in the Hindu expansion of the idea of salvific space.

Visiting salvific space is not considered one of the main ways to salvation in many of the Hindu theological traditions and systems of religious thought, and certainly not the way with most prestige, but it is nevertheless a popular religious phenomenon, probably more important in Hinduism than in any other of the world religions, and it is based on a rich textual and ritual tradition. Hindus might have different motives for visiting sacred sites and participating in pilgrimage rituals and travel. Only some consider salvific liberation or a rebirth in heaven as the main purpose of the pilgrimage, but most are aware of the supposed power of pilgrimage rituals and sacred sites to wash away moral impurity (*pāpa*) and grant religious merit (*puṇya*). This is one reason many of the pilgrims are old people. Hindus might have all kinds of motives for going on pilgrimage, but they are nevertheless aware of the promises to those who visit the sacred sites that their moral impurity will be removed, that they will be rewarded with religious merit and possible rebirth in heaven, and even the attainment of salvific liberation.

The Hindu world is full of *tīrtha*s, sacred places which the pilgrims (*tīrthasevin*, *tīrthayātrin*) visit to have encounters with the divine power of place. The importance of sacred geography and pilgrimage (*tīrthayātrā*, *tīrthacaryā*) varies among religions. The richness of pilgrimage places in Hinduism is due not least to the richness of the divine world – that is, the number of gods and goddesses and sacred narratives are mirrored in the sacred geography. The events of Hindu mythology happened in this world, mostly in India and neighboring areas, and the landscapes with which the mythological events are identified are sacred. The mythology is available not only in texts and narratives but also in landscapes and temples, and pilgrimage to these places plays a major role in the religion. Sacred place is a process, a way to relate to the environment, and new sacred places are continuously being created that give rise to new pilgrimage patterns.[3]

That sites can be sacred, divine and salvific can perhaps be viewed as a defining feature of Hinduism. The idea that the world is divine and not something separate from the divine principle and that, at the foundation of the world, there exists a divine power that is non-different from the world is found in various versions in the different theologies in Hinduism. The world is *brahman*, or the body of Viṣṇu, or a manifestation of the goddess, or the goddess herself; the world is created by god's material principle *prakṛti* or is god's material nature, and so on. The divine is present in the world: gods and goddesses reside in phenomena of nature, such as in rivers and in/on mountains, which in themselves can be divinities or manifestations of divinities, or the divine resides hidden and invisible in many places in the world, ready to be discovered, and their presence might be marked in many ways.

According to many of the Hindu traditions, this world is divine, but the divine is also hidden and this hidden divinity can break forth and reveal itself and thus new sites are continuously created (and older ones may also disappear if the traditions of pilgrimage to them stop for different reasons). In the temples, the divine is present in a particularly powerful way in statues (*mūrtis*), but the divine is everywhere.

Another argument for viewing the sacred, divine and salvific sites as a defining feature of Hinduism is that one of the differences between the religion of the Vedas and the Hindu traditions has to do with conception of divinity and space. The gods of Vedic religion were constantly on the move and they did not belong to particular places. The nomads of early Vedic religion gradually settled down in villages and the religion that slowly developed in the villages is what researchers now call Hinduism. A characteristic view of sacred space, places and temples developed in this tradition. The view that the divine is permanently present at individual sites on earth, at particular, powerful places and in temples, and visiting these sacred spaces, being present at these places of divine power and having a vision of the divine presence there, became a dominant form of religious practice in Hinduism. In Vedic religion, it was the roving gods who moved to where people were performing sacrifice. In Hinduism, on the other hand, gods and goddesses have a permanent presence at particular places, and humans move to these sites to interact with them, to be in their presence and to take advantage of their powers. Pilgrimage is a function of this new conception of divinity and place.

Sacred space, divine space, salvific space and *tīrtha*

Pilgrimage is travel for a religious purpose, religious travel. Pilgrimage places can be designated variously as sacred space, divine space and salvific space, and these words refer to different properties of the pilgrimage places. The word sacred emphasizes the difference between sacred and profane. Sacred space refers to places set apart and points to a differentiation between two kinds of space, sacred and profane, thought of as qualitatively different.[4] Sacred sites often have elaborate entrances or are surrounded by walls to mark the distinction between sacred and profane space. Often, there are separate rules of behavior at sacred places that mark them as different from profane space, and persons will often perform a small symbolic act to signify that they have entered the sacred area. At pilgrimage places, the behavior of the pilgrims is often supposed to follow some of the rules adhered to by ascetics, such as eating only vegetarian food and abstaining from sexual activity. The idea of sacred space set apart from profane space can also be illustrated in pilgrimage processions that can make space sacred as they move (Jacobsen 2008b).

The conception of divine space, on the other hand, emphasizes the presence of the divine at particular sites. In contrast to the concept of the sacred, the concept of the divine is not dualistic. Hindu pilgrimage places are often characterized by the presence of divine powers. Mythic narratives, temples, statues of divinities, priests and rituals are important features of divine space.

Salvific space points to a specific feature of pilgrimage sites, that they are promoted as, and often believed to be, places that are able to grant salvational rewards

– that is, the concept points to the salvific capacity of places of pilgrimage. The salvific goal may also be healing from disease and material prosperity, or to live in the presence of, or in a loving relationship to, god that may be realized here in this life. It does not have to be release from life or rebirth in heaven, rather a salvific goal can also be to live in the divine presence here and now. The salvational goal can then be fulfilled by the pilgrimage site as it offers a divine presence on earth, a certain site where god has become localized in a shrine. If salvation is living in the presence of the divine, the presence of the divine at the sacred sites makes such a life possible. The concept of salvific space signifies the institutionalized pilgrimage traditions. Salvific space is institutionalized space, with rituals and priests. A site can be sacred without space being thought to possess salvific properties, but salvific space refers to space as a source of salvation. In the Hindu traditions, sacred space probably preceded the emergence of salvific space. Salvific power at the places may be explained in narratives, such as the sacred narrative of the descent of the heavenly river Gaṅgā from heaven to earth. No water on earth was pure enough to bring the souls of the sons of King Sagara to heaven, since they had insulted the sage Kapila, who had caused their deaths (Jacobsen 2008a). Only the river Gaṅgā had the salvific power to purify the sons of Sagara. Bhagīratha then performed austerities in the Himālayas, and Gaṅgā showed itself to him and promised to come to earth to save their souls. This salvific power of Gaṅgā, once it has descended to earth, is available to all and the basis for a number of Hindu pilgrimage places. The ability to grant salvific rewards might be a property of space as such, especially bodies of water, such as rivers, lakes and ponds.

In some pilgrimage texts, the salvific power of space is presented as a threat to the other methods of salvation in which humans are dependent on gods. The gods are afraid they will not receive any sacrifices or that heaven will become overcrowded. Salvific space in these texts is presented as a threat to their power and the gods therefore attempted to hide the place because heaven would be too easily available to everyone. In many pilgrimage texts describing the history of the site, the salvific power of place is portrayed, as perceived by the gods, as a danger to other methods of salvation, especially methods that involve transactions with the gods. In some texts, the salvific power of place is presented as something that had been hidden by the gods because the power of place made salvific liberation (*mokṣa*) too easily obtainable, and humans therefore stopped worshipping them.

The Sanskrit word *tīrtha* is derived from the verbal root *tṛ*, which means to cross over (a river), step over or sail across. The causative form of the verb (*tārayati*) denotes to rescue, save and liberate (Monier-Williams 1899: 454) and has the meaning of salvific. The basic intention of calling a pilgrimage place a *tīrtha* seems perhaps to refer to the ability of the place to grant people salvific liberation – the salvific power of place. Perhaps the word also refers to the presence of divinities at the place – that is, their crossing over, in the same meaning as *avatāra*, from the same root *tṛ* (and with the prefix *ava*: "down"). In this way, the meaning of *tīrtha* can be a place where salvific and divine power is available. The term *tīrtha* does not seem to have been etymologically derived from a dualism of sacred and profane. Agehananda Bharati, in his studies of Indian *tīrtha*s, has emphasized that *tīrtha* and *tīrthayātrā* were also understood metaphorically (Bharati 1970). In the *Māhātmya*s propagating the *tīrtha*s, from the earliest texts of the *Mahābhārata*, it is emphasized that just thinking of a specific *tīrtha* or wanting to visit a *tīrtha* gives the same reward as going there (see the section on Kurukṣetra in Chapter 2). Such statements are meant to highlight the great salvific powers of the places.

The idea of salvific space can be illustrated with the sayings that a site (in this case, Kāśī, that is Vārāṇasī) is the "axe for the cutting of the tree of sin" (*pāpataroḥ kāntakuṭhārā*) and "destructive of all seeds of karma" (*karmabījopaśamanī*) and "giver of salvation to all" (*sarveṣāṃ gatidāyikā*).The salvific power of the city of Vārāṇasī grants the salvific goal to all, irrespective of who they are: "A man's mind may be attracted towards worldly pleasures; he may have eschewed devotion and may be unthinking. But if he dies in this holy centre, he does not re-enter the worldly existence (i.e. he attains final liberation)."[5] This salvific power of the places resides even in the dust blowing in the wind from those places. About this dust of Vārāṇasī, it is said: "Even those persons of evil actions who come into contact with the dust particles of Avimukta, and are wafted by the wind towards them attain the greatest goal."[6] This salvific power is the cause of heavenly pleasures as well as salvation.[7] The inclusiveness of the salvific power is expressed in the following verse:

> Brāhmaṇas, Kṣatriyas, Vaiśyas, Śūdras, persons of mixed castes, worms, outcastes, alien tribes, person of sinful birth and of inter-caste origin, germs, insects, ants and all kinds of animals and birds who die (in Vārāṇasī) . . . are remembered as lords of gods.[8]

They rejoice in the vicinity of Śiva, the text says. Although the three quotations are about Vārāṇasī, similar statements about salvific powers are found about many other places in the *Māhātmya*s and *Purāṇa*s.

Distinguishing analytically between these different aspects or ways of perceiving pilgrimage places – sacred, divine and salvific – is important for understanding the characteristics and rituals of Hindu pilgrimage traditions. Space may be sacred, but not all sacred space is salvific. In the Vedic tradition, there was no doubt that sacred space, the ground on which the sacrifice was performed, was sacred during the time of the performance of the sacrifice, but there was no institution of pilgrimage to this space, as pilgrimage is known from Hinduism. There was probably no concept of salvific space in the sense of pilgrimage space. As long as the Vedic people were nomads, there was probably no sense of pilgrimage to places that were designated as permanently sacred in the later Hindu traditions, or a concept of institutionalized salvific space.

Hindu traditions

India has many religious geographies. The sacred geography of Hinduism is just one of several traditions of pilgrimage in India. India has Buddhist, Sikh, Jaina,

Muslim and Christian sacred geographies as well. But in this book, I will analyze the traditions of only one of these sacred geographies, the Hindu traditions.

Is it possible to isolate a history of the Hindu sacred geography from India's other sacred geographies? These sacred geographies are of course related and also somewhat overlap, and the traditions have influenced each other. A Buddhist influence on early Hindu concepts of sacred sites seems undeniable. Nevertheless, a Hindu tradition of salvific space is different from a Buddhist tradition. Although a Hindu tradition can in most instances easily be identified, there are also borderline cases. But that persons from one religious community visit the sacred places of others does not mean that they do not understand that the places belong to religious traditions different from the one they mainly participate in. A Hindu visiting a Muslim *dargāh* for purposes of healing understands that this is a Muslim place, but nevertheless considers that the power of the site is available for everyone, regardless of the identity of their main religious practice.

The use of the word Hindu to refer to religious identities is not ancient, and the word Hinduism is only around 250 years old. However, the term Hindu was used in a religious sense several hundred years earlier. The word, as "Hindooism," was in use among Europeans in Bengal in the 1780s (Oddie 2006). One of the first to popularize the term Hinduism in the English language was the Scottish missionary Charles Grant, who used the term Hindooism in correspondence, documented in 1787 (ibid.: 71). The terms it replaced were the expressions "the Hindoo religion" and "the Hindoo creed," which had a longer history (ibid.). In South European languages, the word Hindu was used with a religious meaning at least as early as 1649 (in Spanish) (Lorenzen 1999: 640). There seems nevertheless to be a number of common patterns that justify applying the name Hinduism or Hindu traditions on religious traditions and religious practices that existed before the invention of the name. An awareness of the pilgrimage texts and traditions has probably something to contribute also to the discussion of the identity of Hindu traditions before the use of the word Hinduism. The traditions of salvific space described in the *Dharmanibandha*s seem to suggest a shared religious tradition, as all the places described are equally recommended for everyone. In the *Dharmanibandha*s, the salvific powers at the different places are not seen as opposed to each other. Each place described is celebrated as supreme. In pilgrimage texts that celebrate individual places, however, harsh statements can sometimes be found about other places and those that visit them. "No one can ever attain salvation at a site not belonging to Viṣṇu" (*nāvaiṣṇave sthale muktiḥ sarvasya tu kadācana*), it is said in a Vaiṣṇava interpretation of the salvific power of Vārāṇasī. Thus this view interprets the salvific power of the site Vārāṇasī to be due to its originally being a city of Viṣṇu.[9] But in the *Dharmanibandha*s, places that are devoted to different gods and goddesses are all promoted as belonging to one pilgrimage tradition. The *nibandha*s on salvific space (*tīrtha*) and pilgrimage (*tīrthayātrā*) seem to suggest that a similar type of salvific power was available on the sacred places in a large geographical area, whether the sacred places were devoted to Śiva, Viṣṇu, the Devī, or other divine beings and powers. But there is also no elaboration in these texts of sacred places that we today would not consider Hindu, but think of as Buddhist,

Jain, Christian or Muslim. The *nibandha*s on *tīrtha* seem to treat the sacred places where the salvific power and vision of the Hindu gods, goddesses and divinities are available as a unity. Claims can also be found in such texts that the many names of goddesses really refer to a single goddess, that Śiva is worshipped under different names at different places but that it is still Śiva that is worshipped there, and the same with Viṣṇu, and that the goal reached by worshippers of Śiva, Viṣṇu and the Devī is the same. The *Dharmanibandha*s tried to treat the phenomenon of pilgrimage and salvific space as a whole. Another connection between salvific space and the developments of the concept of Hinduism is that, at some of the pilgrimage places, the central pan-Indian places, people from all over India came and they recognized that the rituals and their religious concerns had many similarities. Religious traditions that include many gods do have a different approach to religious plurality than monotheistic religions. In the Hindu texts, Śiva and Viṣṇu and other gods and goddesses operate in the same sacred narratives.

In addition, the processes through which the Brahmanical tradition and the ideology of purity and impurity acquired a presence in most of South Asia involve pilgrimage and conceptions of salvific space. This happened through a geographical expansion involving salvific space and pilgrimage. Some uniformity seems to have developed by integration of geographical areas by the Brahmanical tradition in order to create new ritual clients and include new groups in the service of Brahmanical ritual priests (see Chapters 3 and 4). The pilgrimage ritual was presented as open for everyone and the salvific rewards were promoted as easily available. Purity was promised as available to everyone. Since there were so many sources for impurity, and according to the caste system impurity was part of the social ideology, there was a great need for purity. The pattern seems to have been inclusion rather than exclusion of traditions. An important formative period of the Hindu traditions, from the early centuries of the first millennium of the common era, coincides with the expansion of the *Purāṇa*s as a textual category; the *Purāṇa*s seem to have been important for the expansion of the Brahmanical tradition and the texts coincide with the expansion of traditions of salvific space.[10] The Vedic tradition was a limited tradition that represented a single religious strand and manifested an elitist outlook. This tradition developed in an ever-widening horizon and attained a popular base in a large geographical era. The Hindu traditions that are promoted in the *Purāṇa*s were able to include new segments of society, literate as well as preliterate, in an expanding process through its powers of assimilation and synthesis (Nath 2001). Hinduism centers on ritual traditions, and one way it expanded was probably by the inclusion of new geographical areas and social groups into its sacred geography.

Sources

Whole genres of texts were developed to propagate the Hindu pilgrimage places and the benefits enjoyed by visiting them. P.V. Kane, in his renowned *History of Dharmaśāstra*, states that the literature on *tīrtha*s is probably far more extensive than on any single subject of *Dharmaśāstra* (Kane 1973: 581). It is therefore noteworthy that no formal treatment of pilgrimage is found in any of the law books and that the texts on *dharma* usually did not include sections on *tīrtha*s and *tīrthayātrā*. In law books like *Manusmṛti* and *Yājñavalkyasmṛti*, *tīrtha* and *tīrthayātrā* have an unimportant position and are not a topic of discussion. In *Manusmṛti*, it is mentioned in an example as something one does not need to do (*Manusmṛti* 8.92). *Viṣṇusmṛti* devotes one whole chapter, Chapter 85, to a description of the *tīrtha*s which are recommended for performance of *śrāddha*,[11] but the *Viṣṇusmṛti* was probably a late work and, according to Patrick Olivelle (2007), composed between 700 CE and 1000 CE. The lateness of this text explains what happens to be an anomaly – a law text that assigns a whole chapter to the teaching of pilgrimage and *tīrtha*s. That the text deals comprehensively with *tīrtha*s is in fact used as an argument by Olivelle that the text is a late composition (ibid.). It is in the *Mahābhārata* and the *Purāṇa*s that *tīrtha*s are treated extensively, and thereafter in the medieval *Dharmanibandha*s (compilations from *Purāṇa*s and law books with commentaries) on *tīrtha*s and in the numerous texts that glorify particular sacred places: the *Māhātmya*s and the *Sthalapurāṇa*s.

In the earliest descriptions of *tīrtha*s in the *Mahābhārata* and the *Purāṇas*, the *tīrtha*s are compared to the most prestigious sacrifices, which they are stated to supersede. That visiting *tīrtha*s are compared to the sacrifices seems to indicate an attempt to make the pilgrimage traditions Vedic. But the statements could perhaps also be related to particular priestly groups, and they could be evidence of priests associated with the new pilgrimage traditions. There might possibly have been a conflict between the pilgrimage priests and more conservative priests who would not accept pilgrimage and continued with the Vedic sacrifices. The low status of pilgrimage priests compared to other Hindu priests in Hinduism today might reflect a continuous conflict. Such statements may also refer to a time when the sacrifice was perhaps already starting to lose some of its significance due to competition from other religious traditions, such as Buddhism and Jainism, and the Brahman ritual priests were looking for other sources of authority and income. But comparing the rewards of visiting *tīrtha*s to the Vedic sacrifices could also be a way of taking over sacred places of the Brahmanical traditions from the local traditions. By equaling pilgrimage rituals and the salvific power of place with sacrifices, they are made similar to the Vedic tradition and the role of the priests in the rituals is legitimized.

The earliest text to contain sections describing and propagating *tīrtha*s and pilgrimage is the *Mahābhārata*. The *Mahābhārata* received its final form around 400 CE. The longest by far of the *tīrtha* texts in the *Mahābhārata*, the *Tīrthayātrāparvan*, is extensive and constitutes Chapters 78–148 of Book 3, the *Vanaparvan* or *Āraṇyakaparvan*. The extensiveness of this text and the large number of places described seem to indicate that the *tīrtha* tradition at that time had become well established. The text describes a number of different places, promotes pilgrimage by describing the benefits of visiting the sites and narrates the stories associated with the places to explain their salvific power. It names the rituals to be performed and the rewards of each place, often emphasizing that great rewards are promised for little effort. This became the normal structure of the pilgrimage texts: a description of the place with topography and narratives to explain the sacredness, naming or descriptions of the rituals to be performed and stating the rewards. In addition to the *Tīrthayātrāparvan* of the *Vanaparvan* (Book 3) in the *Mahābhārata*, the *Śalyaparvan* (Book 9) contains an extensive *tīrthayātrā* text of 20 chapters (35–54), which constitutes around one third of the book, the *Anuśāsanaparvan* (Book 13) has two chapters (15–16) and the *Ādiparvan* (Book 1) contains Chapters 206–210. These four texts are quite different and several of them probably represent a reworking of earlier texts which describe travels that were originally not conceived within the paradigm of pilgrimage. These parts of the *Mahābhārata* contain more than 3, 900 verses. Vassilkov (2002) even argues that the *Mahābhārata* as a whole is a pilgrimage text, with descriptions of pilgrimage and sacred places in almost all of the 18 books (*parvan*s) of the epos (only in Books 6, 10 and 14 are no *tīrtha*s mentioned), and the last parts of the text are descriptions of the final pilgrimage. Book 17 details the last *tīrthayātrā* of the Pāṇḍavas, *pṛthivīpradakṣiṇā* (circumambulation of the earth), and Book 18 describes the great departure (*mahāprasthāna*) – that is, the pilgrimage to death. These *tīrtha* sections are goldmines of stories and rich sources of information about the religion of the time in a wide geographical area.[12]

To a large degree, the most important textual expressions of traditions of sacred places and pilgrimage are the *Purāṇa*s, and the long *tīrthayātrā* texts in the *Mahābhārata* mark both a transition to and a continuity with the *Purāṇa*s. The completion of the *Mahābhārata* took place in the Gupta era, around 300 CE to 400 CE, and dates from the same period as the production of the early parts of the texts of *Purāṇa*s. The *Purāṇa*s contain very large sections on pilgrimage and sacred geography, many of which are later interpolations in the texts (Hazra 1940). It is not impossible that the *Purāṇa*s as a genre were partly developed for the sake of promoting the traditions of *tīrtha* and *tīrthayātrā*. However that may be, the spread of Hindu conceptions of *tīrtha*s throughout India is probably part of the expansion of the Purāṇic traditions, namely, of the Brahmanical traditions represented in the *Purāṇa*s. This is probably the case both in North and South India. Whole *tīrtha* texts (*Māhātmya*s) have been incorporated into *Purāṇa*s, such as the lengthy *Gautamīmāhātmya* (*Godāvarīmāhātmya*) of the *Brahmapurāṇa* (105 chapters, pp. 759–1, 181) and the longest, the *Kāśīkhaṇḍa* of the *Skandapurāṇa* (99 chapters; in English translation, 992 pages). *Varāhapurāṇa* contains lengthy sections on *tīrtha*s, and of the 3, 182 verses, 1, 400 are about Mathurā; *Matsyapurāṇa* contains 1, 200 verses on *tīrtha*s, especially in the Narmadā region; *Padmapurāṇa* contains 4, 000 verses on *tīrtha*s (see Kane 1973: 582). The last part of *Nāradapurāṇa* includes descriptions (*Māhātmya* texts) of many holy sites and have perhaps been inserted in the text. R. C. Hazra (1940) dates the *tīrtha* chapters in the *Purāṇa*s to 700–1400 CE, but the *Purāṇa*s probably contain chapters that have been composed several centuries later than 1400 CE.

Pilgrimage has most often had a regional or local rather than pan-Indian base and the regional places of pilgrimage, such as the temple to Jagannāth in Purī, the geography of Kṛṣṇa's childhood and youth in Vṛndāvan in Braj (Vraj), the temple to Veṅkaṭeśvara in Tirupati, and so on, have been important for developing the regional identities. The *Purāṇa*s of place, *Sthalapurāṇa*s and *Māhātmya*s, represent regional traditions or local traditions. The number of *Māhātmya*s or *Sthala purāṇa*s and similar texts on one or several *tīrtha*s are "almost beyond reckoning" (Salomon 1985: xx). Such texts usually include descriptions of the sacred place with its different *tīrtha*s, deity, laudatory hymns and statements of the benefit (*phalaśruti*) of visiting the place. Often, each *Māhātmya* or *Sthalapurāṇa* celebrates the site it describes as the place most beneficial to visit. Each is praised as if it is the greatest *tīrtha* of all. This is the particular characteristic of the *Māhātmya*s or *Sthalapurāṇa*s, and a statement about the greatness of a place should be understood in light of this. This characteristic could perhaps be interpreted as an instance of henotheism, a feature of the religious traditions of the Vedas, in which each god that is paid homage to is celebrated as the highest god.[13] The Hindus visiting these places are aware of this tradition.

In South India, where the golden age of *Purāṇa*s started in the sixteenth century, around 2,000 *Purāṇa*s were composed, which were mainly *Sthalapurāṇa*s (in Tamil, *Talapurāṇam*) (Shulman 1980). These Tamil *Purāṇa*s celebrate separate sacred places, and few of them achieved popularity outside of the shrines they celebrate (ibid.). Many of these places are mentioned earlier in the songs of the Tamil *bhakti* saints, the Āḻvārs and the Nāyaṉārs. Their songs are rich in geographical references and constitute a sacred geography, and this was important for the development of the land of the Tamils as a region (Spencer 1970). A similar function is found in the Maratha poet-saints and the pilgrimage to Paṇḍharpūr and the Maharashtrian regional identity. The songs of the poet-saints, while not being pilgrimage literature in themselves, did contribute significantly to pilgrimage and sacred geography.

Tīrtha is a Purāṇic tradition and, interestingly, did not create a sophisticated general *tīrtha* philosophy. No philosopher constructed what could be considered a philosophical system (*darśana*) of sacred space. As mentioned above, *tīrtha*s and pilgrimage were also not general topics in the *Dharmaśāstra*s. It was in the *Dharmanibandha*s, however, that *tīrtha*s became an important theme and became subject of technical discussions that used the methods of philosophical analysis. The multi-volume *Dharminibandha, Kṛtyakalpataru* by a twelfth century scholar on *Dharmaśāstra*, Bhaṭṭa Lakṣmīdhara, a minister in the Gāhaḍavāla who was based in Vārāṇasī, included a volume on *tīrtha*s: the *Tīrthavivecanakāṇḍa*. The *Tīrthavivecanakāṇḍa* primarily promoted Vārāṇasī as a sacred city with hundreds of *tīrtha*s the pilgrim needed to visit. This was not coincidental, since Bhaṭṭa Lakṣmīdhara lived in Vārāṇasī, a city that at that time enjoyed a significant income from pilgrims. *Tīrthavivecanakāṇḍa* was the first independent Dharma text or Nibandha on *tīrtha*s and *tīrthayātrā*, and it is also the first text to give a systematic treatment of pilgrimage and sacred geography. However, *Tīrthavivecanakāṇḍa* mainly includes quotations from the *Mahābhārata*, *Purāṇa*s and *Smṛti* texts, with hardly any comments from the author. The lack of commentary may be because the places described in the text were so well known that no comments were necessary and that the theme itself did not call for a philosophical analysis. The later *Dharmanibandha*s on *tīrtha* imitated the style of the *Tīrthavivecanakāṇḍa*.

The *dharma* texts on *tīrtha*s contain long quotations mainly from the *Mahābhārata*, the *Purāṇa*s and late *Dharmaśāstra*s describing the places and instructions relating to the performance of pilgrimage rituals. The later *Dharmanibandha*s, however, sometimes have long technical discussions on specific topics pertaining to pilgrimage and the pilgrimage rituals. Some of the texts seem to have attempted to superimpose strict normative rules and logical coherence on a diverse popular tradition by trying to ritualize in detail every step of the pilgrim and to calculate the religious merit from the different rituals in exact terms. The merits of various sacrifices are used as units of calculation. Some of the later *nibandha*s attempted to make this into an exact science, equalizing the rewards of each pilgrimage and ritual performed at the pilgrimage place with a percentage or number of a certain sacrifice.[14] Such calculations can hardly have attained much popularity and statements such as "a person who takes ritual bath here gets the merit of a ten-horse sacrifice" were probably never meant to be treated in a mathematical way, but they are more reminiscent of modern advertisements intending to sell a product than scientific factual statements. In these *Dharmanibandha*s, apparent inconsistencies in the rules of pilgrimage are discussed. An issue that is examined is how one should apply the rule of performing tonsure when arriving at a *tīrtha* if one visits more than one *tīrtha* on the same *tīrthayātrā*. Another issue is what one should do when arriving at a pilgrimage place at night. This becomes a theoretical issue since it is said that one should perform *śrāddha* immediately after arriving at a *tīrtha*, but that the night is not a proper time to perform *śrāddha*. The authors of these digests contributed to intricate discussions of rules for pilgrimage. A tendency in the later *Dharmanibandha*s is that they tried to make rules for every act in the pilgrimage. This seems to contradict the popular character of pilgrimage. Perhaps the tendency in the *Dharmanibandha*s to make rules was aimed at gaining greater legitimacy of pilgrimage as an orthodox custom. Another goal was perhaps to gain control of the behavior of the pilgrimage priests. In the general sections of *Tīrthacintāmaṇi* by Vācaspatimiśra of Mithilā (fifteenth century) are discussions of rules for starting a pilgrimage and for the first day of a pilgrimage, and rules about *śrāddha*, tonsure and fasting. The *Dharmanibandha*s are important because they attempt to transform the folk phenomenon of pilgrimage tradition into a *dharmaśāstric* tradition. However, it seems that they had only a limited influence on the pilgrims. They probably do carry some authority as normative texts, but they should certainly not be understood as giving empirical descriptions of what pilgrims actually did. The most important texts for a logical treatment of the details of pilgrimage are *Tīrthacintāmaṇi* by Vācaspatimiśra of Mithilā, *Tristhalīsetu* by Nārāyaṇa Bhaṭṭa (sixteenth century) and the *Tīrthaprakāśa* chapters of *Viramitrodaya* by Mitra Miśra (seventeenth century). *Tristhalīsetu* by Nārāyaṇa Bhaṭṭa is considered the most authoritative Sanskrit text on the subject (see Salomon 1985). Several Sanskrit digests of the *Tristhalīsetu* exist: *Tristhalīsetusārasaṃgraha* by Bhaṭṭoj Dikṣita, *Tīrthakamalākara* by Kamalākara Bhaṭṭa and *Tīrthenduśekhara* by Nageśa Bhaṭṭa (see Salomon 1985). However, *Tristhalīsetu* describes only three pilgrimage places: Vārāṇasī (Kāśī), Prayāg and Gayā, the three sacred bridges (*setu*) indicated in the title. Given the great popularity and influence of the pilgrimage tradition, the number of *Dharmaśāstra* texts that treat *tīrtha* and *tīrthayātrā* as its only subject is surprisingly small. The influence of these texts is also difficult to estimate, but these days most pilgrims do not follow the procedures in elaborate detail as they are described in these texts, and this was probably also the case before the modern period.

Inscriptions are another important source for the study of *tīrtha*s and *tīrthayātrā*, especially for assessing the dates when pilgrimage traditions to particular places originated and when pilgrimage institutions came into existence. They can also say something about the popularity of the places. Giving of *dāna* or donations at pilgrimage sites was an important ritual institution and sometimes inscriptions were made of these donations. In addition, several *tīrtha*s not mentioned in the epics or *Purāṇa*s are cited in inscriptions.

Travel accounts are another important source of documenting the *tīrtha* and *tīrthayātrā* traditions. The Chinese travelers Faxian, who traveled in South Asia between 399 and 412 (Legge 1886) and Xuanzang, who traveled on a pilgrimage to India from 629 to 645 (Xuan and Beal 1884) gave eyewitness accounts of a large number of pilgrimage places. Important for the study of sacred space and pilgrimage are also reports from archaeological excavations and a growing literature of academic publications based on fieldwork or text studies.

The academic study of Hindu pilgrimage has produced a number of important studies. There have been numerous monographic studies and edited volumes of individual Hindu pilgrimage places, such as Ayodhyā (Bakker 1982, 1986; Van der Veer 1988), Badrīnāth (Kumar 1991), Bakreśvar (Chauduri 1981), Braj (Entwistle 1987; Haberman 1994; Hawley 1981), Deoghar (Narayan 1983), Gayā (Vidyarthi 1961), Guruvāyūr (Mathur 2009), Hardvār (Lochtefeld 2010), Janakpur (Jha 1971), Kurukṣetra (Parui 1976), Nāthdvārā (Jindel 1976), Prayāg (Dubey 2001a; McLean 2008), Purī (Banerjee-Dube 2001; Eschmann *et al.* 1978; Patnaik 2006), Rājgir (Narayan 1983), Śabarimala (Sekar 1992), Ujjain (Samanta 1997), Vārāṇasī (Benaras) (Dodson 2012; Eck 1982; Gaenszle and Gengnagel 2008; Gutschow 2006; Gutschow and Michaels 1993; Hertel and Humes 1993; Lannoy 1999; Parry 1994; Schilder and Callewaert 2000; Singh 1993; Sukul 1974; Vidyarthi *et al.* 1979); on particular pilgrimages (Gold 1988; Haberman 1994; Mokashi 1990; Sax 1991); on pilgrimage festivals, such as the *kumbhamelā* (Dubey 2001b; McLean 2008); on pilgrimage places or networks with a focus on a region (Feldhaus 2003; Morinis 1984; Shulman 1980) or a type of divine manifestation (Sircar 1973); on particular sacred rivers (Alley 2002; Feldhaus 1995; Haberman 2006; Stietencron 2010); on pilgrimage texts (Bhardwaj 1973; Kulke 1970; Malik 1993; Salomon 1985); and on professional religious persons at pilgrimage places, such as cremation priests in Vārāṇasī (Parry 1994) and ascetics in Vārāṇasī (Sinha and Saraswati 1978). In addition, there are several edited volumes and important articles (Bharati 1963, 1970; Eck 1981, 1998; Gopal and Dubey 1990; Jha 1991).

There is also a body of literature of quasi-scientific study of Hindu pilgrimage that I will not mention here. Many of these texts are not critical studies but are in fact propaganda or promotional texts with limited academic value. They are part of the field of promotion of Hindu pilgrimage, modern promotion and tourist texts, which also sometimes adapt new values to the ideas of sacred space and pilgrimage, such as contemporary environmentalism, preservation of cultural heritage, New Age philosophy and the values of tourist travel. The academic study of sacred sites and pilgrimage needs to be distinguished from the promotion texts produced from within the religion itself. However, texts in this category are very useful for understanding modern developments of the phenomenon of *tīrtha*s. They are part of the living phenomenon of Hindu pilgrimage and constitute a portion of the empirical material to be studied for the understanding of the phenomenon. Also, modern guide and tourist books are part of the modern pilgrimage phenomenon in which pilgrimage has become joined with, and is increasingly being understood as, spiritual tourism. Visiting temples is an important part of the "the work" of the modern tourist.

There is also in Hinduism a critique of pilgrimage, a skeptical attitude to the often-exaggerated rewards, a suspicion about the motivations of the *paṇḍā*s or pilgrimage priests and a preference for an inner religion. The *Bhāgavatapurāṇa* exclaims that "[J]ust by the sight (*darśanād eva*) of *sādhu*s one is purified, whereas pilgrimage places (*tīrthas*) and gods made of earth or stone purify only after a very long time" (*Bhāgavatapurāṇa* 10.84.11). The critique of pilgrimage constitutes one of many contradictions in the Hindu traditions.

Pilgrimage has probably never been as popular in Hinduism as it is today. Before modern transportation made travel easier, a pilgrimage on foot could take many weeks or even months and promoted ascetic values. Because of the peril of travel, many of those who left for pilgrimage were never expected to return. Now, many reach the sacred places in a day or two of comfortable travel. This is a significant change, and the ascetic quality that characterized pilgrimage travel in the past has now mostly disappeared. Pilgrimage has, to some degree, become a leisure activity associated with tourist values, although this nonetheless still coexists with other more ascetic traditions of pilgrimage.

2 Salvific space, narratives and space as divinity

Salvific power of place and salvific sites as divinities are two remarkable characteristics of Hindu pilgrimage traditions and are of greatest importance for understanding the doctrines and rituals of pilgrimage and the dynamics of pilgrimage traditions, as well as sacred sites in the history of Hinduism. In this chapter, I analyze these two features of Hindu pilgrimage places. To assign the property of salvific power – that is, the possibility of attaining the salvational goal of religion at places of pilgrimage and to have sacred places become personified as divinities in the narratives – probably distinguishes Hindu pilgrimage from the conceptions of pilgrimage of many other religions. These two properties are important for understanding some of the other features of the phenomenon of Hindu pilgrimage.

Salvific space

Traditions of pilgrimage to powerful places are of great importance in several of the religious traditions of South Asia but in the Hindu traditions such powerful places are believed to be not only sacred space – in other words, space that can be distinguished from profane space – but salvific space. In this context, salvific space means a type of geographical site in which the many goals of religion, such as health, wealth, moral purity, divinity, rebirth in heaven and final salvation, *mokṣa*, are promoted as available and attainable for those who arrive there on pilgrimage. Salvific space refers to sites that are believed to possess salvific or salvational power. Such is the salvational power associated with many of the sites that by merely seeing the site one attains *mukti*, salvific liberation (*tasmin muktim avāpnoti darśanād eva mānavaḥ*).[1] The concept of salvific space points to the fundamental fact that pilgrimage places were established as, and were accepted to be, sources of salvation in Hinduism. It is certainly correct, as stated by Surinder Bhardwaj in his famous study of the geography of Hindu pilgrimage, that pilgrimage is mostly "considered an *additional* redemptive practice, an adjunct to other forms of worship" (Bhardwaj 1973: 5), but when he writes that "within the religious armory of Hinduism the emphasis is always on the control of sense and meditation" (ibid.: 5), Bhardwaj might be overstating his case. Merit (*puṇya*) and purification from moral impurity (*pāpa*) are essential in themselves, and the purifying quality of water at salvific sites to remove moral impurity (*pāpa*) is well accepted. Such ritual baths are performed by millions of Hindus daily. The salvific power of place, the ability of the power of place to bring about salvific liberation (*mokṣa*), is well recognized. An acquaintance of mine, a *paṇḍit* living in the Indian city of Vārāṇasī, once told me proudly how he had performed his duty to make this salvific power of place available to his father. When his father, who at this time was old, had become very ill, he had brought him from his village in the state of Bihar to the shores of Gaṅgā in Vārāṇasī in order for his father to breathe his last breath there. Against the strong advice of his father's medical doctor, he decided that it would be better for his father to die in the city of Vārāṇasī with its salvific power than endure the attempts of the doctor to treat him. It is believed that, when death is approaching, the medical doctor has to step aside as now it is no longer about saving life but securing a good death. The *paṇḍit* did not doubt that by dying at the shore of Gaṅgā in Vārāṇasī his father attained *mokṣa* by that very act. He was very proud that he had helped his father attain that goal. The *paṇḍit*'s action was proper according to the tradition, but it was not unique. Thus, the salvific power of place is a reality that does influence the choices people make. Often, old people will travel to the pilgrim festivals associated with salvific space, such as the *kumbhamelā* festivals in North India or the annual Gaṅgā Sāgar festival in Bengal, to wash off their moral impurity, since death could arrive at any moment. The contemporary bus pilgrimage tours organized and sold by companies to customers from both rural and urban India are often filled mostly with elderly people. However, the popularity of the bus pilgrimage tours has expanded to include all age groups. Young people may go to visit pilgrimage places out of curiosity but may postpone further pilgrimage travel until later in life when death might be approaching or they may have other reasons for their pilgrimage.

*Tīrtha*s are associated with purity and the ability to purify the souls of the pilgrims. They are part of social, cultural, economic and political contexts and have many functions related to all these contexts, but as *tīrtha*s are also believed to be sites for the attainment of *mokṣa*/*mukti*, pilgrimage can be a means to salvific liberation. Pilgrimage as a path to salvation, however, in Hinduism did not develop as a view that was systematized and rationally argued in the style of a philosophical school (*darśana*), although there were attempts in the *Dharmanibandha*s to convert it into a rational system. It was perhaps looked down upon by intellectuals, and the priests involved in the pilgrimage trade were often scorned by other Brahmans. But the number of people performing the ritual of pilgrimage and the ritual of purification of the sacred bath at the *tīrtha*s demonstrates that the *tīrthas* as sites that contribute to the attainment of *mokṣa* are an important doctrine in Hinduism. Surinder M. Bhardwaj and James G. Lochtefeld are nevertheless correct when they write about the current state of Hindu pilgrimage:

> Hindu pilgrims come with a wide variety of attitudes, and many are not simple believers. Although religious texts describe the vast religious merit (*puṇya*) generated by visiting pilgrimage places, many pilgrims seem reluctant to claim this. Perhaps this reticence comes from a reluctance to claim benefits for themselves or the notion that what they are doing is not difficult

> enough to "qualify" as pilgrimage . . . for many people this reluctance is more strongly rooted in changing religious paradigms, particularly greater scepticism about literal reality of religious merit. Sanskrit pilgrimage literature reflects the assumptions of an earlier time, and one cannot expect contemporary people to subscribe to these.
>
> (Bhardwaj and Lochtefeld 2004: 492–493)

Assumptions of the pilgrims are always subject to change, and doubt and uncertainty are probably inherent in all lived religions. As the means of transportation has improved, starting with the development of the Indian railway, pilgrimage has become easy and this has influenced the expectation of the rewards of pilgrimage. In many pilgrimages, but still with a number of exceptions, there is no longer any similarity between the wandering of ascetics and the journey of pilgrims. Wealthy pilgrims may now also arrive at pilgrimage places, which, for most pilgrims, demand longer walks, by means of straightforward and fast transportation. To reach some places, such as the cave pilgrimage site in Amarnāth in Kashmir, the mountain Kailās in Tibet and the four *dhām*s in Uttarakhand, transportation by helicopters is organized for those who can afford it and who consider it a valid means of travel to a *tīrtha*.[2] Such technological changes will probably lead to further skepticism about salvific rewards and further transform pilgrimage into a variety of tourism. Some aspect of tourism was perhaps always present in pilgrimage as the pilgrimage meant an escape from daily responsibilities and seeing new places and meeting new people. Nevertheless, new types of travel and the transformation of some *tīrtha*s into tourist places with modern facilities provided for visitors mean that the values sought to be maximized by pilgrimage travel become more and more similar to those of tourism. This also means that findings from contemporary fieldwork and interviews of pilgrims about their expectations of the rewards of pilgrimage and reasons for performing pilgrimage should not be projected uncritically on the past. The Sanskrit texts promoting pilgrimage reflect the assumptions of an earlier time and fieldwork of current belief among pilgrims does not falsify the doctrines of pilgrimage held about the past. Pilgrimage is a historical phenomenon that has always been involved in processes of change. Current views on salvific rewards of pilgrimage should not be transposed onto the past. As we look at salvific space in the history of Hinduism, its origin and development, it is important to be aware of these historical changes and that older texts reflect the view of their time and their validity cannot be falsified by contemporary field studies.

Although travel to the pilgrimage places is becoming faster, easier and more comfortable, there is, nevertheless, in most cases some sort of physical journey involved (but Hindu texts also encourage mental journeys) in order to take advantage of this salvific or salvational power of pilgrimage places. Online *pūjā* is offered by some temples, but performing an online *pūjā* to the divine in a temple of a pilgrimage center can probably not be called pilgrimage in the normal sense of the word.[3] For a ritual act to count as pilgrimage, the persons normally need to visit the place. The model pilgrim is the ascetic, but, surprisingly, especially when compared to Christian pilgrimage texts, the Hindu texts on the particular *tīrtha*s do not deal very much with the travel itself; they deal with the places, especially the narratives that explain the origin of the salvific power, and the rewards the pilgrims gain by visiting the places. The focus of the texts is on the power of the places and the rituals to be performed when at the place, the moving around to the various sub-*tīrtha*s and the rewards. When present at the place, those who want to attain the maximum religious rewards are usually expected to perform some ritual acts, most often involving the ritual services of Brahman priests.

Sacred space is a common translation of the Sanskrit words *tīrtha* (in Hindi, *tīrth*) and *kṣetra*, which I most often translate here as salvific space or pilgrimage place. Pilgrimage is a translation of *tīrthayātrā*, travel (*yātrā*) in order to visit a *tīrtha,* but the word pilgrimage in the English language refers not only to the journey of the pilgrim, but also, writes E. Alan Morinis, to the "socio-cultural institution" – that is, to the "full composite of all relevant features which constitute the socio-cultural ecology of individual pilgrim behaviour" (Morinis 1984: 2). Pilgrimage to a particular place refers to "the total set of symbols, history, rituals, legends, behaviour, deities, locations, specialists," writes Morinis, and the words "Hindu pilgrimage" refer to "the institutional complex of journeys to sacred places as practised and conceived by that cultural or religious group" (ibid.). The concept of salvific space signifies the role of space in that complex institution. Pilgrimage thus refers to a structured institution involving many elements. The word *tīrtha* has a number of additional meanings in Sanskrit texts, such as way, road, advice, instruction, parts of the hand, holy person and virtues.[4] *Tīrtha* in the geographical sense is a place of divine or extraordinary power that is believed to have a particular ability to fulfill wishes and grant salvation, which is a goal for pilgrimage travel (*tīrthayātrā*). In Hinduism, such places are often, but not always, associated with water, such as rivers, lakes and beaches, and also wells and temple basins. In its early meaning, *tīrtha* probably referred more specifically to sacred places associated with water and places where ritual bathing took place. *Tīrtha*s can also be mountains or hills, forests and temples. Whole cities, such as Hardvār, Mathurā, Purī and Vārāṇasī, are also promoted as *tīrtha*s. Larger pilgrimage places can contain a number of *tīrtha*s (in English literature, often referred to as sub-*tīrtha*s and with a modern Sanskrit term *upatīrtha*), which the pilgrims are expected to visit. The whole pilgrimage area, often containing many *tīrtha*s, is called a *kṣetra*. Different routes are organized to help the pilgrims to visit the different sub-*tīrtha*s. One motivation for the expansion of sub-*tīrtha*s has probably been to attempt to prolong the stay of the pilgrims, as the pilgrimage places compete for the economic resources of the pilgrims. The translation of *tīrtha* as "salvific place" is meant to emphasize that visiting the places is associated with removal of moral impurity (*pāpa*) and with religious merit (*puṇya*) and rewards (*phala*). The pilgrimage places promise attainment of salvific goals for those who visit, stay or die at the *tīrtha*. According to the local traditions of numerous Hindu sacred places promoted by local pilgrimage priests (*paṇḍā*), as well as the textual traditions of Hinduism, especially in the traditions represented in the *Mahābhārata*, the *Purāṇa*s, the *Māhātmya*s of place, one's presence at the salvific place is in itself a method to attain the highest salvific goal of religion, *mokṣa,* either freedom from rebirth or a life in some divine heaven, as well as improvements in life, such as health, wealth and happiness. Everything one might wish for is said to be granted at sacred sites. The sites themselves, and especially the sacred water at the sites, have this power.

The power of *tīrtha*s to grant salvific rewards to all regardless of gender, caste or morally impure acts previously performed is a significant fact and is not always sufficiently noted in scholarly presentations of Hinduism, which often favor more conservative or restrictive traditions. The greater the difficulty, the higher the status of the salvific path, it seems. Salvation, *mokṣa*, although often presented in the Hindu sources as something most difficult to attain and that could take a large number of lifetimes, is, according to the ideology of *tīrtha*s, offered as easily accessible. It is portrayed in the texts celebrating the pilgrimage places, the *Māhātmya*s and *Sthalapurāṇa*s, and promoted by priests at the pilgrimage places, as something quite easily accessible and available to all, regardless mainly of a person's moral impurity, lack of restraint or ignorance.

Performance of the ritual of *tīrthayātrā* is not required for the attainment of *mokṣa*, but when performed, it is in the traditions of salvific space presented as a sufficient means to attain whatever one wishes. *Tīrthayātrā* is mostly an opportunity, not a duty, although it may become a duty in connection with rituals such as *śrāddha* (rituals for the ancestors performed at a pilgrimage place) and *piṇḍadāna* (offering of rice balls to the ancestors as part of the *śrāddha* ritual). Many Hindus use the opportunity of pilgrimage to wash off moral impurity in the hope of securing rewards, such as a good rebirth into a rich family, a life in heaven or final salvation, and old people especially, conscious of the fact that death may be approaching, think that it is important to visit *tīrtha*s to wash off moral impurities (*pāpa*) before death arrives. At most *tīrtha*s these days, a visit lasts from a few hours to a few days at most. However, at some places, such as Prayāg (Allāhābad) and Nimsār (a place north of Lucknow that claims to be identical with Naimiṣa/Naimiṣāraṇya described in the *Mahābhārata*) in Uttar Pradesh, people are encouraged to stay for a month and the texts celebrating the greatness of Vārāṇasī encourage people to settle there for life. It is claimed that only a fool leaves the sacred city (see descriptions of Vārāṇasī in *Skandapurāṇa* (*Kāśīkhaṇḍa*), *Matsyapurāṇa* and *Kūrmapurāṇa*). This focus on staying permanently distinguishes Vārāṇasī as a pilgrimage town (although it is not the only one that encourages the pilgrims to settle permanently). The point here is not only to visit, shave off the hair on the head and take a sacred bath, as many pilgrims indeed do, but ideally to stay there for good, never leave and finally die there. As stated in the *Kāśīkhaṇḍa* of the *Skandapurāṇa*: after taking a sacred bath in the waters of other sacred places, a person leaves the sinful and defiled body and becomes a deity in heaven, but after dying in the area of Kāśī, he is completely liberated from *saṃsāra* (30.75). The point of staying permanently in Vārāṇasī reflects the value of dying in this city, which is believed to give the reward of *mokṣa*. In Vārāṇasī, there is a tradition of institutions, called *muktibhavan,* for people from the surrounding villages and sometimes also areas further away who have come to the sacred city to die the good death.[5] Some wealthy families built houses along the river front in order to settle there in old age, and retired persons from other places in India still build houses there to settle in when they retire. A few people spend a lifetime in Vārāṇasī without ever entering outside of the border of the sacred city, although such cases are probably rare.

Dharmakṣetra and the pilgrimage place of Kurukṣetra

The first Hindu text to promote the concept of salvific place (*tīrtha)* and the ritual of pilgrimage is the *Mahābhārata*, from which we get the first written presentations of salvific space. However, the most well-known and celebrated part of the *Mahābhārata* are the chapters called *Bhagavadgītā*, found in Book 6 of the *Mahābhārata*, the *Bhīṣmaparvan*, and in these chapters neither *tīrtha* nor *tīrthayātrā* are mentioned or elaborated on. Nevertheless, it is interesting that the first line of the first verse of the *Bhagavadgītā* mentions one of the most celebrated *tīrtha*s of Hinduism, Kurukṣetra, a well-known salvific place (but without referring to the site as a *tīrtha*). The famous first line of the *Bhagavadgītā* reads: *Dharmakṣetre kurukṣetre samavetā yuyutsavaḥ*, "assembled eager for battle at Kurukṣetra, the field of *dharma*." *Dharma* is one of the central concepts of Hinduism with many meanings, such as the order of things and one's duties. *Dharmakṣetra* could perhaps be translated here as "the field of duty," as the performance of duty with the right state of mind is what Kṛṣṇa stresses in his discourse with Arjuna in the *Bhagavadgītā*. Kṛṣṇa points out that Arjuna should perform his duty without being attached to the fruits of his actions and that the idea of *karma* has to do with the intention of the doer. *Dharmakṣetra*, the field of *dharma*, is a concept. Kurukṣetra, however, is the name of a place; the place where the great battle described in the *Mahābhārata* occurred. Today, this place is identified with the well-known pilgrimage site Kurukṣetra in the Indian state Haryana, just north of the capital of India, New Delhi. Kurukṣetra is one of the important Hindu pilgrimage sites. The exact location where the conversation between Kṛṣṇa and Arjuna is today believed to have taken place, in Jyotisar in modern-day Kurukṣetra, is nowadays marked with a statue of the two and a chariot, and on a board hanging from the sacred tree next to the statue is written: "Immortal Banyan tree. Witness of Celestial Song Bhagwad Gita. *Akṣay vaṭ vṛkṣ śrīmadbhagavadgītā kā sākṣī*" (see Figure 2.1). This illustrates the point that the sacred narratives of Hinduism took place somewhere. The discourse that follows, the content of the *Bhagavadgītā*, is all about *dharmakṣetra*, one's duty performed with the right state of mind, and not about the place Kurukṣetra and the properties of this place. The *Mahābhārata* has a few things to say about Kurukṣetra and quite a lot to say about the tradition of salvific space. Pilgrimages to such places are one of the themes in the *Mahābhārata*. The *Bhagavadgītā* and the story of Kurukṣetra in the *Mahābhārata* have a common theme; both in their own way teach methods to attaining the ultimate goal, *mokṣa*. But the methods that they teach for attaining this goal are very different.

Countless books have been written on *dharma*, the first word of the *Bhagavadgītā*. The theme of salvific space is connected to the second word, Kurukṣetra, and what it entails according to the Hindu traditions – that is, the

Figure 2.1 Banyan tree in Kurukṣetra said to have witnessed Kṛṣṇa's teaching to Arjuna

Photo: Knut A. Jacobsen

properties of salvific space and salvific sites. Although the idea of salvific space and pilgrimage is not elaborated on in the *Bhagavadgītā*, this is a main theme in the *Mahābhārata* as a whole. Among the methods for removing moral impurity (*pāpa*), the practice of pilgrimage to salvific sites receives a lot of attention in the *Mahābhārata*. The portrayal of Kurukṣetra in the *Mahābhārata* introduces, in an instructive way, the topic of space as a source of salvation – that is, the topic of salvific space. A large number of *tīrtha*s are described or mentioned in the *Mahābhārata*, and a plurality of sacred sites without a single supreme sacred center characterizes the pilgrimage tradition from its earliest text to its present configuration (see Chapter 6).

Kurukṣetra

Kurukṣetra can serve as an example of the idea of salvific space. Liberation, states a verse in the *Purāṇa*s, is attainable in four ways: by means of knowledge of *brahman*, by performance of *śrāddha* in Gayā, death while defending cattle and residence in Kurukṣetra.[6] That residence in a place is presented as a way to salvation seems to be a strange form of local patriotism and some implications of this idea will be investigated in Chapter 4. Residency is an important aspect of the idea of salvific space. Kurukṣetra is one among very many Hindu pilgrimage places, but its description in the *Mahābhārata* illustrates several central properties of salvific space. The most prominent sub-*tīrtha* in Kurukṣetra is the large sacred pond Brahmasarovara (see Figure 2.2). The presence of ascetics is a characteristic feature of the place. Bathing in the Brahmasarovara is said to be especially meritorious during the solar eclipses and on the last day of the dark fortnight, when falling on a Monday (*somavatī amāvasyā*). Great numbers of pilgrims assemble at the Brahmasarovara during solar eclipses. The salvific

Figure 2.2 The sacred pond Brahmasarovara in Kurukṣetra

Photo: Knut A. Jacobsen

power of the lake on those days is said, according to the tradition, to give *mokṣa* to all.

The sacred place of Kurukṣetra is referred to several times in the *Mahābhārata*. In the *Vanaparvan*, in homage to the river Gaṅgā, it is said that the river Gaṅgā is equal to Kurukṣetra wherever one may bathe in it (*kurukṣetrasamā gaṅgā yatratatrāvagāhitā*).[7] This comparison shows that the author of this verse viewed Kurukṣetra as the superior sacred place since it is used to promote the purity of Gaṅgā, the foremost of rivers. In this verse, it is the river Gaṅgā that is endorsed, but the fact that it is compared to Kurukṣetra shows that the author considered Kurukṣetra to be a supreme sacred place. The text continues to say that in the *kṛtayuga* all places were sacred, in *tretāyuga* Puṣkara, in *dvāparayuga* Kurukṣetra and in *kaliyuga* Gaṅgā (*sarvaṃ kṛtayuge puṇyaṃ tretāyāṃ puṣkaraṃ smṛtam, dvāpare 'pi kurukṣetraṃ gaṅgā kaliyuge smṛtā* [3.83.82d 13.5–6]). This of course indicates that Puṣkara and Kurukṣetra were the main pilgrimage places according to the view of the unknown author of the verse. Comparisons to the most famous *tīrtha*s are often used to promote individual *tīrtha*s. The sacredness of one place is used to elevate the value of another place. It points to an acceptance of a plurality of sacred sites and the tendency to produce relationships and hierarchies between sacred places. The *Mahābhārata* war took place at the end of the *dvāpara* age at the time when Kurukṣetra, according to this statement, was the most sacred place. But the statement wants to say that the same salvific power that is known to have been present at Kurukṣetra is present nowadays in all the water of the Gaṅgā.

One sacred narrative in the *Mahābhārata*, in the *Śalyaparvan*, tells how Kurukṣetra became a salvific place – that is, a *tīrtha*. According to the narrative, a royal sage named Kuru ploughed the field there for many years, and therefore it became known as Kurukṣetra, the field of Kuru. *Kṣetra* means "field," but also a sacred area. The god Indra came down from heaven and asked why he tilled the field with such perseverance. "What is the purpose, what do you want to accomplish with the tilling of the soil?" asked Indra. Kuru answered that what he wanted to ensure was that those who died on the field should be cleansed of their moral impurity and should proceed to the blessed regions – that is, to heaven. In other words, he wanted the site to become endowed with salvific powers. That tilling the soil would endow the site with salvific power is strange indeed. Indra ridiculed Kuru's wish and went back to heaven. King Kuru continued to plough the soil. Indra went to Kuru repeatedly and asked him the same question, but he received the identical answer every time and Indra left mocking him. But Kuru did not become depressed from this, and Indra started to get worried. The god Indra then called the other gods together and informed them what was going on. The gods, after hearing this, said to him:

> We have to stop him! Indra, stop him by offering him a boon if you are able to. If humans were to come to heaven by means of only dying at Kurukṣetra without having performed sacrifice to us, our very existence would be endangered!

Hence, no-one would sacrifice to the gods in order to attain the reward of going to heaven, and since the gods lived from the offerings of the sacrifices, this would be catastrophic. That the gods feel threatened by the easy access to *mokṣa* at the *tīrtha*s is a common theme in the narratives of pilgrimage places (see pp. 32–34). Indra therefore went back to Kuru and told him: "Do not till anymore! Those men that will die here having abstained from food and with their senses awake, and those that will die here in battle shall come to heaven, O king." Thus, ascetics who die there and warriors who perish there in battle attain the reward of heaven, but not everyone. By consenting, the gods limited the salvific power of the place from applying to everyone. But Kuru was satisfied and answered, so be it! In this way, the salvific power of Kurukṣetra is explained.

Historically, pilgrimage gradually replaced the sacrifice to the gods (see Chapter 3), and the story tells of the tension between salvific power of place and the ritual of sacrifice. The gods manage to limit the salvific power of place to grant *mokṣa* only to warriors and ascetics. The idea that people who died in battle at Kurukṣetra attained heaven might perhaps be older than the idea of pilgrimage, but it means that not only is the power of pilgrimage equal to the sacrificial power of the Brahmans but it is also equal to the highest salvific rewards offered to the *kṣatriya*s who perform their duty (Bigger 2001: 159–160). It is interesting that the salvific power of place is contrasted with and presented as a challenge to the salvific power of sacrifice to the gods, and not only presented as a ritual with salvific rewards equal to sacrifices. Pilgrimage is looked on here as a threat to the sacrificial religion, and this is probably historically correct. Ploughing the soil is also presented as a challenge to the sacrificial tradition. That tilling of the soil creates salvific space is perhaps a reference to the connections between agricultural expansion and the expansion of traditions of sacred space and pilgrimage that took place from the third and fourth centuries CE. Agricultural growth was probably one important cause for the expansion of the teaching of salvation by means of sacred sites of Hinduism (see Chapter 4). Geographical and agricultural expansion was probably an important way for the Hindu tradition to spread in India from the fourth to the eighth or ninth centuries CE. Hindu mythological frameworks were in many instances probably merged with traditions of sacred places belonging to a variety of local contexts. However, the connection of the myth of Kurukṣetra with agriculture and salvific power is intriguing. This connection will be further investigated in the next chapters.

Mahābhārata, then, after having described Indra's consent, portrays Kurukṣetra as the most powerful salvific site on earth. *Mahābhārata* states that those who give away their fortune at this place will have their wealth doubled. This provides a connection to the ritual of *dāna*, gifting, with the concept of salvific space, which is important and will be examined in the following chapters. The expansion of salvific space was part probably of the expansion of the ritual of *dāna* as an important form of economic exchange. The text continues to say that those who always live at Kurukṣetra will never have to visit the region of Yama – that is, hell.[8] The king who performs a sacrifice there will reside in heaven as long as earth exists. The god Indra is said, according to the *Mahābhārata*, to have composed the following verse about the sacred place of Kurukṣetra:

> *pāṃsavo 'pi kurukṣetrād vāyunā samudīritāḥ,*
> *api duṣkṛtakarmāṇaṃ nayanti paramāṃ gatim*
>
> Just the dust of Kurukṣetra blown by the wind shall take even persons of wicked acts to the highest salvific goal.[9]
>
> (*Mahābhārata* 3. 81.174 and 9.52.18)

The salvific power of place belongs here to the ground, the place itself, which is a common pattern, here symbolized by the tilling of Kuru. Salvific space is not only the individual shrines but may include large areas (*kṣetras*), especially in North India, with hundreds of shrines, which might take many days to visit or circumambulate. The twelfth-century text Lakṣmīdhara's *Tīrthavivecanakāṇḍa*, in the description of Vārāṇasī, lists more than 200 *liṅgas*, wells and ponds, their salvific powers and the benefits (*phala*) from visiting each of them. Sacred space, especially in North India, is often larger landscapes, even whole cities, with hundreds of sacred centers containing healing, enriching and salvific power. Examples of such *kṣetras* in contemporary North India are not only Kurukṣetra, but Ayodhyā, Vṛndāvan, Nimsār, Citrakūṭa, Vārāṇasī, Gayā, Haridvār, Ujjain, Oṃkāreśvar, Tryambak (Tryambakeśvar) and many others. Rivers and mountains also constitute entire sacred regions. The whole of the river Narmadā is a sacred area and probably the longest pilgrimage in India performed regularly by lay

Figure 2.3 Pilgrims performing the Narmadā *parikrama* in Amarkaṇṭak

Photo: Knut A. Jacobsen

pilgrims is along this river. The pilgrims first walk to the ocean from its source, Amarkaṇṭak, on one side of the river and return on the other side (see Figure 2.3). A similar pilgrimage around the Gaṅgā has also been created but hardly any pilgrims perform this walk. However, the salvific power of place is also transportable, as the dust from Kurukṣetra still contains the salvific power of the place even when not at Kurukṣetra. Transportability becomes an important feature of Hindu salvific space. The site is not limited only to its original setting, but can also be established at many other places. Kurukṣetra has also been set up in Vārāṇasī and other places, the Jagannāth of Purī is worshipped at many places other than Purī and Veṅkaṭeśvara of Tirupati is based at numerous sites, although his main place is nevertheless in Tirupati. The place has been reduplicated. In the same way as a god can be present in many statues, but nonetheless does not become diminished, a sacred place can be present at many places. That the god Indra is said to have composed the verse is of significance because it reverses the Vedic tradition. Indra is the most important god revered in hymns of *Ṛgveda*. These hymns were used in the ritual of sacrifice, the central ritual of the Vedic tradition. In the tradition of pilgrimage, on the other hand, the god Indra composed a hymn paying homage to the salvific power of a sacred site. The roles are, in other words, inverted. The gods now pay homage to the salvific power of place. Humans praise gods; gods praise salvific sites. The supreme powers are now the sites. This verse is quoted twice in the *Mahābhārata*, in *Vanaparvan* and *Śalyaparvan*.

So sacred is the Kurukṣetra that warriors (*kṣatriya*s) slain in battle there obtain access to the sacred regions and eternal salvation, and here we have a quite different reason why warriors (*kṣatriyas*) who were killed at the battle at Kurukṣetra would go to heaven than the arguments presented in the teaching of Kṛṣṇa in the *Bhagavadgītā*. According to Kṛṣṇa, it was because the warriors performed their duty with a disinterested state of mind that they attained *mokṣa*. As Kṛṣṇa states in *Bhagavadgītā*:

> *yadṛcchyā copapannaṃ svargadvāram apāvṛtam*
> *sukhinaḥ kṣatriyāḥ pārtha labhante yuddham īdṛśam*
>
> Presented by mere luck, an open door to heaven –
> happy are the warriors, son of Pārtha, that get such a fight.
> (*Bhagavadgītā* 2.32, trans. F. Edgerton, slightly modified)

But according to the statements about Kurukṣetra, it was not through the performance of their warrior duty that they attained heaven, but due to the salvific power of place that promised attainment of the reward of heaven for all warriors that died there. After Indra had composed the above quoted verse about Kurukṣetra, which stated that the dust of Kurukṣetra blown by the wind would take everyone to the highest salvific goal, the text declared that this was approved by Brahmā, by Viṣṇu and also by Śiva. Thus the salvific power of Kurukṣetra had become an absolute truth.

The salvific power of Kurukṣetra is further praised in the *Mahābhārata*. It is stated in the *Vanaparvan* about Kurukṣetra:

> *manasāpy abhikāmasya kurukṣetraṃ yudhiṣṭhira*
> *pāpāni vipraṇaśyanti brahmalokaṃ ca gacchati*
>
> If one desires to go to Kurukṣetra, even in thought, all his moral impurity (*pāpa*) disappears and he goes to the world of Brahmā.
> (*Mahābhārata* 3.81.5)

Here, just thinking about the place Kurukṣetra and possessing the desire to go there is enough to attain heaven (the world of Brahmā). Again, the site itself has become the ultimate salvific power. Belief in its powers purifies all moral impurity.

In *Vanaparvan* 81.173–176, it is said: "On earth Naimiṣa is sacred, in the sky Puṣkara, but in all three worlds Kurukṣetra stands out." The text states that those who dwell in Kurukṣetra south of the river Sarasvatī and north of the river

Dṛṣadvati dwell in heaven. Even if a person only utters the sentence, "I shall go to Kurukṣetra. I shall live in Kurukṣetra" (*kurukṣetraṃ gamiṣyāmi kurukṣetre vasāmy aham*), that person is released from all moral impurity and is liberated (*pramucyate*).

pṛthivyāṃ naimiṣaṃ puṇyam antarikṣe ca puṣkaram
trayāṇām api lokānāṃ kurukṣetraṃ viśiṣyate
pāṃsavo 'pi kurukṣetre vāyunā samudīritāḥ
api duṣkṛtakarmāṇaṃ nayanti paramāṃ gatim
dakṣiṇena sarasvatyā uttareṇa dṛṣadvatīm
ye vasanti kurukṣetre te vasanti triviṣṭape
kurukṣetraṃ gamiṣyāmi kurukṣetre vasāmy aham
apy ekāṃ vācam utsṛjya sarvapāpaiḥ pramucyate

(*Mahābhārata* 3.81.173–176)

How the Hindu pilgrims in the early days of Hindu pilgrimage understood such statements about the salvific power of place is not clear. Judging from the documented numbers of people visiting the sacred places when such figures became available in the sources, the statements represent not only the views of the pilgrim priests but also the hopes of the pilgrims. However, in the later *dharma* texts dealing with the topic of *tīrtha* and *tīrthayātrā*, in addition to presenting the promises of sacred space, the restrictions on the salvific rewards were also elaborated on. There was also a tendency to make the attainment of the fruits of pilgrimage depend on the person's control of the senses, ritual performance and moral purity. There is a continuous tension in the Hindu tradition between the easy access to salvific rewards promised by the textual and ritual traditions (and presumably the priests) of the individual places and the restrictions on the rewards promoted by the *dharma* texts on pilgrimage. Such restrictions are already found in the *Mahābhārata* but are discussed in detail in the medieval *Dharmanibandha* texts on pilgrimage (for more on this tension, see Chapter 7).

Sacred places as divinities

The Hindu doctrines of salvific space and pilgrimage mythology contain some unique characteristics. Kurukṣetra is not the only place that is salvific – that is, has power in itself to provide human beings with their salvific goals unmediated by a god. The salvific power of many sacred places rests on the principle that the sites in themselves have power. The sacredness of many of the sites is probably older than the myths that are linked to them today. Some of the places were Buddhist sacred places, and some were sacred places for local communities. Traditions have merged at the sites, some of which were multi-religious sites. At some places, the power is not mediated by a personal god, but is a property of the site itself. At the confluence (*saṅgama*) of Gaṅgā and Yamunā (and according to the Hindu belief, the subterranean river Sarasvatī) in Prayāg (Allāhābad), there is no temple that needs to be visited by all the pilgrims or a *mūrti* they need to worship in order to obtain the salvific rewards. It is the natural phenomenon of the place, the confluence itself, not a human-made structure that constitutes the place. It is the merging of the white water of Gaṅgā with the dark water of Yamunā and the surrounding sand banks that form the sacred site. The place itself is the basis for attaining the results, not the grace of a personal god. Gaṅgā and Yamunā are considered goddesses, but there are no temples with statues of them at the confluence which all pilgrims need to visit.

The theme we encountered in the case of the Kurukṣetra – that sacred places can be competitors to the gods – is found in narratives about several other places as well and seems to be a unique feature of the Hindu pilgrimage mythology. In the case of Kurukṣetra, we saw that the god Indra tried to stop the creation of Kurukṣetra as a *tīrtha* because it would become too easy to attain heaven, and humans then would no longer need the gods and they would stop sacrificing to them. This is a common theme in narratives of many salvific sites. In several *Māhātmya* texts on *tīrthas*, the gods do in fact complain that salvation for humans has become too easy. The gods bemoan that, since salvation is so easily attained by visiting a *tīrtha*, no-one cares to worship them anymore. The gods, therefore, attempt by different ways to remove this possibility of bypassing the worship of the gods. The place might then be hidden by the jealous gods and revealed later for the benefit of humans. This theme is presented in a typical way in the tradition about the pilgrimage place Kolāyat in Rajasthan and its sacred lake. According to the tradition of Kolāyat in Rajasthan, told in the text *Kolāyat Māhātmya* (*Śrī Kapilamāhātmya Kolāyatjī*, 1999), the gods became jealous of that site. Instead of undergoing the hardships of *tapas* and sacrifice or undertaking long journeys to places of pilgrimage, such as to Ayodhyā and Vārāṇasī, the local people would attain *mokṣa* the easy way, by just taking a dip in the holy lake at Kolāyat. Hence, the gods contemplated hiding Kolāyat from humanity and moving themselves to the place. However, the god Skanda felt sorry for humanity and brought this sacred place to light for the benefit of all, so that everyone can easily obtain *mokṣa* in the dark *kali*-age (Jacobsen 2008a). Another version of the same theme is found in a Tamil temple narrative. The gods complained to Śiva that no-one worshipped them anymore since salvation had become so easily available at Muttūrkūṟṟam (Shulman 1980). The gods complained that hell had become deserted and heaven too crowded. However, Śiva answered the gods by reminding them that they indeed had reached their current positions as gods by performing *tapas* at the sacred place Muttūrkūṟṟam, and that it would not be right to stop others from worshipping there. Instead, he advised the gods to go there and worship to attain the *muktipada*, salvific liberation, for themselves. The gods then went to the temple, bathed in the river and meditated on Śiva. David Shulman concludes: "The power of the shrine has become an absolute. The shrine must offer salvation to all" (Shulman 1980: 21). In this Tamil temple narrative, the other gods were reminded by Śiva that they should also attain the salvific goal of *mokṣa* and that the site itself had the power to give salvific liberation. In another myth illustrating the same theme, a theme Shulman calls "the gods' war against a shrine" (Shulman 1980: 55), a drop of *amṛta* fell from Garuḍa's pot into the temple tank at Puṣpagiri and the temple tank thereafter granted everyone immortality. The god

Brahmā became nervous about this and Nārada told Hanumān to drop a hill on the tank, presumably to hide it. But the hill just floated on the water of the temple tank like a flower. In another narrative, the god Indra attempts to prevent humans from attaining the salvific power of the place Tiruvārūr. Indra saw that evil persons were going to heaven and reaching *mokṣa* by worshipping at Tiruvārūr. He disliked this and wanted to stop it. He "called Anger, Lust, Covetousness, Hatred, Fear, Sexual Pleasure, Delusion, Addiction, Jealousy, and Desire and said: 'You must prevent any man or woman who is going to the shrine from reaching it'" (Shulman 1980: 24). Here, it is not the place that is hidden, but it is humans who become degenerate by the forces Indra called on and therefore do not visit the place. The gods protect themselves from the salvific power of the site by making humans immoral so that they do not go to the place. The gods were afraid of losing their power to the sacred site. Humans should, therefore, try to overcome their disinclination not to visit and make every effort to go to the shrine and take advantage of its salvific power. And when some do not visit the shrine, it is because they have become evil due to the forces called on by Indra. Perhaps there were, at some point in time, very few visitors to the place and this narrative tried to explain that. More probable is that the story fits the pattern of the gods trying to make the salvific power of place unattainable for humans. A further example is from Vārāṇasī (Kāśī), which is said to be the city Śiva never leaves (see Figure 2.4). Śiva dwells in Kāśī, the first three *yuga*s, and in the *kaliyuga* that city goes into hiding while the city of humans again exists (*Brahmāṇḍapurāṇa* 2.3.67.63–64, *Vāyupurāṇa* 2.30.25–55;

Figure 2.4 The river Gaṅgā and *ghāṭ*s of the city of Vārāṇasī

Photo: Knut A. Jacobsen

see Shulman 1980: 78). Here, the narrative of hiding the shrine explains the existence of the human city, the historical Kāśī. The idea is that the human city of Kāśī can exist only if Śiva's Kāśī is in some way hidden. The salvific power of Kāśī, however, is in no way absent.

Since the *tīrtha*s themselves have salvific power – the power to grant heaven or salvific liberation to humans and, at some places such as Kolāyat, even animals – in some narratives they become personified as divine powers. In several accounts of salvific space, the *tīrtha*s are presented as individualized divinities. One theme in the narratives is that the *tīrtha*s accumulate so much impurity (*pāpa*) from pilgrims washing off their impurity there, that the places themselves need to go on pilgrimage to become pure. In the narratives, therefore, *tīrtha*s go to other *tīrtha*s to take sacred baths and wash off all the moral impurity they have accumulated from people washing off their impurities at the places. According to one pilgrimage mythology, during the month of Māgh (January–February), all the other *tīrtha*s and all the auspicious cities arrive in Prayāg to bathe at the confluence of the three rivers to wash off the *pāpa* they have received that year. In the *satyayuga*, all *tīrtha*s were white, the narrative continues, but in the *kali*-age their white complexion was concealed and they became black due to contact with morally impure people. But when they take a bath in Prayāg (see Figure 2.5) in the month of Māgh, they become white again

Such claim to superiority, as being the place all the *tīrtha*s travel to on pilgrimage, is not unique to Prayāg. The narratives of *tīrtha*s traveling intend to say that the

Figure 2.5 Pilgrims at the *saṅgam* in Prayāg during the *kumbhamelā* in 2001

Photo: Knut A. Jacobsen

pilgrimage place being described is superior to all others. A claim of *tīrtha*s going on pilgrimage to a superior place to wash away moral impurity is made about the river Gautamī in Maharashtra. This river is so sacred that, at a particular holy time, all the other sacred rivers come there to take sacred baths, according to a narrative. In the *Brahmapurāṇa* 7.32–33, it is said: "When the sun is in the Leo zodiac the rivers Gaṅgā, Narmadā, Yamunā, Sarasvatī, Bhīmarathī and others come (to the river Gautamī) for taking baths." The purpose of the assertion is stated in the verse that follows: "When the sun is in the Leo zodiac if foolish persons avoid Gautamī Gaṅgā and go to other rivers for ablution they are sure to fall into hell."

The pilgrimage places themselves need to go on pilgrimage, and during the festival time of Gautamī Gaṅgā, the other rivers go on pilgrimage to Gautamī Gaṅgā. Those who do not understand this and travel at this time on pilgrimage to bathe in the other rivers end up in hell, according to these verses. The last statement, the threat of hell, leaves little doubt what these statements are about and seems to reflect the competition between pilgrimage places (presumably between the priests at these places) for the pilgrims.

In the *Prayāgamāhātmya* in *Matsyapurāṇa*, the idea that *tīrtha*s are present at other *tīrtha*s is also found in the description of Prayāg. This narrative also reflects a competition between the priests at the different *tīrtha*s:

> *daśatīrthasahasrāni ṣaṣṭikoṭyas tathā parāḥ*
> *teṣāṃ sānnidhyam atraiva tatas tu kurunandana*
>
> (*Matsyapurāṇa* 106.23)

> At Prayāga there are sixty crores and ten thousand *tīrtha*s gathered, Kurunandana

> *śṛṇu rājan prayāgasya māhātmyaṃ punar eva tu*
> *naimiṣaṃ puṣkaraṃ caiva gotīrthaṃ sindhusāgaram*
> *gayā ca caitrakaṃ caiva gaṅgāsāgaram eva ca*
> *ete cānye ca bahavo ye ca puṇyāḥ śiloccayāḥ*
> *daśatīrthasahasrāṇi triṃśaṭkoṭyas tathāparāh*
> *prayāge saṃsthitā nityam evam āhur manīṣinaḥ*
>
> (*Matsyapurāṇa* 110.1–3)

> Listen King again about the glory of Prayāg. The sages have said that Naimiṣa, Puṣkara, Gotīrtha, Sindhusāgara, Gayā, Gaṅgāsāgara and other sacred places along with ten thousand and three hundred crores and of other *tīrtha*s are always present in Prayāg.

In the month of Māgh, additional *tīrtha*s go and stay in Prayāg:

> *daśatīrthasahasrāṇi tisraḥ koṭyas tathāparāḥ*
> *māghamāse gamiṣyanti gaṅgāyāṃ bharatarṣabha*
>
> (*Matsyapurāṇa* 112.16)

> Ten thousand *tīrtha*s and three crores of rivers go and dwell in the Gaṅgā during the month of Māgh.

In these verses, the peculiar phenomenon of *tīrtha*s staying at or going to other (superior) *tīrtha*s is promoted. This is a different way of thinking of sacred space than in, for example, mainstream Buddhist or Christian Catholic pilgrimage. In this thinking, a sacred site is something more than a site. The relationship of a *tīrtha* and its presence at other sites parallels, to some degree, the relationship of a god and his *mūrti*. In the same way as a Hindu god is present in multiple statues, the sacred site is present at multiple sites.

That *tīrtha*s travel on pilgrimage to other *tīrtha*s was part of the understanding of pilgrimage already mentioned in the *Mahābhārata*. According to *tīrthayātrāparvan* (*Mahābhārata* 3.81.165–170), one should go to the *tīrtha* Saṃnihiti. At that place, all *tīrtha*s on the earth and in the atmosphere, all the rivers, streams, wells, ponds, holy sanctuaries, are all assembled every month, no doubt about it![10] The *tīrthayātrāparvan* became the model for many of the later descriptions of *tīrtha*s, and that the idea that *tīrtha*s going on pilgrimage to other *tīrtha*s is already presented in this text probably shows that it is part of the fundamental understanding of *tīrtha* and pilgrimage. This understanding combines in an interesting way the idea of the mobility of the Vedic gods – that is, that gods travel – with the idea of the divine power being present permanently at a sacred site, which is fundamental to the Hindu temple tradition.

In a tradition from Ayodhyā, the city of Ayodhyā claims superiority to Prayāg by claiming that Prayāg comes to bathe there. According to this story, Vikramaditya, when he came to Ayodhyā in search of Rāma, set up his camp on the banks of the river Sarayū and rode around on his horse. There he saw a man on a black horse dressed as a king and totally black. Vikramaditya saw him descend from the horse and take a bath in the Sarayū and, when he came up from the river, he was totally white. Vikramaditya asked who he was and how he had changed from black to white. The king then revealed that he was Prayāg, the king of *tīrtha*s (*tīrtharāja*), that he had become black by absorbing the moral impurity of so many impure people and that by taking a bath in the Sarayū he had become pure again. Vikramaditya was surprised that the king of *tīrtha*s needed to come to this place, but Prayāg answered that this spot was the Gopratara, the place where Rāma had left the world. Prayāg thereafter showed Vikramaditya all the sacred spots in Ayodhyā and Vikramaditya drew a circle around them (van der Veer 1988). This story seeks to legitimate the *tīrtha*s of Ayodhyā and tries to promote Ayodhyā as even more powerful than Prayāg. The prestige of Prayāg makes the comparison implied in the pilgrimage narrative meaningful.

Another innovative way to claim superiority over all other *tīrtha*s is found in Braj. There is a narrative about Braj that says that, when all the *tīrtha*s had gathered in Prayāg, Braj was absent. Prayāg is also called *tīrtharāja*, "the king of *tīrtha*s," to indicate that Prayāg is indeed the most important of all *tīrtha*s. The absence in the gathering of Braj angered Prayāg and the other *tīrtha*s and they decided to attack Braj. However, when they arrived at the border of Braj, they saw Kṛṣṇa.

Prayāg complained to Kṛṣṇa that Kṛṣṇa himself had made him the king of *tīrtha*s, but that Braj did not obey him. Kṛṣṇa replied that it was he that made Prayāg the king of *tīrtha*s, but that Braj was his *dhām* (sacred place), and he did not make Prayāg king of his *dhām* (Haberman 1994: 72). In the *Māhātmya* of Mathurā in *Varāhapurāṇa*, it is said that Yamunā is a hundred times more sacred in Mathurā than where it meets Gaṅgā in Prayāg (152.30). This story achieves two things. Obviously, it makes Braj superior to all *tīrtha*s, but it also makes all *tīrtha*s subservient to Kṛṣṇa. In the story of Śiva in Vārāṇasī the opposite is accomplished. Śiva had cut off the fifth head of Brahmā and, as punishment for this sin, the head of Brahmā was stuck to his palm and Śiva had to beg for food using the skull. To get rid of the sin of cutting off the fifth head of Brahmā and remove the skull stuck to his hand, he had to come to Vārāṇasī. When he entered Vārāṇasī, the skull dropped off. Here, Śiva is made subservient to the place. This is a strong argument for the salvific power of place: even the most powerful of gods, Śiva, needs its power.

In an illustrative narrative about pilgrimage in the Arbuda (Mount Ābū) in the *kali*-age, it is explained why all places of pilgrimage traveled to Arbuda. The narrative starts by stating that the pilgrimage places Gaṅgā and Kedārnāth, and many others, joined the gods such as Indra and together with sages traveled to god Brahmā, where they engaged in different religious discourses (*Skandapurāṇa*, *Prabhāsakhaṇḍa*, *Arbudakhaṇḍa*, Chapter 10). It is said that "all places of pilgrimage, regions, forests, and gardens belonging to gods were present at this congregation." It is notable that the pilgrimage places are treated here as divine and mobile, like the gods and sages. They are both localized and universal, as are the gods! Indra asked Brahmā to explain the *yuga*s, and Brahmā therefore explains the qualities of the different *yuga*s. Some usual characteristics of *kaliyuga* are mentioned, such as greater prevalence of sins and cheating, jealousy, greed, anger and fear prevail. Gaining wealth is a main concern – the earth gives fewer crops, cows provide less milk, Brahmans no longer tell the truth, people get gray hair at the age of 16, women become pregnant at the age of 12 and all *āśrama*s and *varṇa*s become one. Then, with respect to *tīrtha*s, the text states that all places of pilgrimage become meaningless because of their coming in contact with non-*āryans* (*Skandapurāṇa* 7.3.10.30). The pilgrimage places, having heard this from Brahmā, answered him: "You have stated what our position will be in the difficult *kaliyuga*. With no place for us, god, please tell about the places that could always be ours in this yuga" (*Skandapurāṇa* 7.3.10.32–33). Brahmā answered: "There is the best of mountains by name Arbuda where *kali* cannot prevail. Hence, that is the destination for all centres of pilgrimage to have their station" (33). Then all the *tīrtha*s went to Arbuda in the *kaliyuga*.

> The rivers Gaṅgā, Yamunā, Sarasvatī and even the ponds and places of pilgrimage such as Kurukṣetra, Prabhāsa, Brahmāvarta, including all other pilgrim centres spread over three and a half crore lands, went to the Arbuda mountain out of fear for *kaliyuga*. This is how every pilgrim centre could have its place of fixation on the Arbuda mountain and this is how Gaṅgā and Sarasvatī also came there.
>
> (*Skandapurāṇa* 7.3.10.36–38, trans. S. Balooni and P. Panda)

Every pilgrim who goes there, the text says, also those who have committed great sins, attain *mokṣa* there; they become free from all the shortcomings of the *kaliyuga* and all the ancestors of a family go to heaven if *śrāddha* is performed there for them. The story fits one pattern of claiming superiority of a *tīrtha* over all others; that all the other *tīrtha*s are really included in the superior *tīrtha*, and this inclusion is explained by the pilgrimage places having left their sites and becoming settled or fixed at the superior place. Here, the *tīrtha*s are thought of as movable as the gods. Their salvific power now became available at their new place. In these stories, the salvific place with its salvific power and the secular geographical place seem to be thought of as separable. It is also noteworthy that the salvific places are not thought of here as reduplicated in Arbuda, but have been moved to Arbuda.

A famous and often-quoted verse, known by many Hindus and found in the *Garuḍapurāṇa*, claims that there are seven sacred cities:

> *ayodhyā mathurā māyā kāśī kāñcī avantikā/purī dvāravatī caiva saptaitā mokṣadāyikāḥ*
>
> Ayodhyā, Mathurā, Hardvār (Māyā), Vārāṇasī (Kāśī), Kāñcīpuram, Ujjain (Avantikā), and Dvārkā (Dvāravatī) – these seven cities are the givers of salvific liberation.
>
> (*Garuḍapurāṇa* 2.38.5)

It seems to be implied in this verse that the seven cities are equal. However, each place claims superiority and, after the statement of a similar verse in the *Skandapurāṇa*, *Kāśīkhaṇḍa*, 1.23.7 (*kañcyavantīdvāravatīkāśyayodhyā ca pañcamī, māyāpurī ca mathuryaḥ saptavimuktidāḥ*), the *Māhātmya*, the propaganda text in favor of Vārāṇasī, states in the next verse (1.23.8) that the salvific power to grant *mokṣa* has abandoned the other cities, but not Kāśī. This follows the same logic as in the above examples. Each place wants to present itself as superior to the others and the salvific power is seen as movable. According to the propagation texts of Vārāṇasī, the salvific power of all the pilgrimage places is found in Vārāṇasī, and therefore there is no need to go to other pilgrimage places! The claim about Vārāṇasī is the same as those made by the promotion texts of many other places. But the promotion text of Vārāṇasī goes even further: "The salvation attained by the residents of Avimukta cannot be attained by residing in Kurukṣetra, Gaṅgādvāra or in Puṣkara."[11] And in the *Kāśīkhaṇḍa*, it is said that "those who consider Vārāṇasī as equal to other pilgrimage places, despite the fact that the power of Kāśī is unrivalled and divine, are sinners. No-one should even talk to them" (30.86). Once arrived in Vārāṇasī, a person should stay because if they wish they can easily attain learning, wealth, houses, elephants, horses, servants, garlands, sandal paste, women of exquisite beauty and even heaven, but the Vārāṇasī that gives salvific liberation even to locusts and moths is not easily available (30.88). A person who has arrived in Vārāṇasī and decides to stay should be revered like the god Śiva (30.90). In Vārāṇasī, Śiva whispers the salvific mantra in the ear of the dying and they attain liberation. In the *Māhātmya* of Mathurā, however, it is said that all the *tīrtha*s and sacred lakes in the world make their presence in Mathurā (*Varāhapurāṇa* 152.18) and a person, by just hearing the name of Mathurā uttered by another, receives release (*Varāhapurāṇa* 152.17).

According to a Tamil temple myth (see Shulman 1980: 18), a man was bringing the bones of his father for cremation in Vārāṇasī and he decided to stop for the night at the Tamil sacred place of Tiruvaiyāṟu. The next morning, when he woke up, he discovered that the bones had grown into a *liṅga*. But when he started to walk towards Vārāṇasī, the bones separated again. In that way, he discovered that Tiruvaiyāṟu was a greater *tīrtha* than Vārāṇasī.

Pilgrimage places are also typically named in contrast to or in imitation of the most famous sites. For example, Madurai is the Mathurā of the south. Shulman (1980) mentions Teṅkāśī, Tirukkūṭalaiyāṟṟūr (Dakṣiṇaprayāga), Maṉṉarkuṭi (Dakṣiṇadvārakā), Vetāraṇiyam (Dakṣiṇamānasā) and several Dakṣiṇakailāsas, among them Aruṇācalam. This is typical of regional pilgrimage traditions (see Feldhaus 2003 for a similar pattern in Maharashtra).

Not only are the divine present on earth as *tīrtha*s, the *tīrtha*s are also located in the divine world. In a reversal of the common pattern, a mythologization of *tīrtha*s places the sites in the divine worlds. In one *Purāṇa*, the *Bṛhaddharmapurāṇa*, in the *Madhyakhaṇḍa* (Chapter 20), the sacred sites are located on objects of the gods: Ayodhyā is situated on the tip of Rāma's bough, Mathurā is placed on Kṛṣṇa's Sudarśana disc, Māyā (here Kāmarūpa) rests on the Śivaliṅga, Kāśī perches on Śiva's trident together with Kāñcī (which is twofold, a Śivakāñcī and a Viṣṇukañcī), Avantī is on Hari's lotus and Dvāravatī rests on Kṛṣṇa's conch shell (Hazra 1979: 522). The text then states that Gaṅgā is equal in glory to all these sacred cities. The purpose of identifying the salvific cities with places associated with the divine seems to stress the divine nature of the place and associates them with the divine powers of these gods.

The problem of the localization and universalism of the places is dealt with in the *Śivapurāṇa*, about the Tryambakeśvara Jyotirliṅga. When sacred places go to other sites, their original places lose their salvific power: ". . . whenever Jupiter enters Leo, the holy rivers, sacred centres and the gods come here" (*Śivapurāṇa, Koṭirudrasamhitā*, 26.51); "The holy lakes Puṣkara, and others, the sacred river Gaṅgā and others, Vāsudeva and other gods stay on the banks of Gautamī river" (26.52); "While they are here they lose the sacredness in their original places. They will have it back when they return there" (26.53).

The idea that, when sacred centers leave their places, the sacredness of their original places is temporarily lost is an intriguing thought, as the site and the *tīrtha* become two separate things. As god is present in the statues but also is different from them, the site is also different from its salvific power. Its salvific power becomes a transcendent and salvific personification who is himself able to travel. The sites are also salvific powers that transcend the visible material places.

Tīrtha seems to have played an important role in the transfer from sacrifice to *pūjā* and *bhakti* – that is, from religion of Vedic sacrifice to Hindu worship of gods manifested in concrete matter, such as stones or statues. Pilgrimage ascribed divinity and salvific power to the tangible forms of nature, such as water, trees, caves and mountains, and could have prepared the foundations for the worship of gods in *mūrtis*. In the *tīrthayātrā* section of the *Vanaparvan*, shrines and statues of gods are described several times, along with visions of gods and recitation of hymns at the *tīrtha*s the Pāṇḍava brothers visit. Worship at *tīrtha*s of divinity in concrete form can very well have been an important step in the development of worship of gods in statues.

In the next chapter, I will look at the historical origin and early development of the Hindu traditions of salvific space and pilgrimage. How did the belief in the efficacy of salvific space and the tradition of the ritual of pilgrimage originate? How did the concept and tradition spread throughout the Indian subcontinent? And how did salvific space come to dominate the Hindu tradition?

3 The origin of the Hindu traditions of salvific space

Given the importance of salvific space and pilgrimage in Hinduism, it is quite remarkable that, in the early Vedic tradition, there was no tradition of assigning a permanent divine presence to particular places which could be the basis of pilgrimage. The ancient etymological dictionary of words in the Vedas, Yāska's *Nirukta*, does not list pilgrimage as one of the meanings of *yātrā*, "travel" (Bharati 1963: 137). The view of sacred sites as salvific space, as divine and as sources of salvific rewards and the object of pilgrimage travel, is important in the Hindu tradition, but this view of sacred sites differs dramatically from those found in the early Vedic tradition. In the early Vedic tradition, there were probably no temples and no statues of gods and goddesses that could be objects of pilgrimage travel. It seems most likely that the emergence of sacred sites and pilgrimage was in some way connected to the processes that led to the existence of temples and statues of gods. They all involve a view of the embodiment of the divine that differs from the one found in the early Vedic tradition.

In this and the next chapter, I will look at some of the reasons why salvific space and pilgrimage attained such a central role in Hinduism. One important part of the answer lies in understanding how salvific space originated, how the change came about, and in this chapter I will consider a number of suggestions of the origin of Hindu salvific space and pilgrimage. I shall address the question of origin and discuss possible antecedents to the Hindu pilgrimage traditions in the Vedic tradition and the Indus civilization. I will also analyze and consider the significance of the emergence of Buddhist sacred sites and pilgrimage traditions for the Hindu traditions of pilgrimage, the possible role of pre-Buddhist divine figures associated with particular places, the role of the appearance of temples and statues of gods and the role of a new type of priest associated with the performance of rituals for the statues in the development of the Hindu pilgrimage traditions. The chapter will only put forth some suggestions and it does not in any way claim to present a final answer to the question of the origin of salvific space and pilgrimage in the Hindu tradition. Questions of origins are always intriguing, although the question of why a phenomenon becomes successful is often historically more important. As significant as understanding the origin of salvific space is understanding the reasons for its success. Why did the conception and rituals of salvific space succeed to such a degree that it became a dominant form of religious life in Hinduism (as well as in South Asia in general)? In the next chapter, therefore, we will look at the great expansion of the Hindu pilgrimage tradition.

One difficulty with attaining knowledge of the origin of Hindu pilgrimage is that the idea of sacred place – that is, the idea that divine powers are present at particular sites – although probably not universal, is common to a large number of cultures. The belief that particular sites possessed divine powers could, therefore, have been common to many pre-Vedic or non-Vedic cultures of India of which we do not have any written sources. To identify an origin of sacred space in South Asia would then be impossible. That pilgrimage and conceptions of the permanent presence of divine powers at particular sites were absent in the Vedic tradition – but dominate the Hindu traditions – make the question of the roots of Hindu conceptions of salvific space and pilgrimage traditions a particularly interesting and intriguing one. Identifying an origin of the conception and rituals of divine and salvific space in South Asia is most probably not possible, as such conceptions and rituals might have existed for thousands of years before they became available in written sources. However, the question of how the conception and rituals of divine and salvific space and pilgrimage became part of the Brahmanical tradition, the tradition based on the Vedic tradition, and dominant in the Hindu tradition is different and perhaps a question that *can* be answered. In this chapter, some answers will be suggested.

The answers to the questions of the origins of traditions of salvific space and pilgrimage given by critical research often differ dramatically from those given by the pilgrimage traditions themselves. Critical research gives different accounts of the origin and is interested in social and cultural processes; the pilgrimage traditions present their origin in narratives about sages and divinities. The promotion texts of sacred places (*Māhātmya*s and *Purāṇa*s) are about salvific power and the power and legitimacy of rituals. In contemporary India, however, politicians, political parties and other groups and organizations have sometimes attempted to reconcile these approaches and to connect religious identity and secular history to the promotion texts of salvific space and sacred geography, of which Ayodhyā is the most well-known case (see Chapter 7). This reflects a development in which the religious identity of the site, for some, has become more important than the salvific and divine power of the pilgrimage places.[1] Historical research, nevertheless, has attempted to go beyond the sacred narratives and understand sacred sites and pilgrimage traditions as part of social and cultural processes that involve human intentions, interests and conflicts, as well as religious devotion and aesthetic experience. According to a Purāṇic tradition stated in the *Brahmapurāṇa* (70.16–19), *tīrtha*s are, however, classified into four divisions according to who created them: *Daivya*, created by the gods; *asura*, associated with Asuras; *arśa*, established by sages (*ṛsis*); and finally *manus*, created by kings. In this scheme of the origins of pilgrimage places, the historical origins of the places are made to coincide with the sacred narratives that are told about them. The *Brahmapurāṇa* assigns each of these four types of pilgrimage places to a separate *yuga*, *kṛta*, *tretā*, *dvāpara* and *kali*, respectively. *Daivya tīrtha*s are places such as Prabhāsa, Kāśī and Puṣkara, and the rivers Gaṅgā, Yamunā, Narmadā, Sarasvatī, Beas and

Godāvarī. Gayā is an example of an Asura *tīrtha*. Many *tīrtha*s are associated with *ṛṣis*, such as the number of places connected with the sage Kapila for different reasons (see Chapter 5). The sacred narratives about the origin of many places often contain stories about divinities and powerful ascetics, but there is a great variety of foundation myths which are more complex than the verses from the *Brahmapurāṇa* would suggest. Often, the creation stories of pilgrimage places describe how a divine power made itself known to humans so they could realize the sacredness of the place. A case in point is the discovery of the spiritual center of Vṛndāvana. In 1534, one of the Gosvāmīs, Rūpa Gosvāmī, noticed a cow shedding milk on a hillside. The hill is the *yogapīṭha*, the place for the union of Kṛṣṇa and Rādhā. He dug at the spot and unearthed the black stone figure of Kṛṣṇa as Govinda, the protector of cows, and a temple was built on the site (Case 2000: 98). Which came first, the sacredness of the place or the narratives of the divine manifestation, is often difficult to decide, but in many cases the traditions of pilgrimage to places seem to be older than the particular sacred narratives and the deities attached to them today. Sacred narratives might change according to the groups or religious traditions (*sampradāya*) that dominate the pilgrimage places.

The origin of South Asian pilgrimage traditions and the Vedic traditions

While the origin of Hinduism is usually traced to developments in the Vedic tradition, although influenced by a number of other traditions, it is of significance that there seems to be agreement among most researchers who have done *critical* research on Hindu pilgrimage that pilgrimage was a non-existent institution in the Vedic tradition (Bharati 1963) and that there is no textual evidence of pilgrimage in the Vedas (Bharati 1970). Surinder M. Bhardwaj thinks, however, that two elements of Hindu pilgrimage, the merit of travel and reverence for rivers, are continuities from the Vedic times (Bhardwaj 1973: 4). In the early Vedic tradition, though, both gods and humans are continuously on the move, but being on the move is not in itself pilgrimage. Pilgrimage traditions are absent in the Veda, but the praising of rivers as holy and purifying and as deities to be worshipped is found (*Ṛgveda* 7.47.49, 10.9.4; *Taittirīya Saṃhitā* 4.5.11.1–2, 6.1.1.1–2; *Atharvavaveda* 6.24.1–3, 19.10.8). The *avabhṛta* bath at a ford (*tīrthe snāti*) at the conclusion of a Vedic sacrifice is mentioned in *Taittirīya Saṃhitā* (6.1.1.1–2). Reverence for rivers and worship of them as deities is of course one important aspect of Hindu notions of salvific space and pilgrimage, but reverence for rivers does not in itself constitute pilgrimage rituals or the establishment of individual sacred sites. Even though the word *tīrtha* appears in the *Ṛgveda*, it is not used in the sense of a sacred site and object of pilgrimage. *Tīrtha* in the *Ṛgveda* meant way and path (1.69.6, 1.173.11, 4.29.3) and high bank of a river (8.47.11, 146.8) (Kane 1973), but not a pilgrimage place.

The idea of *tīrtha* can in one sense be thought of as an extension of the practice of seeing divinity in nature, and the ability of seeing divinity in nature is an important presupposition of Hindu pilgrimage conceptions of the salvific power of places and rewards for visiting them. But reverence for nature does not in itself explain the move in the Hindu tradition to ascribe salvific power to geographical places, the claim that the rewards of those visiting such places are superior to the rewards attained by Vedic sacrifices, and the extraordinary geographical and ritual expansion of the pilgrimage traditions. No doctrine in the early Vedic tradition stated that particular sites in nature were enduringly filled with sacred power, since in the Vedas there is no conception of sacredness attached permanently to particular places. One important reason for this absence of a doctrine of salvific power of place is that the Vedic gods were not connected to places. The gods of the Vedic tradition did not inhabit specific places and they had no clear links with any specific location. The implication of this fact is that "there can be no question of pilgrimage in the Vedas. To go on pilgrimage you must have somewhere to go!" (Angot 2009: 48). The Vedic religion and the Vedic gods were, therefore, placeless. They preferred open space and did not like locations (ibid.: 63). Significantly, in the Vedas, hardly any sites or locations are mentioned. Personal names abound in the Vedic texts, but there is an almost total absence of place names. In the whole of the Veda, there are just a few places mentioned. "In all of the extensive Vedic literature," Michel Angot notes, "you never come across a sentence 'He went to X' where X would be the name of a place" (ibid.: 52). This is quite remarkable and points to a fundamental difference between the religion of the Vedas and the religion of the earliest Hindu pilgrimage texts. In the *Brāhmaṇa* texts, there are many questions and answers of when it is right and most effective to perform an act, but there is no mention of where an act should take place (ibid.: 54). The vocabulary in the Vedas reflects the high value given to the movement and travel of the gods, and the religion of the Veda reveals that the composers of the *Saṃhitās* were nomads, or nomads who slowly became settled. The gods in the Vedic religion were also "nomads," permanently on the move and were, therefore, not connected to particular places. One reason the most central Vedic gods, such as Indra, Agni, Varuṇa, Mitra or Yama, did not become the great gods of Hinduism (Viṣṇu played a minor role in the Veda, and Śiva developed from several traditions, one of which was the Ṛgvedic Rudra) was perhaps because "the mobility of the Vedic gods and the fact that they were not fixed in the locations and the lands of 'Indian' society might have counted against them" (ibid.: 91). Indeed, one major difference between Vedic religion and Hinduism is that, in the Vedic religion, gods were not tied to locations, while in Hinduism the gods are localized and their most powerful manifestations are attached to particular localities.

The rituals of salvific space and the belief in the ability of gods to be fixed in particular locations are important factors in explaining the religious changes that transformed the Vedic tradition into the religion of the Epics and Purāṇas. The great gods of Hinduism are connected to places and many of them have particularly powerful forms that are identified with specific sites, such as Kāśī Viśvanāth in Vārāṇasī, Jagannāth in Purī and Veṅkaṭeśvara in Tirupati, and so on. The city of Vārāṇasī is also named Avimukta, which means "never abandoned (by Śiva)," meaning that Śiva is always located there; he is never absent, his presence is absolutely permanent. Even when the world dissolves between the periods of creation,

Vārāṇasī does not disappear, so even during the time of world dissolution, Śiva, with his wife, Pārvatī, stays at this place, according to the traditions that promote Vārāṇasī as a pilgrimage place. The popularity of the great gods of Hinduism might very well have been caused by their association to particular localities, which gave them material, powerful presences, and the festival culture that developed at the sites. The contrast between these Hindu gods who have permanent presence in particular, powerful forms at specific sites and the placelessness of the Vedic gods is striking and makes it difficult to support a view that traditions of salvific space and pilgrimage should have its roots in Vedic religion.

Some researchers have nevertheless suggested that there is a possible Vedic forerunner for the Hindu *tīrtha* ritual, the Vedic ritual *sarasvatīsattra* – a ritual that involves a journey along the river Sarasvatī (Oberlies 1995). This would make Hindu pilgrimage traditions an extension of pastoral nomadism, of the nomadic practices of moving with their animals for pasture. The ritual journey was supposed to start where the river Sarasvatī disappeared into the earth and move upstream to the source at Plakṣa Prāsravaṇa. It implies a journey in which the place of the sacrifice is moved everyday in an easterly direction. The movement eastward perhaps had a symbolic meaning of moving towards an afterlife in heaven (ibid.). Hindu pilgrimage is usually to a particular place, but there are also pilgrimage traditions that do have some similarity with *sarasvatīsattra*, although they are not identical, such as the pilgrimage around the Narmadā river. The Narmadā pilgrim is a circumambulatory (*pradakṣiṇā*, *parikrama*) ritual that starts at Amarkaṇṭak at the source of the Narmadā (but people today start the *parikrama* from many places along the river) and heads towards the ocean; having reached the ocean, the pilgrimage continues towards Amarkaṇṭak on the other bank of the river, but the pilgrims do not perform sacrifice. There is no movement towards an afterlife in heaven but a circumambulation that, in principle, can be repeated. A few persons perform this pilgrimage several times. The influence of the *sarasvatīsattra* on the later circumambulation pilgrimage of sacred rivers is of course difficult to evaluate. There are also Hindu pilgrimages to the sources of rivers such as Yamunā and Gaṅgā. That there is some similarity with the Vedic ritual of *sarasvatīsattra*, a ritual which involved traveling along the Sarasvatī river, and Hindu pilgrimage travel cannot be denied, as both rituals involve travel, but the differences between most Hindu pilgrimages and *sarasvatīsattra* are also striking. Most Hindu pilgrimage places and pilgrimage texts emphasize the arrival at the site, not the travel. The salvific space is emphasized, rather than the journey *per se*. The pilgrimage of Baladeva described in *Mahābhārata* 9.34–9.53 (*Baladevatīrthayātrāparvan*, see below) is a pilgrimage along the Sarasavatī river and the argument that the literary description seems to have been modeled on the Vedic ritual of *sarasvatīsattra*, a ritual the author of this text seems to have known about, seems convincing (Bigger 2001; Oberlies 1995). However, the concept of pilgrimage and vocabulary of *tīrtha* and *tīrthayātrā* may have been added, since what is described in the *Baladevatīrthayātrāparvan* differs from the later pilgrimages. As described in the *Mahābhārata*, this is a procession in which a large number of people walk together led by hundreds of Brahmans, and the description focuses on lavish offerings of wealth and cows to Brahmans and ascetics at the pilgrimage places and the performance of daily sacrifices. The focus is on conspicuous gift-ing, economic redistribution, sacrifice and procession. S. Einoo has suggested that the *sarasvatīsattra* was "a ritualization of cattle rearing" (Einoo 2001: 617) and that it had nothing to do with pilgrimage, and Andreas Bigger has admitted that in the references to *sarasvatīsattra* (in *Taittirīya Saṃhitā* 7.2.1; *Jaiminīya Brāhmaṇa* 2.297–299) there are no *tīrtha*s in the classical meaning of the term (ibid.: 158). Another possible interpretation is that it described the expansion of the Vedic sacrificial rituals along a river. However, Catherine Ludvik (2007) argues that the description in the *Baladevatīrthayātrāparvan* of the *Mahābhārata* is an expansion of the description of *Pañcaviṃśa Brāhmaṇa* 25.10 and that the *sarasvatīsattra* in the *Brāhmaṇas* is "a kind of Sarasvatī pilgrimage" (ibid.: 87), and Bigger is convinced that:"das *sarasvatīsattra* einer der Vorläufer der klassischen *tīrthayātrā* ist, auch wenn man Entwicklungsstufen zwischen *sarasvatīsattra* und *tīrthayātrā* nicht mehr rekonstruiren kann" ("the *sarasvatīsattra* was one of the precursors to the classical *tīrtayātrā*, even if the stages of development between the *sarasvatīsattra* and *tīrthayātrā* can not be reconstructed" [2001: 158]). Bigger argues that the *sarasvatīsattra* served as a model for the description of Baladeva's pilgrimage in the *Śalyaparvan*. Another possibility is to argue that, when the rituals of pilgrimage and salvific space became part of the Hindu traditions, they were adapted to and were attempted to be understood in terms of Vedic sacrificial ideas, which so often happened with innovations and influences from other traditions on the Brahmanical tradition (Jacobsen and Smart 2006). The salvific rewards of pilgrimage are most often compared to the rewards of sacrifices, which they are also said to supersede. Some Brahmans, and perhaps those Brahmans that became the ritual specialists of *tīrtha* and *tīrthayātrā,* may have wanted to emphasize the continuity of the pilgrimage ritual with the Vedic tradition. This would be important for making pilgrimage orthodox and for the status and prestige of the priests involved in pilgrimage.

The *sarasvatīsattra* could possibly be interpreted as one Vedic influence on the Hindu pilgrimage tradition. In an interesting study of pilgrimage in the *Mahābhārata,* Yaroslav Vassilkov states that he would prefer to speak "not about the 'Vedic source' of the Hindu practice, but rather about common survivals of the archaic Indo-Aryan and IE [Indo-European] mythical cosmology patterns both in Vedic rituals and in Hindu pilgrimage practice" (2002: 134–135). His conclusion, however, is that "there is no trace of any kind of pilgrimage in the Vedas" (ibid.). So, although the argument has been made that *sarasvatīsattra* is a precursor to Hindu pilgrimage, this view does not have the unanimous support of researchers. It is also notable that Hindu pilgrimage in other contexts in the *Mahābhārata* is presented as a ritual for those who cannot afford the sacrifices; a ritual that is also the opposite of the *sarasvatīsattra* and includes a critique of the sacrifice (see pp. 51–53).

Vassilkov suggests another source for the Hindu pilgrimage tradition and gives an interesting interpretation of an early Vedic passage (*Kauṣītaki Brāhmaṇa* 12.1.8–14), which says that "the Rākṣasas, confounders of the sacrifice, used to watch the waters at the fords (*sma . . . tīrtheṣvapo gopāyanti*), . . . whosoever came to the waters they killed them all." He suggests that the Rākṣasas here represent non-Vedic people who controlled the fords and supported popular rituals before they were brahmanized. He also points to the view of E. W. Hopkins that pilgrimage was recognized but not approved by the early Vedic texts, which admitted only the efficacy of sacrifice at a holy place. The Vedic worship of sacred rivers was limited to the performance of Vedic sacrifices on their banks and their confluences. It was only later that the Vedic tradition accepted the pilgrimage tradition in which belief in the purifying power of water was a central element, argues Vassilkov (2002: 135).

Salvific space is the idea that particular places have divine and salvational power. For those not settled at these places, visiting them involves travel. Hindu pilgrimage traditions are about the salvific power of particular places. The origin of traditions of salvific space and pilgrimage seems, therefore, probably to be sought in the idea of a permanent presence of salvific power at particular places.

The Indus Valley Civilization, pre-Vedic India and pilgrimage

While there is an almost general agreement among researchers that the concept of salvific space and the ritual of pilgrimage in India did not have its origin in the Vedic tradition, some arguments have been presented that pilgrimage was a tradition of the Indus civilization and the pre-Vedic cultures of India (Bharati 1963; Ensink 1974; Parpola 2003). One argument in favor of perceiving the origin of Hindu pilgrimage in the Indus civilization is presented by Vassilkov (2002). The argument is interesting, but speculative. Vassilkov suggests that the practice of pilgrimage was perhaps widespread in the Indus Valley civilization and proposes that the most widespread type of artifacts in the Indus civilization, the seal impressions, were associated with pilgrimage (ibid.: 133). They were, he suggests, tokens certifying pilgrims' visits and donations given to temples (ibid.: 133–134). This is a fascinating argument and a suggestive theory, but it is difficult to evaluate since the written language of the Indus civilization is not known and, therefore, such interpretations cannot be confirmed. Vassilkov supports his argument by referring to the similar use of tokens associated with pilgrimage in other ancient cultures.

The majority of Hindu pilgrimage places have been and continue to be associated with water. Many of the main Hindu pilgrimage places are along rivers, and the places where rivers meet are especially sacred. A lot of sacred places are next to lakes and a few are also close to the ocean. The temples that are pilgrimage places often have pools or wells for taking baths or for providing holy water for the rituals. Ritual bathing is often a central element of a pilgrimage. At many *tīrtha*s, there has been worship of *nāga*s, divine serpents thought to be associated with the subterranean water world. These *nāga*s were pre-Vedic and there might be a connection between the *nāga*s and pilgrimage places and the Indus civilization (see Vassilkov 2002). Vassilkov refers to interpretations of archaeological remains in Bihar from 3000 BCE that archaeologists interpret as *nāga* worship. This argument implies that pilgrimage traditions were part of the pre-Vedic cultures of India which continued to flourish alongside the traditions of the Vedic cultures. At some point in time, some Brahmans decided to make pilgrimage to these places of worship part of their ritual traditions as well.

Asko Parpola has argued that the Hindu pilgrimage tradition developed from the Indus civilization and that the *avabhṛta* bath, a marginal phenomenon in the Vedic tradition, was an influence from the Indus civilization. Parpola writes:

> the *avabhṛta* bath and the few references to it being performed on the banks of sacred rivers are relatively marginal aspects of the Vedic religion. The enormous popularity of the *tīrthayātrā* in later Hinduism would be difficult to comprehend if one assumes that it developed from the Vedic religion alone. On the contrary, this later popularity rather suggests that the Vedic religion got the *avabhṛta* bath from an earlier South Asian religion where the *tīrtha* cult occupied an important position. . . . There is indeed good reason to assume that the *tīrtha* cult goes back to the Harappan religion, for water and bathing clearly played a very important role in the Indus Civilization.
>
> (Parpola 2003: 525)

Parpola presents a philological argument and argues that some of the most important terms associated with Hindu pilgrimage, such as *ghāṭ* (bathing place, steps leading down to a bathing place), *kuṇḍa* (sacred pond, bathing place) and *tīrtha* were in their origin Dravidian terms (Parpola 2003).The Pāli term *titthakara* (Sanskrit: *tīrthaṅkara*) is used derogatorily as a founder of a sect but is also used in a positive sense and "appears to have been originally an honorific (rather than pejorative) title of the leading ascetics of all religious orders" (ibid.: 542). In the Hindu traditions, the term *tīrtha* is used not only for places, but also for good qualities and for venerable persons, such as in the *Manusmṛti* 3.130 in the sense of "a person worthy of receiving religious gifts or offerings" (ibid.: 542). Parpola suggests that:

> the *tīrtha* cult of Hinduism may well represent the basic and more "primitive" background in which "heterodox" religious systems of the Jaina, Buddhist and other ascetic orders too developed. I would be inclined to think that *tīrthakara-* is more original than *tīrthaṅkara–* "maker of fords", . . . so *tīrthakara* may have originally meant "one who frequents sacred bathing places, one who abides at a *tīrtha*."
>
> (ibid.: 543–544)

Parpola seems to suggest that one important source for the later Hindu pilgrimage was travel to visit the holy ascetics living at these places, *tīrtha* dwellers. For Jainism, *tīrtha* is not a bathing place but a religious title and visit to *tīrtha*s means also visit to places associated with the *tīrthaṅkara*s, as well as the living ascetic community. Parpola suggests that *tīrthakara* could be a borrowing from early Dravidian for a holy man. These are intriguing suggestions. In Jainism, "every locale that 'hosts' an eminent monk or nun is capable of becoming a holy place"

(McCormick 1997: 236). This is especially the case during the four months of the monsoon season when the monks stop wandering and reside with lay people and become the focus of local religious activities. This might develop into pilgrimage (ibid.). The development of Buddhist pilgrimage to the places associated with the life of the Buddha seems to be an extension of this idea of pilgrimage, travel to where the salvific power of ascetics is present. The presence of ascetics is a dominant feature at many Hindu pilgrimage places. According to Parpola's suggestions, one reason for travel on pilgrimage would be the merit associated with visiting ascetics, the dwellers at *tīrtha*s.

A number of the places of pilgrimage described in the *Mahābhārata* are associated with *nāga*s, *yakṣa*s and *yakṣī*s/*yakṣinī*s. The connection between *nāga*s, *yakṣa*s, *yakṣī*s/*yakṣinī*s and *tīrtha*s is intriguing. The pilgrimage tradition was probably influenced by a tradition associated with pre-Vedic divine beings, such as *nāga*s and *yakṣa*s, beings identified with owning and guarding specific territory (Eck 1981: 334; Kessler 2009). The *yakṣa*s and *yakṣī*s/*yakṣinī*s were likewise worshipped as guardians at several pilgrimage places, such as Kurukṣetra, also after the places had become identified with narratives of Hindu gods. Some *yakṣa*s were also transformed into Hindu divinities and sages. The worship of *yakṣa*s reached its peak under the Maurya empire, which also saw the expansion of Buddhism and Buddhist sacred space. In the descriptions of pilgrimage in the *Mahābhārata*, *yakṣa*s, *yakṣī*s/*yakṣinī*s and *nāga*s are associated with territory. The *yakṣa* Macakruka owns a lake at the border of Kurukṣetra and is recognized as the mighty gatekeeper of that country. When a person goes there, even if it is only in thought, all his evil deeds disappear and he will obtain the reward equal to the gift of 1, 000 cows, but especially when he salutes the *yakṣa* Macakruka states the *Mahābhārata* (*Mahābhārata* 3.81.7, 3.81.178). In the *Mahābhārata*, the *yakṣa*s, "as *kṣetrapāla*s ('protectors of the field') or *dvārapāla*s ('door guardians'), are signposts on the pilgrimage trail and guardians of ancient, sanctified grounds and pools" (Sutherland 1991: 121–122).

*Nāga*s and *yakṣī*s/*yakṣinī*s are divine beings associated with sites which they guard. The worship of them, therefore, is bound to places. There was probably a close relationship with the worship of *nāga*s and *yakṣī*s/*yakṣinī*s and the idea of sacred places – that is, of sacred power associated with places. The *nāga*s and *yakṣī*s/*yakṣinī*s were guardians of treasures thought to be hidden at the sites. Thus, there were invisible riches at the sites. We have here, therefore, the idea of divine power of place and invisible treasures being available there. Diana Eck, who underplays the radical newness of gods and goddesses being permanently present at localities and instead interprets *tīrtha*s in continuation with ideas of Vedic sacrificial religion and Upaniṣadic philosophy of "crossing" (Eck 1981), nevertheless admits that the *tīrtha*s are also grounded in the tradition of *yakṣī*s/*yakṣinī*s, *nāga*s and other non-Vedic divinities of place. *Yakṣa*s, *nāga*s, *gaṇa*s and *mātṛkā*s, she writes:

> were associated with groves and pools, hillocks and villages. Many of the deepest roots of India's traditions of pūjā and *tīrthayātrā* are here in this

> place-oriented cultus. Although the myths associated with these places have changed, layering one upon the other through centuries, pilgrims have continued to come with their vows and petitions, seeking the sight (*darśana*) and tokens of blessings (*prasāda*) of the deity of place.
>
> (Eck 1981: 334)

The contrast between the placelessness of the Vedic gods and the territory-based *nāga*s, *yakṣa*s and *yakṣī*s/*yakṣinī*s is significant. The hidden treasures of the places seem to connect also to the salvific rewards present at the Hindu places of pilgrimage, and the idea of salvific power of place may perhaps be connected to the earlier idea of such hidden treasures. The salvific power of a site is in some ways similar to its hidden treasure, and the rewards of heaven, a good rebirth or *mokṣa* can perhaps be understood as extensions of this idea.

An important feature at some sacred places is devotion to natural phenomena, such as trees, which are said to be immortal (at *tīrtha*s such as Gayā, Prayāg and Purī), and mountains, which are circumambulated in rituals (for instance, the mountains Govardhana, Aruṇācalam and Citrakūṭa). In such tree or mountain worship, it is perhaps possible to discover ancient tribal traditions older than the Hindu traditions that overlay them. Possibly some of the importance of the place was the worship of the tree or the mountain, and the places were then redefined as centers of Hindu gods. That the statues of Kṛṣṇa, Balarāma and Subhadrā in Purī, according to the foundation stories, were fashioned from a tree cut down by the king on the orders of the gods refers perhaps to such ritual takeover of the place.

Mahābhārata and the beginning of the textual tradition of pilgrimage

The earliest pilgrimage texts in Hinduism are found in the *Mahābhārata* (400 BCE–400 CE).[2] The pilgrimage texts in the *Mahābhārata*, especially the lengthy *Tīrthayātrāparvan,* are the earliest descriptions of pilgrimage places in Hindu texts and provided a pattern for the subsequent genre of pilgrimage texts (*Sthalapurāṇa*s, *Māhātmya*s). The largest pilgrimage texts in the Hindu traditions are found in the *Purāṇa*s, but these pilgrimage texts are often based on the same principles as the texts in the *Mahābhārata*. In the *Mahābhārata*, we get the first descriptions of the popular culture of pilgrimage, particularly to places of water, and of the purifying ritual role of the sacred bath and the worship of divine beings whose presence at the *tīrthas* is an important reason for the sacredness of the places. The *tīrtha* sections of the *Mahābhārata* probably belong to the most recent layers of the text – that is, from around 200 to 400 CE, the period around the beginning of Gupta empire (320–550 CE). *Tīrtha* sections were probably inserted into the text, and older narratives of travel were most likely also transformed into pilgrimage travel. The erotic adventures of Arjuna in *Ādiparvan* are presented in a pilgrimage framework, but the pilgrimage context of his exploits has perhaps been added to the story. The focus of the story is erotic adventure, not salvific purification. By including the *Tīrthayātrāparvan* to the *Āraṇyakaparvan*, the exile in the forest of the *Āraṇyakaparvan* was transformed into a pilgrimage, a meaning that was perhaps also added.

It is significant that in the *Mahābhārata*, in the *Āraṇyakaparvan* (*Vanaparvan*), it is a fully developed pilgrimage tradition that is presented, with a large number of pilgrimage places being described. The *Mahābhārata* is the first Hindu text that presents pilgrimage traditions but it is not a tradition in the making; rather, it is a complete tradition that is portrayed. Pilgrimage traditions, therefore, seem to have flourished for some time before they were described in the written records. This probably meant that, at the time of the final redaction of the *Mahābhārata*, assuming that the main pilgrimage texts in the *Mahābhārata* were composed at this very late stage of the editing of the text, a vibrant and geographically widespread pilgrimage tradition existed. The text might of course also have continued to influence and popularize the idea of salvific space and the rituals of pilgrimage, but it seems reasonable to assume that the tradition did not start with the *Mahābhārata*, and that the *Mahābhārata* depicted existing traditions of pilgrimage. The pilgrimage texts were probably partly based on oral traditions told or sung by bards (*sūta*s) or Brahmans at the *tīrtha*s and were subsequently inserted into the text (see Vassilkov 2002: 149).

The longest of the pilgrimage texts of the *Mahābhārata* is the *Tīrthayātrāparvan* of the *Āraṇyakaparvan* (*Vanaparvan*) (Chapters 78–148). The other major pilgrimage chapters are in the *Śalyaparvan* (Chapters 35–54) and the *Anuśāsanaparvan* (Chapters 25–26), but there are a number of other shorter texts that describe pilgrimage travel, such as in the *Ādiparvan* (Chapters 206–210), the *Udyogaparvan* (Chapter 187), the *Mahāprasthanikaparvan* and the *Svargārohaṇikaparvan* (*pṛthivīpradakṣiṇā* and *mahāprasthāna*). *Ādiparvan* (Chapters 206–210), as already mentioned, focuses on Arjuna's erotic adventures at certain places as part of a journey and might originally have described travel and not pilgrimage. A full list of every mention of the *tīrtha*s and pilgrimage in the *Mahābhārata* has been collected in Vassilkov (2002), and the list shows that some verses on pilgrimage are found in almost all of the 18 books (the exceptions are Books 6, 10 and 14). However, two types of pilgrimage texts in the *Mahābhārata* can perhaps be distinguished – promotion texts and description texts. Promotion texts center on the rewards of pilgrimage, while description texts describe persons on a journey identified as pilgrimage, focusing instead on the activities of the protagonists rather than the rewards. The focus on the description texts is on the persons as part of a larger narrative. Promotion texts are probably composed for the sake of attracting pilgrims to a place, perhaps by bards (*sūta*s) who were wandering with pilgrims and by the Brahmans serving the place and attaining their income from it, and point to the presence of the full institution of pilgrimage. The promotion texts show that pilgrimage had become an important institution. The later pilgrimage texts are generally promotion texts.

The difference between the *tīrtha* texts of the *Āraṇyakaparvan* and *Śalyaparvan* is striking. The *Āraṇyakaparvan* states that pilgrimage is the poor man's ritual, while the *Śalyaparvan* describes a kingly procession whose main function seems to be the redistribution of wealth. Two different rituals seem, in fact, to be described. *Āraṇyakaparvan* states:

> *na te śakyā daridreṇa yajñāḥ prāptuṃ mahīpate*
> *bahūpakaraṇā yajñā nānāsaṃbhāravistarāḥ.*
> *prāpyante pārthivair ete samṛddhair vā naraiḥ kva cit*
> *nārthanyūnopakaraṇair ekātmabhir asaṃhataiḥ.*
> *yo daridrair api vidhiḥ śakyaḥ prāptuṃ nareśvara*
> *tulyo yajñaphalaiḥ puṇyais taṃ nibodha yudhāṃ vara.*
> *ṛṣīṇāṃ paramaṃ guhyam idaṃ bharatasattama*
> *tīrthābhigamanaṃ puṇyaṃ yajñair api viśiṣyate.*

> A poor man cannot obtain the fruits of sacrifices, O king, for they require many implements and a great variety of ingredients. Kings can perform them and sometimes rich people, not individuals lacking in means and implements and not helped by others. But hear, O King, of the practice accessible even to the poor, which equals the salvific rewards of sacrifices (*tulyo yajñaphalaiḥ puṇyais*). This is the secret of the sages, O King, the meritorious practice of visiting *tīrtha*s (*tīrthābhigamana*), which even excels the sacrifices.
> (*Mahābhārata* 3.80.35–38).

Claiming something as a secret is often a way to attempt to get legitimacy for a new teaching. This description can be compared to a description of Baladeva, the brother of Kṛṣṇa, moving with his entourage in the procession described in the *Śalyaparvan*. Preparing for his pilgrimage ritual, Baladeva ordered his servants to:

> Bring all things that are necessary for a pilgrimage . . . Bring gold, silver, kine, robes, steeds, elephants, cars, mules, camels, and other draft cattle. Bring all these necessaries for a trip to the sacred waters, and proceed with great speed towards the Sarasvatī. Bring also some priests to be especially employed, and hundreds of foremost Brahmans . . . he visited all the sacred places along her course, accompanied by priests, friends, and many foremost Brahmans, as also with cars and elephants and steeds and servants, O bull of Bharata's race, and with many vehicles drawn by kine and mules and camels. Diverse kinds of necessaries of life were given away, in large measures and in diverse countries unto the weary and worn, children and old, in response, O king, to solicitations. . . . At the command of Rohinī's son, men, at different stages of the journey, stored food and drink in great quantities. Costly garments and bedsteads and coverlets were given for the gratification of Brahmans, desirous of ease and comfort. Whatever Brahman or *kṣatriya* solicited whatever thing, that O Bharata, was seen as ungrudgingly given to him. . . . That chief of Yadu's race also gave away thousands of milch cows covered with excellent cloths and having their horns cased in gold, many steeds belonging to different countries, many vehicles and many beautiful slaves.
> (Translation by K. M. Ganguli, modified, *Śalyaparvan*, 97–98)

The Hindu pilgrimage tradition is connected to the ritual of gift giving. In the descriptions of pilgrimage places in the *Mahābhārata,* gift giving to Brahmans is mentioned repeatedly as a way for the pilgrims to accumulate more merit. The most important acts at the *tīrtha*s seem to be gifts to the Brahmans and the ritual contact with purifying water. Giving of considerable wealth to the Brahmans at the pilgrimage sites and the sites' ability to grant the pilgrims fruition of every wish seem to be related. Giving money and other valuables to Brahmans at the *tīrtha*s is promoted in the texts of the Hindu pilgrimage tradition. However, what is described in the *Śalyaparvan* is obviously not the poor man's ritual pointed at in the *Āraṇyakaparvan*. The travel described in *Śalyaparvan* seems to be a procession ritual of redistribution of wealth and conspicuous gifting. It is also notable that, in the *Śalyaparvan* chapters, we are told about the performance of sacrifices on the *tīrtha*s (*Śalyaparvan*, Chapter 41), while in the *Āraṇyakaparvan* pilgrimage is presented as an alternative to the sacrifice ("a poor man cannot obtain the fruits of sacrifices, O king, for they require many implements and a great variety of ingredients"). The *Śalyaparvan* focuses on the sites, the narratives and the gifting, but not on the rewards of the individual sites, in contrast to the *Āraṇyakaparvan*, which focuses on the rewards of visiting the individual sites.

The *Tīrthayātrāparvan* of the *Āraṇyakaparvan* is a promotion text of the pilgrimage places. The text advertises pilgrimages and visits to the sites by focusing on uncomplicated rituals and the great rewards of visiting the place. The texts of the *Tīrthayātrāparvan* of the *Mahābhārata* are strikingly similar in form to the later genre of *tīrtha* texts and seem to have initiated a whole genre of texts. This genre of texts has been produced for 1, 500 years and dominates the *Purāṇa*s. Pilgrimage and the promotion of salvific space were perhaps important reasons for the flourishing of the text category of *Purāṇa*s. A larger number of places have been included and there has been a growth in the length of the descriptions of the individual places. That the *Māhātmya*s of place as found in the *Purāṇa*s or circulating as independent texts have similarities to the *Tīrthayātrāparvan* in the *Mahābhārata* indicates that, by the time of the composition of the later parts of the *Mahābhārata*, traditions of sacred sites and pilgrimage had become part of the Brahmanical ritual system. Traditions of sacred sites have probably existed outside of Brahmanical ritual tradition before their inclusion in the *Mahābhārata*. Their inclusion in the *Mahābhārata* means that narratives of sacred sites and their salvific rewards had become part of the ritual complex of Brahman priests who made a living by performing rituals for the pilgrims at the sites.

The *Tīrthayātrāparvan* starts with Pulastya answering questions about the awards (*phala*) of pilgrimage. Yudhiṣṭhira asked Nārada: "If a person makes a circumambulation of the earth to visit pilgrimage places, what award does he get? Tell me in full, Brahman!" (*pradakṣiṇaṃ yaḥ kurute pṛthivīṃ tīrthatatparaḥ, kiṃ phalaṃ tasya kārtsnyena tad brahman vaktum arhasi* [3.80.10]). Nārada then related what answer Pulastya gave Bhīṣma when he lived as an ascetic on the bank of the Gaṅgā and asked Pulastya a similar question: *pradakṣiṇaṃ yaḥ pṛthivīṃ karoty amitavikrama, kiṃ phalaṃ tasya viprarṣe tan me brūhi tapodhana* (a person who makes a circumambulation of the earth to visit pilgrimage places, Brahman of unbounded valor, what award does he get, tell me that ascetic! [3.80.28]). Pulastya begins his answer to Bhīṣma by stating that he will talk of the rewards (*phala*) of pilgrimage. The text emphasizes the idea of salvific space, with stress on the fruits of visiting the places. This is typical of the promotion texts. The contrast with the *tīrtha* text in the *Śalyaparvan* is noteworthy. The *Śalyaparvan* text starts by highlighting the gifts given to the Brahmans. The focus in the *Śalyaparvan* text seems to be on the redistribution of wealth, but the *Tīrthayātrāparvan* of the *Āraṇyakaparvan,* on the other hand, reads as a series of advertisements for pilgrimage places. The topic, it seems, of the *Tīrthayātrāparvan* is on a particular aspect of pilgrimage, the rewards of visiting the places – that is, the salvific power of place. The stated purpose is not to give a description of the route, but a description of the rewards (*phala*) of pilgrimage. The text then describes some of the presuppositions for attaining the rewards, again emphasizing that the rewards of pilgrimage are the focus. Pulastya describes ascetical values, such as control of the senses and being content, restrained, without selfishness, free from vices, without anger, truthful and seeing oneself in all beings. Pulastya explains that the salvific power of place is the same as the rewards of sacrifices (*tulyo yajñaphalaiḥ puṇyais* [3.80.38]), but that going (*abhigamana*) to *tīrtha*s also surpasses them (*ṛṣīṇāṃ paramaṃ guhyam idaṃ bharatasattama, tīrthābhigamanaṃ puṇyaṃ yajñair api viśiṣyate* [Going to sacred places which even surpasses the sacrifices is the greatest secret of the seers], 3.80.39). Pilgrimage is a ritual that is available to poor persons, the texts says, and the poor attains rewards that the rich do not attain, not even by their sacrifices. The comparison and the statement that pilgrimage surpasses sacrifice perhaps points to a rivalry between two types of priests – those involved with sacrifice and recitation of the Vedas and those involved in pilgrimage rituals (see the section Temples and *Tirtha*s below). Thereafter, the text starts presenting the individual pilgrimage places, but the places themselves are mostly not described in great detail. The emphasis is on the rewards. A common pattern is that the places are named, the story that explains its salvific power is told, the number of days one should stay there mentioned and the reward is described.

The first place that Pulastya promotes is Puṣkara. Several elements of the conceptions of salvific space that become important in the genre of *tīrtha* texts are already presented in this earliest text. The text starts by saying that at sunrise, midday and dawn millions and millions of pilgrimage places (*daśa koṭisahasrāṇi tīrthānāṃ* [3.80.42]) are present in Puṣkara. The statement is meant to emphasize its importance and salvific power. In other words, other pilgrimage places, *tīrtha*s, travel to Puṣkara. This is a remarkable statement and shows that, already in this early pilgrimage textual tradition, pilgrimage places were looked upon as able to move from their sites. The *tīrtha*s are thought of as having a movable form (see also *Śalyaparvan,* Chapter 45). The statement shows that there was probably a competition between the priests at the pilgrimage sites for pilgrims and pilgrim donations (*dāna*) and a conception of a hierarchy of pilgrimage places. Also, divine beings other than *tīrtha*s are present at the site Puṣkara: Adityas, Vasus, Rudras, Sādhyas, the Maruts, Gandharvas and Apsarases are always present (*adityā vasavo rudrāḥ sādhyāś ca samarudgaṇāḥ, gandharvāpsarasaś caiva nityaṃ saṃnihitā vibho* [3.80.43]) and Brahmā (*pitāmahaḥ*) also stays there. Significantly, the text says that it was by performing asceticism at Puṣkara that the many divine beings attained their divine status (*yatra devās tapas taptvā daityā brahmarṣayas tathā, divyayogā mahārāja puṇyena mahatānvitāḥ* [3.80.44]). The place is the absolute, and the divinities are dependent on it. The power of the place surpasses the power of gods. So strong is the salvific power of place in Puṣkara that by simply having the desire to go there one is freed from all moral impurity and is honored in the highest heaven (*manasāpy abhikāmasya puṣkarāṇi manasvinaḥ, pūyante sarvapāpāni nākapṛṣṭhe ca pūjyate* [3.80.45]).

The economic importance of the sacred places for the Brahman priests is also detectable in the same text on Puṣkara. Pilgrimage became an important source of income for the Brahmans and the ritual clients at the pilgrimage places probably became the most significant source for the priests associated with the pilgrims. In North India, a whole class of pilgrimage Brahmans who obtained a living from the pilgrimage traffic arose.[3] Pulastya states that the person who is devoted to gods and ancestors and carries out ablutions there attains the fruit equal to ten horse sacrifices (*aśvamedha*s). Additionally, if he feeds a single Brahman, he is rewarded in this life and in the afterlife. Even if he himself lives on only herbs, roots and fruits, if he gives that to a Brahman, he attains by that single act the fruit of a horse sacrifice. It is noteworthy how closely the rewards of bathing are connected to the rewards of giving gifts to Brahmans and the comparisons of these rewards with the rewards of sacrifice.

According to the *tīrtha* texts of the *Mahābhārata*, the rewards are: freedom from all evil, being honored in heaven, attaining the same rewards as various sacrifices as the *aśvamedha* and *agniṣṭoma*, such as going to the heaven of Viṣṇu, reaching the rank of a Gaṇapati, the award of ascending a celestial chariot (*vimāna*), attaining the fruit equal to the giving away of 1, 000 cows or 100 brown-red (*kapilā*) cows, glories in the world of heaven, gaining a lot of gold, attaining the world of Brahmā, attaining the world of Indra, and so on. The rewards at some places are unique. To give an example, bathing at the *yoni* at the place of Bhīma will ensure one will be born as the son of a goddess with earrings of gold and receive the fruit of giving away 100, 000 cows (*tato gaccheta dharmajña bhīmāyāḥ sthānam uttamam, tatra snātvā tu yonyāṃ vai naro bharatasattama* [3.80.100]; *devyāḥ putro bhaved rājaṃs taptakuṇḍalavigrahaḥ, gavāṃ śatasahasrasya phalaṃ caivāpnuyān maha* [3.80.101]).

A characteristic of the pilgrimage texts of the *Mahābhārata* is the criticism of the sacrifice. Just by visiting Puṣkara at *kārttika pūrṇimā* (full moon day of the month of kārttika [October–November]), the text states a person gains the same merit as he who performs the *agnihotra* sacrifice for 100 years (*yas tu varṣaśataṃ pūrṇam agnihotram upāsate, kārttikīṃ vā vased ekāṃ puṣkare samam eva tat* [3.80.57]). This comparison not only gives high value to pilgrimage but at the same time implies that sacrifice is more or less meaningless, since the fruit one gains for performing a costly sacrifice for 100 years can be attained in a much easier way by bathing at a pilgrimage place. The rituals that replaced the sacrifice for attaining rewards at the pilgrimage places were bathing, offerings to the ancestors, worshipping gods and feeding Brahmans. The comparison with the sacrifice can also be understood as stating that pilgrimage is Vedic. Such statements try to link pilgrimage to the Vedic tradition and to show that the pilgrimage ritual is a Vedic tradition by making the rewards of pilgrimage comparable to the rewards of sacrifice. It gives Vedic legitimacy to the pilgrimage tradition. The text states that pilgrimage is hard. Places are difficult to reach, one lives on little food, austerities and gifts are hard, but the rewards fully match the hardships.

The pilgrimage texts in the *Mahābhārata* say that the pilgrimage places are visited by gods, seers and ancestors. Also, divine beings utilize the sacred power of the sites. It is also said that the gods and the *ṛṣi*s attained perfection at the places. That the power of the sacred places is the source of the power of the gods becomes an important theme in the narratives of the salvific space. Places become the supreme powers and the gods are dependent on them. The gods also travel to pilgrimage places to get rid of moral impurity. Viṣṇu travelled to the *tīrtha* Dṛmi to clean himself of impurity after he had killed the rivals of the gods, according to the *Mahābhārata* (*jitvā yatra mahāprājña viṣṇunā prabhaviṣṇunā, purā śaucaṃ kṛtaṃ rājan hatvā daivatakaṇṭakān* [3.80.91]). At the confluence of the Sarasvatī, the gods, led by Brahmā, the seers, Siddhas and Cāraṇas go once a month to worship Janārdana (Kṛṣṇa) (*yatra brahmādayo devā ṛṣayaḥ siddhacāraṇāḥ abhigacchanti* [3.80.131]) and, presumably, become purified.

It is said about some places that visiting this particular *tīrtha* is equal to visiting all. In the lake of Miśraka, Vyāsa mixed water from all the *tīrtha*s; hence bathing in the lake at Miśraka is like bathing in all the *tīrtha*s (*tato gaccheta rājendra miśrakaṃ tīrtham uttamam, tatra tīrthāni rājendra miśritāni mahātmanā* [3.81.76]; *vyāsena nṛpaśārdūla dvijārtham iti naḥ śrutam, sarvatīrtheṣu sa snāti miśrake snāti yo naraḥ* [3.81.77]) (identified with modern Miśrik; see Figure 3.1). In a well in Svastipura, there is the equivalent of 30 million sacred places (3.81.153). At Samnihiti, all the *tīrtha*s on the earth or in the sky, male and female rivers, tanks and streams, wells, ponds and holy sanctuaries come together every month (*pṛthivyāṃ yāni tīrthāni antarikṣacarāṇi ca, nadyo nadās taḍāgāś ca sarvaprasravaṇāni ca* [3.181.168]; *udapānāś ca vaprāś ca puṇyāny āyatanāni ca, māsi māsi samāyānti saṃnihityāṃ na saṃśayaḥ* [3.181.169]). Going to one *tīrtha* is equal to visiting them all. This is a common pattern utilized in the promotion texts of many pilgrimage places.

Sacred places are often mentioned in a hierarchical manner in the *Mahābhārata*. *Mahābhārata* 3.81.125 states that it is said that Kurukṣetra is meritorious, Sarasvatī is more meritorious than Kurukṣetra, Prayāg is more meritorious than Sarasvatī, but better than Prayāg is Pṛthūdaka (*puṇyam āhuḥ kurukṣetraṃ kurukṣetrāt sarasvatīm, sarasvatyāś ca tīrthāni tīrthebhyaś ca pṛthūdakam*). *Mahābhārata* adds that it is stated in the Veda that one should go to Pṛthūdaka (*vede ca niyataṃ rājan abhigacchet pṛthūdakam* [81.127]). Even criminals (*pāpakṛta*) who bathe in Pṛthūdaka go to heaven (*tatra snātvā divaṃ yānti api pāpakṛto janāḥ* [81.129]). In 3.81.173, it is said that Naimiṣa is the most holy place on earth, Puṣkara is the most holy place in the atmosphere, but Kurukṣetra is the most sacred in the three worlds

Figure 3.1 The pool in Miśrik

Photo: Knut A. Jacobsen

(*pṛthivyāṃ naimiṣaṃ puṇyam antarikṣe ca puṣkaram, trayāṇām api lokānāṃ kurukṣetraṃ viśiṣyate*).

Places of pilgrimage are places to acquire visions of god. Pilgrimage, in other words, represents not only a change from a religion of placelessness to a religion of place, but also a change from the audible to the visible at the center of the rituals. The emphasis has moved from invisible to visible gods, from placelessness to divine sites. Pilgrimage is a religion of *darśan*, of seeing the places and their divine presence. At Rudrakoṭi, ten million seers came to see a vision of god, to see Śiva, and Śiva resorted to yoga and created a crore (ten million) of Rudras, one before each seer, so that each thought they had seen him first (*Mahābhārata* 3.80.125–128).

The general context of the *Tīrthayātrāparvan* is the rewards of pilgrimage and the text as a whole is a promotion text. But there are other texts about *tīrthayātrā* in the *Mahābhārata* that are not promotion texts – that is, they describe travel and *tīrtha*s, but do not focus on the rewards. However, the promotion text became the model for the later pilgrimage genre of texts. The other two long descriptions of *tīrtha*s in the *Mahābhārata*, the *Śalyaparvan* and the *Ādiparvan*, each have a different focus. *Śalyaparvan* focuses on places along the Sarasvatī and stories, and since in this description the pilgrims perform sacrifices at each place, the rewards are not focused upon. *Ādiparvan* (Chapters 206–210, Arjuna's *tīrthayātrā*), and also *Udyogaparvan* (Chapter 187, Princess Ambā's *tīrthayātrā*), describe pilgrimage, but do not emphasize rewards. These texts focus on narratives. *Ādiparvan*

Chapters 206–210 give an account of Arjuna's stay in the forest for one year, a punishment for having entered the room of Yudhiṣṭhira and Draupadī to fetch his weapons in order to help a Brahman whose cows were stolen by thieves. He was then consecrated to live the life of a hermit and thus went to live in the forest. However, he did not go alone; he walked in a procession with great spirited Brahmans, scholars of the Veda, philosophers and devotees, reciters, bards, storytellers, forest-dwelling hermits and Brahmans telling divine stories (*taṃ prayāntaṃ mahābāhuṃ kauravāṇāṃ yaśaḥ karam, anujagmur mahātmāno brāhmaṇā vedapāragāḥ* [1.206.1]; *vedavedāṅgavidvāṃsas tathaivādhyātma cintakāḥ, caukṣāś ca bhagavad bhaktāḥ sūtāḥ paurāṇikāś ca ye* [1.206.2]; *kathakāś cāpare rājañ śramaṇāś ca vanaukasaḥ, divyākhyānāni ye cāpi paṭhanti madhuraṃ dvijāḥ* [1.206.3]). He saw beautiful woods, lakes and *tīrtha*s and settled at the Gate of Gaṅgā (*gaṅgā dvāra*), perhaps Hardvār. The priests offered *agnihotra*s and Arjuna bathed in the river and made offerings to his ancestors. When he was about to rise up from the river to perform fire rituals, he was pulled under the water by Ulūpī, the daughter (*kanyā*) of the king of the snakes (*nāgarāja*), Kauravya. Then Arjuna saw a high-piled fire in the palace of Kauravya and performed the ritual. He laughingly asked Ulūpī about the meaning of this and who she was. She identified herself and confessed her love for him. Arjuna spent the night in the palace and the next day he continued the pilgrimage. He gave a donation of 1, 000 cows and dwellings to the Brahmans at the various *tīrtha*s. Arjuna then went to the southern ocean, "ornamented with ascetics." These ascetics avoided the five *tīrtha*s there, explaining to Arjuna that five crocodiles guarded these *tīrtha*s and that they dragged ascetics into the ocean. Arjuna went to one of these *tīrtha*s, dived into the water and a crocodile seized hold of him. However, Arjuna pulled the crocodile to the shore, whereby it transformed itself into a beautiful woman. She explained to Arjuna that she was an Apsaras. She explained that the five Apsarases fell in love with a Brahman ascetic who was studying alone in the forest, which was illuminated by the light of his austerities. The Apsarases sang and laughed and tempted him and, in anger, the Brahman condemned them to be crocodiles for 100 years. If a man could pull them out of the water, they would become Apsarases again. Arjuna then visited all the *tīrtha*s on the south and in the west, and in Prabhāsa he again met the other Pāṇḍavas and Kṛṣṇa, in whose house he stayed for many days.

The pilgrimage story in *Udyogaparvan* 187 is about Sikhaṇḍin, who was originally born a girl. He had been born in an earlier lifetime as a woman called Ambā. Bhīṣma rejected her because of his promise of celibacy and Ambā felt humiliated and wanted revenge. She performed penance for succeeding in killing Bhīṣma and was reborn as Sikhaṇḍin. Her father heard a divine voice that ordered him to raise her as a boy. On the wedding night, her wife insulted her but she was saved by a *yakṣa*, who exchanged gender with her. She bathed and did penance at a number of *tīrtha*s, one after the other. It is said that, because of her greed for *tīrtha*s (*tīrthalobhāt* [5.187.38]), she became a river in Vatsabhūmi, known as the river Ambā, with half of her body, "a mere monsoon stream, teeming with crocodiles, and with miserable fords and crooked," and the other half remained a woman (5.187.39–40).

The length of the *tīrthayātrā* texts in the *Mahābhārata* signifies that pilgrimage around this time had become an important institution. A great number of pilgrimage places distributed in a very large geographical region are described in the *Mahābhārata*. Salvific space and pilgrimage entered the Hindu texts as a complete tradition and as a tradition that is extended to a widespread geographical area. It described a development that had been ongoing for some time, perhaps a Sanskritization, or better Hinduization of older non-Vedic traditions of pilgrimage and salvific space. The *Mahābhārata* contains several pilgrimage texts, but it has been argued that the text as a whole contains elements that make it possible to see even the whole text as a pilgrimage text (Vassilkov 2002). This would mean that persons involved in the composition of the narratives at the pilgrimage sites were actively shaping the text as a whole. Vassilkov has argued that, in the *Mahābhārata*, there is evidence of a transition from performance of the text in a warrior's milieu to performance at *tīrtha*s and temples (ibid.). It is generally accepted that the *Mahābhārata* was created in the *kṣatriya* social milieu and in the oral-poetic tradition and was then taken over by Brahmans and finally put into writing. Vassilkov writes:

> In the epic's base historical layer we see, for example, the figure of the *sūta* Saṃjaya who improvises, in typical heroic poetical style, the descriptions of battle events for the king and his retinue as an audience at the royal court. But the late epic directly refers to the *sūtas* wandering together with pilgrims from one *tīrtha* to another.
>
> (ibid.: 143)

The *Mahābhārata* is of great importance as a source for understanding the transition of the religion of Vedic sacrifice to one based on *tīrtha*s, *pūjā* and temples. The full transition is found in the *Purāṇa*s, texts that seem partly to have been composed for the sake of the integration of sacred sites in the repertoire of Brahmanical rituals – that is, to secure income for the pilgrimage and temple priests (and perhaps income in the form of tax for the rulers).

Stūpas, early art and pilgrimage

The beginning of Hindu pilgrimage depends on the idea that salvific, divine power was fixed to particular sites. This permanent presence of power became marked by symbols and statues. The origin of the idea of a permanent presence of salvific power at particular sites and the origin of Hindu pilgrimage are interconnected. Buddhist pilgrimage was probably an important influence on the early Hindu traditions of pilgrimage places. They are clearly different pilgrimage traditions, although the same persons perhaps participated as ritual clients of both. The patrons were probably different – Buddhist monks and nuns in the Buddhist tradition and Brahman priests serving the Hindu sites. From the descriptions of pilgrimage and pilgrimage places in the *Mahābhārata*, it seems that many of the early Hindu pilgrimages were along rivers or lakes. Buddhist pilgrimage places, on the other hand, were at places associated with the Buddha and his relics, which were not beside rivers. Buddhist pilgrimage involved, in particular, *stūpa*s, burial monuments and places associated with the key events in the life of the Buddha. Pilgrimage described in the *Mahābhārata* is a tradition that is already well established. One reason for this might be that pilgrimage had existed for some time as a folk religion phenomenon and that it had now, for the first time, entered the Sanskrit textual tradition. The phenomenon of pilgrimage was perhaps being brahmanized; the tradition was now promoted by, and perhaps taken over by, Brahman priests. Nonetheless, what is described does not seem to be a new phenomenon; what seems to be new is the description of the phenomenon in Sanskrit.

One of the early forms of pilgrimage in South Asia, and certainly one of the early forms that can be documented, was to the Buddhist *stūpa*s. The word *tīrthayātrā* is not found in the sense of pilgrimage in the Pāli literature (Upasak 1990). In the Pāli canon, the term *cetiya-cārikā* is used for pilgrimages to sacred sites that preceded the Buddhist places, as well as pilgrimage to the places associated with the Buddha. *Dharmayātrā* later becomes a term for Buddhist pilgrimage. *Cetiya* is the name for the place where a *stūpa* of bone-relics of sacred persons stood and *cetiya-cārikā* means traveling to such *cetiya*s. There are references to Pre-Buddhist *cetiya*s in the Pāli canon. According to the Pāli scripture, Buddha himself witnessed many of these *cetiya*s. When Buddha instructed his disciples about pilgrimage to the places associated with main events in his life, he used the term *cetiya-cārikā* (*Mahāparinibbānasutta* 5.8). However, studies of inscriptions show that already at the time of Aśoka (third century BCE) Buddhists had established their own sacred sites (Schopen 1997). The most characteristic element of Buddhist sacred sites in India was the presence of a *stūpa* (Schopen 1994: 273). The Buddhist *stūpa*s were burial mounds of the relics of the Buddha, his main disciples and other persons. The Buddhist sacred sites of Lumbinī and the *stūpa* of the past Buddha Konākamana, both probably pre-Aśokan, were already centers of pilgrimage. The relics of the Buddha and the *stūpa* symbolized his presence and were objects of worship and preceded that of Buddhist image worship.

The *stūpa* was, in contrast to the placelessness of the Vedic gods, a site containing the permanent presence of sacred power. The *stūpa,* writes Romila Thapar, "was in many ways the antithesis of a Vedic sacred enclosure. Unlike the temporary sanctification of the location of an area for the sacrifice, the *stupa* was a *permanently demarcated sacred place*" (Thapar 2003: 264, italics added).The relics were meant to be seen and touched (Colas 2010: 531), and this was only possible by pilgrimage to these permanently demarcated sacred places. There was an emphasis on *darśan* of the place itself, and this *darśan* of the place implied a "direct, intimate contact with a living presence" (Schopen 1997: 117). According to Gregory Schopen, the relics were seen to represent a living presence of the person and, in the case of the Buddhist *stūpa* pilgrimage places, there was an identity between the place and the person, and "wherever there is a *stūpa* . . . there is the Buddha" (1994: 289). Schopen has also argued for a close similarity between the Hindu idea of *tīrtha*s and Buddhist *stūpa* places as living deities. When the Buddha began to be represented in statues, the Buddha image was also considered a living person, according to Schopen (1994). The idea of the living presence of the Buddha at the *stūpa* was transferred to the image, and the image of the Buddha, from around the third century CE, was considered "a kind of relic" (Colas 2010: 531). The permanent presence of the Buddha at sacred places in the form of relics or statues led to the identification of place and deity, and here there might perhaps be Buddhist influence on Hindu pilgrimage sites. The salvific power that was thought to be characteristic of the deity was identified with the site itself, and the site became salvific space. The emphasis was on *darśan* of the places as a living presence. There is a similarity of the text of the *Mahāparinibbānasutta* to the inscriptions at the Buddhist sites (Schopen 1997: 117). There was a belief that, although the Buddha could be no longer contacted after his *parinibbāna*, he was nevertheless present at the places in some way and present in the form of salvific power. At the Buddhist sites, it was the relics especially that possessed this power, but power also belonged to places, in particular where Buddha had been present. They had retained some of the same qualities as the living Buddha – morality, concentration and wisdom. The blending of the salvific power of the Buddha and the sites made sacred by his presence has some intriguing connections to the Hindu sacred sites endowed with salvific power. Could this salvific power present at the Buddhist sites have been the model for the salvific power thought to be present at Hindu *tīrtha*s or was there a parallel development? The Buddhist sites were probably established a century or more earlier than Aśoka. The confirmed evidence of inscriptions at the Buddhist sites dates from Aśokan times and is earlier than the *tīrtha* texts of the *Mahābhārata*. The Buddhist pilgrimage seems to have been well established before the Hindu pilgrimage. The sudden expansion of Hindu pilgrimage places in the *Tīrthayātrāparvan,* which encompasses large parts of India, could perhaps be a textual manifestation of the response to the expansion of Buddhist pilgrimage.

The textual evidence of Buddhist pilgrimage is also earlier than the Hindu pilgrimage texts. In the Pāli canon, in the *Mahāparinibbānasutta* of the *Dīghanikāya*, the *sutta* about the last days of the Buddha, the famous instructions for Buddhist pilgrimage are found (in *Dīghanikāya* 2.140.7–8). Buddhist pilgrimage has its origin, perhaps, in the Buddha himself. In this story of the *Dīghanikāya*, Ānanda explains that the monks used to come and see the Buddha after the rainy season, during which they had spent time in different districts. But when he was no more, he would "not be able to receive those very reverend brethren to audience." Buddha then explained that people should come to pay homage to four inspiring places (*saṃvejanī ṭhānāni*) with the same emotional fervor that they displayed to the Buddha. The four places were Lumbinī, his birth place; Bodhgayā, the place of the awakening of the Buddha; Sārnāth, where the Buddha held the first sermon (see Figure 3.2); and Kusinārā, where he attained *parinibbāna*. The monks, nuns and lay people are encouraged to go to these places and receive religious merit from visiting these places.

> There are these four places, Ānanda, which the believing human should visit with feelings of reverence. Which are the four?
>
> The place, Ānanda, at which the believing human can say: "Here the Tathāgata was born!" is a spot to be visited with feelings of reverence.

> The place, Ānanda, at which the believing human can say: "Here the Tathāgata attained to the supreme and perfect insight!" is a spot to be visited with feelings of reverence.
>
> The place, Ānanda, at which the believing human can say: "Here was the kingdom of righteousness set on foot by the Tathāgata!" is a spot to be visited with feelings of reverence.
>
> The place, Ānanda, at which the believing human can say: "Here the Tathāgata passed finally away in that utter passing away which leaves nothing whatever to remain behind!" is a spot to be visited with feelings of reverence.
>
> And there will come, Ānanda, to such spots, believers, brethren and sisters of the order and will say "Here was the Tathāgata born" or "Here the Tathāgata attained to the supreme and perfect insight!" or "Here was the kingdom of righteousness set on foot by the Tathāgata!" or "Here the Tathāgata passed away in that utter passing away which leaves nothing whatever to remain behind!"
>
> (trans. Rhys Davids, 1903: 90–91, modified)

Concluding the topic, the Buddha promises a rebirth in heaven as the reward of the pilgrimage:

> *Ye hi keci, Ānanda, cetiya-cārikaṃ āhiṇḍantā pasannacittā kālaṃ karissanti, sabbe te kāyassa bhedā param maraṇā sugatiṃ saggaṃ lokaṃ uppajjissantīti*

Figure 3.2 The stūpa in Sārnāth

Photo: Knut A. Jacobsen

> And they, Ānanda, who shall die while they, with believing heart, are journeying on such pilgrimage (*cetiya-cārikaṃ*), shall be reborn after death, when the body shall dissolve, in the happy realms of heaven.
>
> (trans. Rhys Davids, 1903: 91)

Here pilgrimage to the *stūpa*s is represented as a replacement of travel to the revered teacher of salvific knowledge. So the origin of this pilgrimage is perhaps the tradition of visiting sacred persons. This was probably an important element in the development of pilgrimage. In Jainism, lay people travel to where the monks and nuns are, and Asko Parpola (2003) has indeed argued that this travel to places where sacred persons stayed was an important element in the pilgrimage traditions. That the Buddha is stated to have said that those who made the pilgrimage and died at a sacred site will be reborn in heaven seems to express that the sites have the salvific power. At these sites, argues one researcher, "the Buddha was thought to be actually present and alive" (Schopen 1997: 126).

Some Buddhist influence on the origin of Hindu traditions of salvific space seems hard to deny, while a Hindu influence on the Buddhist tradition is more difficult to identify. A. Bharati writes:

> The desire to keep and perhaps display the Buddha's relics cannot be explained from any known Hindu precedence – nothing of the sort is mentioned in any pre-Buddhist literature. The building of memorial *stūpas* over them, following the distribution of the relics, cannot be traced to anything older – in fact, the Buddhist *stūpas* and *caityas* are the oldest instances of relic worship in India.
>
> (Bharati 1963: 152)

The emergence of the Buddhist tradition of *stūpa* worship had probably great consequences for the development of salvific space in South Asia. The Buddhist pilgrimage tradition probably encouraged the Brahmans to promote other sacred places. One reason seems to have been a Brahmanical competition with the Buddhist monks for ritual gifts. It seems likely that some of the typical characteristics of Hindu pilgrimage developed as a response to, and was influenced by, Buddhist pilgrimage. That Hindu pilgrimage gives merit equal to or superior to sacrifices might be an influence from, or response to, the Buddhist critique of the sacrifice and the popularity of Buddhist pilgrimage rituals. Under the dominance of the Śramaṇa traditions, the ritual of sacrifice was weakened and the ritual of *dāna* became dominant.

The origin of statues of gods in South Asia is probably also connected to the development of *tīrtha*s and pilgrimage. Sculpture in this period "began as an adjunct of architecture, being essentially ornamental on gateways, railings and entrances, where deep relief was mixed with some free-standing sculpture" (Thapar 2003: 268). The free-standing figures were of *yakṣa*s and *yakṣī*s, and these, suggests Thapar, encouraged an increase in the worship of, and donation of, images. The competition between Hindu Brahmans and the Buddhist *saṅgha* for ritual income was probably important for the development. In the competition between Hindus and Buddhists for ritual income and support, it has been suggested that "art helped attract devotees" (Falk 2006: 159). Harry Falk argues that the Buddhists were the first to benefit from the use of good art to attract devotees, and "all other groups were obliged to follow suit" (ibid.: 160). Anthropomorphic figures of semi-divine figures came "as a reaction to the Buddhist monopoly" (ibid.). The first pieces of Hindu art were of *yakṣa*s. These colossal figures were probably raised to compete with the Buddhists for donations and support. Perhaps the gods of Vedic religion were not considered proper to be shaped in stone, and therefore the local divinities associated with sites were used. Falk suggests that the *yakṣa*s were too low in status to offend Vedic Brahmans, but that they were regarded "as so useful for the adorant that they keep major parts of the population from giving all their donations at the Buddhist sites" (ibid.: 159). The Buddhists responded by producing statues of the Buddha and, predating the Guptas, Hindus started presenting their gods in the arts. The *yakṣa* statues competed with the Buddhist picture walls, according to Falk.[4] The construction of *stūpa*s was a means to expand the sacred space and influence of Buddhism undertaken under Aśoka. Some of the *stūpa*s were decorated with Aśoka pillars. These *stūpa*s, coupled with a *bodhi*-tree within a railing, "developed a certain touristic quality" (ibid.: 158). Art was one part of the attraction of the *stūpa*s and art developed as an integrative part of the religious sites, which led to further artistic developments. Competitiveness arose between Buddhists and Hindu communities and the development of art for the purpose of attraction. The *yakṣa* figures attempted to compete in attractiveness with the Buddhist sacred places. The linear development for the arts can be imagined as follows: stone art for the Buddhists and Jainas, then semi-divine anthropomorphic figures for the Hindus, then divine anthropomorphic statues for the Buddhists and Jainas, and finally divine anthropomorphic statues for the Hindus. The driving force was competition for donations and the desire to make the Vedic tradition survive. This then led to the Hinduism of the Epics and the *Purāṇa*s. Pilgrimage and salvific space dominate Hindu traditions of medieval India. The sacred sites were important for *dāna* and donations and thus became the arena for the competition for economic means and support. On the basis of the study of inscriptions, G. Schopen agrees that the new Buddha statues were closely related to the *yakṣa* figures, that a characteristic of both the *yakṣa* statues and the first Buddha statues was their huge sizes, and that there was:

> an intentionally organized, even coordinated distribution of early images from a central point. The earliest cult of images at three of the most important Buddhist sites – almost certainly came from Mathurā, where scholarly opinion is more and more inclined to locate the production of the first Buddha images.
> (Schopen 1997: 248)

Schopen further argues that the production, transportation and installation of all these images, which were the first at these sites, were effected by at least two monastics who knew one another. These monastics were scholarly and were propagating a new cult in a systematic fashion. Hindus responded by making divine anthropomorphic figures.

The origin of Brahmanical pilgrimage traditions – that is, Brahmans as priests of pilgrimage places – seems to be found in the religious pluralistic cultures of the Gaṅgā Valley in the centuries around the beginning of the Common Era. Buddhist pilgrimage might very well have been a model for the development of Hindu pilgrimage.[5] The period of Buddhist dominance in parts of North India was the time in which Vedic religion was transformed into Hinduism. Buddhism grew at the expense of the Vedic religious tradition and the Buddhist monks and monasteries received much of the income that had previously gone to the Brahman priests (Eliot 1957). *Tīrtha* and its ritual of giving (*dāna*) are two important elements in the emerging Hindu religion. Traditions of *tīrtha* and *dāna* probably became important in the Brahmanical tradition after the critique of the Vedic sacrifice by the Buddhists and the decay of the sacrifice and the rise of Buddhist pilgrimage. Brahmanical *tīrtha*s might have been a response to the success of Buddhism and the religion of *stūpa*s, which was a religion of salvific space, and competition for economic support from the gift (*dāna*) system. *Tīrtha* traditions provided income and a livelihood for the Brahman priests, and by making *tīrtha*s equal to, or superior to, and not opposed to the sacrifice, it supported the Brahmanical system and at the same introduced this new type of ritual.

Himanshu Prabha Ray has, on the basis of analysis of the archaeological material, pointed out the importance of multiple religious affiliation of sacred sites (Ray 2004, 2009). She claims that "multiple affiliation was the norm rather than the exception" and refers to the Caves of Ellora, where in the sixth century CE the earliest caves, dedicated to Śiva, were excavated, followed by Buddhist and Jaina caves over the centuries. She notes that the close association among religious architecture, Buddhist, Jaina and Hindu, also points to shared spaces. She agrees in understanding the religious expansion as acculturation and Sanskritization, suggesting integration of local cults, but also warns that it might be a simplification of the process. She wants to understand the history in terms of "sharing and negotiations rather than hegemony and integration" (Ray 2004: 367). The community that supports the shrine should be in focus to understand the development. She is right to point to the importance of analyzing the understanding of those who use the shrine, and not only those that founded it or donated to it. Shared sacred spaces, however, are often contested and sources of conflict. That a site is sacred to more than one community does not necessarily in itself promote intercommunal understanding or a deeper awareness of the faith of others (Sikand 2003). Persons from different religious communities that share a sacred space are also quite aware that they follow different religious traditions.

Temples and *Tīrthas*

The Vedic gods were invisible presences in the ritual. Pilgrimage to sacred places builds on the idea that divinity is fixed to particular sites. In Hinduism, the temples give the gods a permanent presence at particular places. One difference between sacred space in North and South India is that in the north it is the area that is sacred, regardless of whether or not there are temples, while in the south it is the temples that make an area sacred (Saraswati 1985). Most pilgrimages are to temples and most *tīrtha*s have temples. Nevertheless, the idea that an area is sacred is fundamental to the idea of pilgrimage and this seems perhaps to point to the idea in the tradition of salvific space that the *tīrtha*s are deities. The site is sacred irrespective of the presence of a temple there.

The Hindu *tīrtha*s were promoted by Brahmans who had moved away from the placelessness of the Vedic gods and the rituals of sacrifice to the worship of divinities present permanently at particular sites. However, many Brahmans were probably opposed to the new rituals of temples at the *tīrtha*s and there was most likely a conflict between those Brahmans who chose to function as priests at the temple sites and those that were against the concept of a permanent presence of the divine at specific sites (Olivelle 2010; Stietencron 1977). That there is an almost total absence of the temple in early Hindu legal literature, the *dharmaśāstra* literature (Olivelle 2010), seems to point to a strong Brahmanical opposition. Patrick Olivelle writes that "in the religious life of a good Brahmin . . . the temple or anything resembling it plays no significant or even a secondary role" (ibid.: 193). None of the principal *gṛhya-* and *dharmasūtra*s contains any procedures of consecration of images in a temple (ibid.). The *dharmaśāstra* literature follows the path of the Vedic ritual life in which no public structure of worship or ritual played any role (ibid.). Olivelle documents that the most common term for temple in legal literature is *devagṛha*/*devatāgṛha* (but there are only 13 occurrences!), followed by *devāyatana*/*devatāyatana* (11 occurrences), *devālaya* (two occurrences), *devāgāra*/*devatāgāra* (two occurrences) and *devakula* (one occurrence) (ibid.: 192). Olivelle also notes that the term *devālaya* occurs only in the late text *Vaikhānasa Dharmasūtra* (sixth or seventh centuries CE) and *devāgāra* in *Viṣṇusmṛti* (seventh century CE). *Devāyatana*/*devatāyatana* most probably meant a roadside shrine situated at a crossroads to attract the highest number of people, but temples were in general situated outside of the village, according to Olivelle. Regarding the archaeological material, Olivelle comments that "there is no archaeological evidence for temples in what could be termed the mainstream Brahmanical tradition, as opposed to the Buddhist and Jain, until at least the time of the Kushana, that is, the second century CE" (ibid.: 194). The ritual specialist connected to the temple, the *devalaka*, is first mentioned in *Manusmṛti*, a text from the same period. Olivelle's statement that "the temple/shrines were small structures located along roads and removed from human habitations" (ibid.: 195) seems to suggest that the earliest temples were connected to travel and perhaps even to pilgrimage. In order to reach temples that are "removed from human habitations," travel is involved as well as a purpose for visiting the temple, and this is close to the definition of pilgrimage.

There is a close relationship between Hindu pilgrimage and asceticism, since the ascetics were people on the move. The most common religious function of a *devāyatana* given in the legal literature "relates to the place where wandering ascetics are expected to spend the night" (ibid.: 197). The Hindu *sāṃnyāsin* was the model pilgrim. According to the sacred narrative of the salvific power of Kurukṣetra, which was examined in Chapter 2, it was the warriors and the ascetics who die there that were promised attainment of *mokṣa* at that place. The *sāṃnyāsins* were without a permanent home and they must have played an early role in developing aspects of the pilgrimage traditions.[6] Some think that Vārāṇasī became the holiest city of Hindu India because it managed to become a pilgrimage center both for pilgrims pursuing happiness, health and religious merit and ascetics pursuing the aim of salvific liberation (Bakker 1996).

Clear references to temples in the *dharmaśāstra* literature are found only from the middle of the first millennium CE (Olivelle 2010: 197). The evidence in the *dharmaśāstras* seems to also point to some connection at the outset between pilgrimage, and shrines and temples. In the legal literature, temples do not form part of a social, religious or legal system. In *Vasiṣṭha Dharmasūtra*, there is a list that mentions *grāmasīmānta* (the outskirts of a village), *devagṛha* (a temple), *śūnyāgāra* (an abandoned house) and *vṛkṣamūla* (the foot of a tree), which are all places far from human habitation, and Olivelle notes that this list "raises interesting questions about the geography of temples during this period" (ibid.). Temples, according to this list, were located far from villages and towns or any human habitation and the role they are expected to serve is as shelter for the wandering ascetics. Also, in *Arthaśāstra*, temples are thought to be located in isolated places (ibid.). It is mentioned (2.36.13) that the king should have secret agents in woods, cemeteries, shrines or places held sacred (*puṇyasthāna*) (Buddhist places?) and temples (*devagṛhas*), and arrest anyone loitering there with weapons. Similarly, in the *Nāradasmṛti*, areas where thieves are thought to gather, such as at crossroads, *Caitya* trees, vacant houses, forests and temples, are included in a list (ibid.: 198).

That the temples were away from human habitation made some travel necessary to visit them. The contrast with the ritual of Vedic sacrifice is substantial. In the Vedic sacrifice, the gods traveled to where the sacred ritual took place. With regards to the temples, humans traveled to the places where the divine was thought to be present. This change, argued Heinrich von Stietencron, has come about "because the god has now taken his residence in an image which is permanently installed in a shrine somewhere at a distance from the village" (1977: 129). In other words, to meet god personally, it was now necessary to go to the shrine or temple and, this could be a pilgrimage. Images of gods could also be worshipped in the home, but assumedly the more powerful presences of the gods were in the shrines and temples located, for most people, at a distance. Somebody had to take care of the worship at these places and this task belonged to the *devalakas*, who were the functionaries at the temples. Stietencron refers to Pāṇini 5.3.99 (*jivikārthe cāpaṇye*), a *sūtra* interpreted by the commentators as an intention to regulate the formation of the names of divine images. The commentators explain that the rule was based on a distinction between two types of images, those that were meant for sale and those taken care of and worshipped by a *devalaka*, a custodian, who oversaw the worship of them. The images were not of the Vedic gods, but new gods, such as Śiva, Skanda, Vaiśravaṇa (Kubera), Samkarṣaṇa or Rāma and Vāsudeva or Keśava (Stietencron 1977:130).

There seems to have been a conflict between Vedic Brahmans and the Brahmans, who had started to worship statues, and a split took place in the Brahman class. Axel Michaels (2004) has argued that the low status of temple priests relates to the permanent presence of the divine, as compared with the Vedic priests, who summoned the gods for the sacrifice. Because gods had permanent places, the priests were required to leave the house and thus become susceptible to pollution, unlike the Vedic priests, who were able to summon them where they were. Serving the gods at the temple involved contact with strangers. Acceptance of gifts from devotees of the god is ritual polluting because the gifts were seen as polluted. That there was a Brahmanical opposition to temple worship and statues is well documented in the *Dharmaśāstra* literature. The functionaries of the temples, the *devalaka*, were despised by the *dharmaśāstra* tradition and were "ostracized by the Brahman community" (Olivelle 2010: 202). However, other Brahmans tried to integrate the worship of images and shrines into the Brahmanical tradition. Stietencron argues that the custodians of images, the *devalaka*s, were *śūdra*s but that some Brahmans started to perform services for the shrines (Stietencron 1977). The Vedic Brahmans then turned their backs on them and also called them *devalaka*s and considered them fallen Brahmans. Stietencron interprets the statements in the *Mahābhārata* and the *Purāṇa*s about the rewards of visiting *tīrtha*s being compared to the sacrifices and the exaggerated rewards, as well as the comparison of the rewards with the sacrifices which the viewing of the image was supposed to supersede, as a function of the conflict between the two groups of Brahmans and the need to devaluate the Vedic sacrifice for the priests who took care of images. The escalation of the conflict was, argues Stietencron, to a large degree, economic and concerned the gifts to the Brahmans. Stietencron argues that, with the development of statues, shrines and temples, the gods and goddesses had a presence on earth and gifts could be given directly to them. Thus, the priests of the shrines, statues and *tīrtha*s accumulated great wealth, whereas the priests of the sacrifices lost out. Also, the shrines and *tīrtha*s were open to a much larger part of the population than the sacrifices, so the number of donors increased. The priests then used the wealth to arrange festivals that attracted more pilgrims. The donations of the pilgrims more than covered the expenses of the festivals. With growing wealth, the temples were expanded and the fame of the place also increased. The greatest temples – temples that accumulated wealth – became important centers of pilgrimage.

In the *Manusmṛti*, the *devalaka* are accused of offering their services for money, like physicians, meat-sellers and shop-keepers:

> *cikitsakān devalakān māṃsavikrayiṇas tathā*
> *vipaṇena ca jīvanto varjyāḥ syurhavyakavyayoḥ*
>
> Doctors, priests of shrines, people who sell meat, and people who support themselves by trade are to be excluded from offerings to the gods and ancestors.
>
> (*Manusmṛti* 3.152)[7]

The person mentioned in *Manusmṛti* 11.26, "an evil-hearted man who greedily seizes what belongs to the gods" refers to the priest of the shrine, implying that while serving the shrine priests take for themselves the goods which were offered to the gods (Stietencron 1977: 133). Stietencron thinks that the "traditionalists" also tried to prohibit the temple priests from using the wealth of the temples in sacrifices and that the attempts of the traditionalists to stop the temple and the temple priests failed. The success of the priest serving shrines contributed to the growth of pilgrimage:

> The *devalaka*s proved to be good managers. They were successful in increasing the fame and power of many temples to such an extent that they gained far more than regional importance. *Tīrthayātrā*, the pilgrimage to distant sacred places, became increasingly popular and the major temples became centres of interregional communication.
>
> (Stietencron 1977: 135)

The critique of the temples by the "traditionalists" did not include the merit of pilgrimage. The critique was against the priests. The "traditionalists" claimed the *devalaka* simply pretended to sacrifice by offering for a second time what had already been given to the god:

> The only merit lay in the field of propaganda, in the spread of the god's fame and glory and in the opportunity given to the devotees who had come from afar on the occasion of the festival in order to approach the deity and to win his grace.
>
> (Stietencron 1977: 135)

Devalaka refers in general to persons who worship a god for a living. Temple priests, for a long time, had a low status among the Brahman sub-castes and the term *devalaka* was used pejoratively to label them (Hüsken 2009: 54). A negative connotation became attached to the term and, even today, temple priests have low status among the different Brahman castes, with only funeral priests having lower status. The critique of the sacrifice by the Buddhists and others probably also made the Vedic priests criticize the temple priests for abandoning sacrifice (Hüsken 2009). Also, in the *Purāṇas*, the *devalaka* are mentioned in lists of persons that were to be excluded, for instance, from participation in the *śrāddha* (see *Matsyapurāṇa* 16.14–17). In spite of this criticism and loss of status, the pilgrimage tradition expanded to include a large number of sites and came to dominate Hinduism in the medieval age. In the next chapter, we will look at this expansion.

Gods in statues meant that gods became located in space, contrary to the Vedic gods, and this made it possible to travel to where a god was present. It gave rise to a geography of statues, shrines and temples. The shrines were outside the villages and often at places away from human habitation – for example, at crossroads and along roads. Pilgrimage expanded with the development of shrines. The goal of the priests at the shrines was to lead as many people as possible to the presence of god and this continues to be the basic ideology of pilgrimage places: it is open to everyone and it gives great rewards for very little. The places compete for visitors by outbidding each other with respect to rewards. The success of a pilgrimage is measured by the number of people participating and visiting, and fairs and festivals are organized in order to attract more people. This ideology is opposite to the Vedic sacrificial ideology.

The growth in number of Brahmans and a strong decline in people willing to offer donations for the large and costly sacrifices led to a difficult economic situation. The greatest sin of the *devalaka* was to accept gifts as a source of income, according to the Vedic priests. The change might very well have been motivated by the need to compete with the Buddhists monks and nuns for donations, but the condemnation of the *devalaka* by other Brahmans shows that there was also competition between the Brahmans. A competitive situation for attracting devotees continued for several centuries. H. Falk has suggested that the statues of *yakṣa*s were produced to compete with the Buddhists for *dāna*, and this created the demand for life-size statues of the Buddha in order to attract the devotees. The Vaiṣṇava and Śaiva statues of their gods in full figure emerged only under the Guptas, and these anthropomorphic statues were perhaps, to some degree, reactions to the Buddhists' statues of the Buddha. Competition for donations seems to have been one of the dominating forces in this development. The origin of temples and statues – that is, a god's permanent presence in particular locations – and the origin of pilgrimage – that is, visits to particular places in which gods and divine power are present permanently – seem to be closely related. The transformation of religious life in ancient India that is associated with the beginning of Hinduism is closely connected to the worship of gods belonging to sites. The land of the temple became identified with the divine and was divinized, and thus the temple and the god merged. The central Vedic gods, which were placeless, lost their importance. While Vedic religion involved the worship of gods without places and was a religion of placelessness, Hinduism is the religion of sacred places, places associated with particular manifestations of divine power.

4 The growth and omnipresence of the Hindu traditions of salvific space

In the last chapter, we looked at possible origins and early manifestations of the Hindu tradition of pilgrimage. A dramatic change took place in the Brahmanical tradition in the understanding of the relationship between divinities and space from the time of the Vedas to the period of the composition of the *tīrthayātrā* chapters of the *Mahābhārata*, a text that has been called the religion of *tīrtha*s (Patil 1983: 28). The composition of the *tīrthayātrā* chapters most probably coincided with the composition of the earliest *Purāṇa*s, a genre of texts that seems to have been a product of the same change in religion that the *tīrthayātrā* chapters exemplified. Notions of the divine as permanently present at particular sites became a dominant feature in religious life. In the Vedic tradition, the gods were not worshipped at sites at which they were thought to be permanently present; the Vedic gods were placeless. In the religious traditions represented in the *tīrthayātrā* chapters of the *Mahābhārata* and in the *Purāṇa*s, descriptions of numerous *tīrtha*s are a characteristic feature. One significant transformation that had come about in India before the composition of the *tīrthayātrāparvan*, which was an important source for the new perception of divinity and space, was the belief in the permanent presence of the power of the Buddha in the *stūpa*s and at the places associated with key events of his life, and perhaps a similar development took place in the Jaina traditions with respect to Mahāvīra and other *tīrthaṅkara*s. These *stūpa*s were thought to contain parts of the salvific power of the Buddha, present in his remains and the sites, and worship at these places of power was thought to give religious merit (*puṇya*). The *stūpa*s attracted visitors from afar. Pilgrimage to the *stūpa*s was thought to have salvific implications. Visiting *cetiya*s was a pre-Buddhist practice in some parts of the eastern region of the Gaṅgā Valley but was spread to a wider area when transformed into the worship at *stūpa*s in the Buddhist religion. Hindu pilgrimage possibly arose partly as a response to Buddhist pilgrimage and the Śramaṇa critique of the ritual of sacrifice (*yajña*), and was a part of the competition for support and for the economic resources and the donations (*dāna*) of the pilgrims. The beauty of the art at the places of the *stūpa*s was perhaps also a reason for these sites attracting visitors (Falk 2006). The first Hindu statues made in stone, which most probably were the large statues of *yakṣa*s, were perhaps in response to the Buddhist pilgrimage to *stūpa*s and an attempt to attract donations from pilgrims. The *yakṣa*s were early examples of divinity permanently present at particular sites that attracted visitors – that is, pilgrims. In the descriptions of *tīrtahyātrā* in the *Mahābhārata*, the presence of *yakṣa*s is a feature at some of the pilgrimage places. According to the *Mahābhārata* 3.81.7, when a person arriving at Kurukṣetra has saluted the *yakṣa* Macakruka, the gatekeeper, he will receive merit equal to having given away 1, 000 cows.[1] In Mount Mandara dwell the *yakṣa*s Maṇicara, Maṇibhadra and Kubera, who is the king of *yakṣa*s. Also, *nāga*s belonged to particular places at which they were worshipped. In the Vedic tradition, rivers were sacred and the Hindu ritual of pilgrimage is closely connected to sacred rivers and bathing rituals. There is a connection between Hindu pilgrimage and the Vedic *sarasvatīsattra* ritual, which implied a ritual journey with cattle along the river Sarasvatī and a performance of a ritual sacrifice each day. However, Hindu pilgrimage seems to presuppose a permanent presence of the divine at particular sites and particular rituals at the sites performed by pilgrimage and temple priests, and these characteristics seem to indicate that the *sarasvatīsattra* was a different ritual. The sacredness of rivers, however, also points to continuity, as rivers, and not least the confluences of rivers (*saṅgama*), are important in the Hindu pilgrimage traditions. The transformation of the Vedic culture from placeless divinities to the permanent presence of divinities at particular sites is probably best explained by the greater pluralistic context, which includes Buddhism and also other Śramaṇa traditions, such as Jainism, and not as an internal transformation of the Vedic tradition. Although some aspects of pilgrimage, such as sacredness of rivers, had precursors in the Vedic tradition, pilgrimage to places permanently endowed with divine and salvific power nevertheless represented something new. In the sacrificial religion of the Veda, the gods were thought to move to where the humans performed their rituals. In the Hindu tradition, in contrast, in order to perform rituals, humans moved to where the gods had a permanent presence. Pilgrimage is an expression of that change.

The belief in the presence of the divine at particular places was often accompanied by the worship of statues (*pratimā*, *mūrti*) at these places. The narratives of these places may have varied but narratives associated with sages and divinities were probably connected to the locations. Performance of *darśan* and *pūjā* were established as rituals to be performed to pay homage to the presence of the divine in statues, but a number of other rituals, such as *śrāddha*, *vrata*, *dāna* and *snāna*, were performed at pilgrimage places. The most powerful sites with statues of the divine undoubtedly attracted visitors from far and wide. Pilgrimage, thus, was an important element in the larger transformation of religion into *bhakti*, devotion to the divine presence on earth in temples and statues, as the dominant form of Hindu religious life.

A number of the pilgrimage sites were perhaps places that the people who belonged to the pre-Vedic or non-Vedic religious traditions believed possessed a divine presence and were incorporated into Hindu traditions as part of its geographical expansion. Once the possibility that the divine could be present permanently at particular sites was accepted, claiming such presence could be a way to expand a tradition – that is, to mobilize new ritual clients – and also to claim land for one's own tradition. Pilgrimage partly replaced sacrifice (*yajña*), and in the *Mahābhārata* and the *Purāṇa*s the rewards of pilgrimage are often compared to the rewards of sacrifices, which they are similar to and often surpass. I am not aware of textual evidence of the opposite, the rewards of sacrifices (*yajñā*s) being compared favorably to the rewards of pilgrimage. The central role of pilgrimage priests and the importance of gifts or donations (*dāna*) to Brahmans, not least in the pilgrimage economy, also indicate that pilgrimage took over from the ritual of sacrifice. Establishment of Hindu pilgrimage places and sacred sites seems to have been an important means for the expansion of Hinduism. In addition, giving land grants to Brahmans or the establishment of Brahman villages (*brahmadeya*) for the support of temples expanded Hindu rituals to new geographical areas and led to a Brahmanization (some use the term Sanskritization) of tribal deities and the spread of temple Hinduism, and in turn these temples also became centers of pilgrimage.

This geographical expansion marked a new approach to the areas peripheral to the Gaṅgā-Yamunā *doab* and the middle Gaṅgā Valley, which was the center of the Brahmanical culture. In *dharma* literature, the *Dharmaśāstra*s, pilgrimage was in general not a key topic before the composition of the *Dharmanibandha*s from the twelfth century CE. The first text, the *Tīrthavivecanakāṇḍa*, was composed to promote Vārāṇasī as a pilgrimage destination but also became a model for further texts that also favored other destinations. On the contrary, penance was prescribed for visiting places outside of the Brahmanical area, many of which were viewed not only as peripheral but also as antagonistic (*Baudhāyana Śrautasūtra* 18.13 and *Baudhāyana Dharmasūtra* 1.1.2.15; see Roy 1993). Feelings of superiority in the case of Brahmanical culture, as well as hostility in the case of the people in the areas peripheral to the expansion of the Brahmanical tradition, might explain this attitude. Nevertheless, geographical focus was widened and "the development of the Brahmanical tradition occurred in and was related to a context of expanding geographical horizons" (Roy 1993: 32). A. Bharati is certainly correct about medieval pilgrimage when he writes that its expansion is "due to Brahmin revival, and to ruralization of religion in the Hindu Middle Ages through its partial absorption into local, non-Brahminic cults" (1963: 137). The composite of salvific space and pilgrimage can be said to be the fundamental feature of Hinduism. But how and why did this Brahman revival and ruralization happen and how did this bring about the expansion of Hindu pilgrimage? Why did the Hindu tradition of salvific space achieve such a great success? How did salvific space attain such a dominant role in the Hindu tradition?

Urbanization, de-urbanization and geographical expansion

Several historians, foremost among them the Indian historians R. S. Sharma, R. N. Nandi and V. Nath, have in a number of studies argued that the remarkable success of the Hindu pilgrimage traditions was brought about by responses to economic changes with far-reaching consequences (Nandi 1979/1980, 1986; Nath 1987, 2001, 2007, 2009; Sharma 1965, 1987). S. M. Bhardwaj also suggested early on that "the evolution of specific sacred places as economic enterprises is a legitimate hypothesis and may shed light on their relative prominence" (1973: 5). The historians argue that the geographical expansion of the pilgrimage tradition was related to two periods of dramatic urban decline in the Brahmanical core areas and a subsequent agrarian expansion and the feudalization of the economy. The first period of degeneration took place after the end of the Kuṣāṇa empire, which was founded in the first century CE and lasted to the third century. The second period of decline took place during the centuries after the end of the Gupta empire, which lasted from around 320 CE to 550 CE. The Kuṣāṇa and Sātavāhana urban centers declined suddenly in the second half of the third century CE and during the fourth century CE and coincided with the fall of the Kuṣāṇa and Sātavāhana kingdoms. As mentioned previously, the second phase of urban decay coincided with the fall of the Gupta empire. Both periods of urban decay were associated with a decline in trade (Sharma 1987: 180, 182). After these periods of urban degeneration, urbanization did not become a dominant process in India until perhaps the fourteenth century (ibid.: 185). However, old towns and cities did not completely disappear and new urban centers continued to develop throughout this period, but probably on a smaller scale than during the periods of strong urbanization (Chattopadhyaya 1994; Ray 2009). Urban decay led to, on the one hand, the migration of numerous Brahmans from the towns and cities to villages and the expansion of the Brahmanical cultural area, whereby thousands of new sacred places were included in the Brahmanical tradition. On the other hand, the Brahmans who remained in the towns during the period of urban decline promoted the cities as *tīrtha*s in order to attract clients to their rituals. The urban decay, in other words, had a double effect on salvific space and pilgrimage. It contributed to the great geographical expansion of the Brahmanical pilgrimage area and to the redefinition of old towns as *tīrtha*s. New towns also developed as sites for temples, and places for pilgrimage encouraged urbanization (Thapar 2003: 458).

One of the pioneers of these studies was R. S. Sharma, who, on the basis of the study of coins, could show the decay of the money economy and a possible feudalization of the Indian economy. This was dealt with in *Indian Feudalism* (1965), *Urban Decay in India* (c. 300–c. 1000) (first published 1987), *Early Mediaeval Indian Society* (2001) and a number of other publications. The decline of trade, which had been the basis for the economic development of the second period of urbanization in South Asia, is explained as the cause of urban decay and the subsequent feudalization. The period from 200 BCE to 300 CE was the most prolific in the production of coins (Sharma 2001: 23), and the disappearance of coins points to dramatic changes in the society. The expansion of Hindu pilgrimage happened in the Gupta and the post-Gupta period, in the same period as the *Purāṇa*s became an important genre of religious texts. R. S. Sharma argues that early historic urbanism reached its peak between 200 BCE and 300 CE and that the peak of urbanism was associated with growing trade and commerce in this period and that this growth in commerce was related to the presence of money (Sharma 1987). Money made trade and economic exchange simple.

R. S. Sharma, R. N. Nandi and V. Nath all emphasize economic arguments to explain social and religious changes. In traditional pilgrimage, most of the money spent by the pilgrims was for services to the priests, who depended on the income and offered the pilgrims lodging and food in addition to the ritual services.[2] However, while the success of the religion of *tīrtha*s in their works is linked to economic change, they do not discount that other factors were also involved. Certainly, there is no contradiction in arguing for the importance of economic factors in the expansion of the tradition of temples and *tīrtha*s and the idea that people perceived the temple "as an abode of spiritual power" (Ray 2009: 77). If people had not perceived the spiritual power of the places, the expansion could not have happened. The growth of the traditions of temples and *tīrtha*s was possible precisely because of the religious views of the ritual clients of the pilgrimage priests. The ritual expansion depended as much on the ritual clients as on the Brahman ritual performers. Without the perception of salvific power at the sites, there would be no pilgrimage.

From around 300 CE, towns and cities in India suffered decline and desertion (see Sharma 1965, 1987, 2001). The following period, from 300 CE to 1000 CE, was an age of feudalization in India. Cities and monetary economy in large areas mostly disappeared, although new cities were also founded, and there was an agrarian expansion. Agriculture and exchanges based on other means than money took over. The value of land increased and land grants became a form of payment. This was probably the period when the *jajmānī* system became dominant. The *jajmānī* system was a method of exchange based on the duty of individuals and groups (based on caste) to provide services in a patron–client system. R. S. Sharma writes:

> Urban decline led to the regrouping and reorganization of social relationships, albeit within the broad ideological framework of the *varṇa* system. Guilds fossilized into castes. On account of the scarcity of markets and moneyed consumers urban occupations came to be viewed with contempt.
>
> (Sharma 1987: 165)

However this may be, the decay of towns also caused Brahmans to move to rural areas where "they lived on the income from the land donated to them by the chiefs and princes" (Sharma 1987: 167). The settling of Brahmans in rural areas strengthened state authority and contributed to the development of agriculture. Artisans took up agriculture but were also involved in new types of trade in which they "produced for temples and monasteries goods of a ritualistic nature, especially a large number of bronze images"; merchants were ruralized and "earned their living by managing land"; "professionals and various kinds of state functionaries came to be paid through land grants" and the "identity of the decaying towns was maintained by converting them into places of pilgrimage" (Sharma 1987: 167). This last point is especially relevant to this study. The "new urban" phenomenon was marked by garrisons, palaces, pilgrim centers and temple establishments, writes Sharma (1987: 177). Buddhism, which was a religion connected to cities, slowly disappeared after the last period of urban decay in the eighth century.

R. S. Sharma's arguments in support of the view that a feudal-like system developed as a result of the crumbling of the money economy, which led to urban decay and agricultural expansion, are based on archaeological material and inscriptions, as well as textual sources, but it is primarily the archaeological material he utilizes that reveals direct evidence of urban decay. However, in the literature of ancient India, "a celebrated ancient town being deserted and becoming inhabited by wild animals was a literary *topos* at least since the fifth century AD" (Bakker 2004: 10). In Kālidāsa's *Raghuvaṃśa* 16.12–22, in the description of the deserted Ayodhyā, jackals, wild buffaloes, peacocks in a poor condition, lions and snakes dominate. Grass and cobwebs have overrun the buildings and there are no rituals being performed:

> *balikriyāvarjitasaikatāni snānīyasaṃsargam anāpanuvanti*
> *upāntavānīragṛhāṇi dṛṣṭvā śūnyāni dūye sarayūjalāni*
>
> I am grieved to behold the waters of the Sarayū not obtaining contact of the perfumed powders (used in ablutions), with the sandy beds bereft of the rites of Bali offerings and on whose banks are huts made of live canes (now) deserted.
>
> (*Raghuvaṃśa* 16.21, translated by Nandargikar 1982: 502)

Sharma identified the following marks of urbanization in archaeological remains: metal coins, foreign coins, seals, sophisticated forms of pottery, molds of stone and terracotta, dies of copper, bronze, stone and ivory for the manufacture of gold, silver and copper, ivory and glass goods, and iron artifacts, which all signified trade and urban prosperity (Sharma 1987). The disappearance of these items in material remains excavated by archaeologists shows evidence of urban decay. The evidence, according to Sharma, illustrates a de-urbanization in two phases – the first after the third century CE and the second after the sixth century. Sharma concludes that "[F]ar more towns decayed in the first than in the second phase" (Sharma 1987: 130). The decay of the towns was part of a transformation of the economy, from one in which trade, merchants and artisans played important roles to one based on agriculture, in which central institutions depended primarily on agricultural surplus collected from the countryside. Cities that had flourished from trade and the production of artisans decayed and many of the artisans were forced by economic necessity to leave the cities. Sharma argues that the decay and disappearance of urbanism can be explained in the context of the same social upheaval that created the descriptions of the *kali*-age in the *Purāṇa*s (Sharma 1982, 1987, 2001). Sharma explains this as feudalization. Towns were deserted or converted into fiefdoms; villages were granted by rulers for the support of priests and officials; artisans left the cities, while some merchants became managers of land granted for religious or other purposes, reduced their trading activities and no longer had urban functions. Urban decay generated scorn for artisans, argued

Sharma, and their status changed from high to low. The economy in which they functioned was demonetized. The artisans migrated from the towns to the hinterland, where the raw produce that supported them and their skills was disseminated to the villages. The Brahmans of the towns had lived on gifts (*dakṣinā* or *dāna*), offered by kings, officials, merchants and artisans, and the decay of towns led the Brahmans to move to the countryside to find sources of sustenance (Nandi 1986: 80–89; Sharma 1987). Migration from towns peaked in the sixth to eighth centuries and also continued in the following centuries. There were still towns, but they were not based mainly on trade but were garrisons and administrative centers, as well as pilgrimage centers and religious establishments (Sharma 1987: 152). That at this time new towns also developed does not disprove the main argument (Chattopadhyaya 1994). Notable, from a religion point of view, are the numerous and large land grants to temple institutions. The period of feudalization was not without non-agriculturalist settlements, but Sharma notes a change in the composition of the population and the pattern of their occupation: "Now we find more people who managed religion, administration and military affairs, apart from a good number of soldiers. The number of artisans and traders substantially decreased. Capitals, garrisons, temples, monasteries, pilgrim centres became primarily centres of consumption" (Sharma 1987: 157). The non-agricultural settlements were no longer centered on trade. Hindu pilgrimage centers developed into the major form of religious life in this period.

During the period of de-urbanization, many old commercial cities in northern India, such as Champa, Vaiśālī, Kauśāmbī, Śrāvastī and Rājghāṭ (Vārāṇasī), ceased to be towns. R. S. Sharma compares the list of pre–Kuṣāna towns (26 towns) with the list of towns in Al-Biruni's descriptions of India (Sharma 1987: 120) and shows that only five of the pre–Kuṣāna towns appear in Al-Biruni's list, namely Ayodhyā, Mathurā, Pāṭaliputra, Ujjain and Vārāṇasī. Sharma notes that "these existed as religious centres," which "developed when towns lost their urban character" (ibid.: 120). Ayodhyā, Mathurā, Pāṭaliputra, Ujjain and Vārāṇasī, in other words, were transformed from centers of trade into centers of pilgrimage and were thus rebuilt as sacred centers based on pilgrimage economy. R. N. Nandi gives a similar description:

> The more important urban centres which declined between the third and fifth centuries A.D.. and from which most brāhmaṇas migrated subsequently include such prosperous ancient cities as Mathura, Varanasi (Rajghat), Kurukshetra (Rājā Karṇa kā Qila), Śrāvastī (Sahet-Mahet), Prayag (Bhita), Kauśāmbī, Ujjain, Vidiśā (Bhilsa), Tripurī (Jabalpur), Hastināpura, Pāṭaliputra (Kumrahar), Champā (Bhagalpur), Vaisali (Basarh), Chechar (near Hajjpur) and Chirand (near Chapra). In respect of a great majority of urban sites in the peninsular region the phase marked by a long period of decay is not very distinct and the towns which were in a prosperous state between 250 B.C. and A.D. 250 appear to have been deserted rather suddenly about the close of the third century A.D.
>
> (Nandi 1979/1980: 75)

This urban decay has been explained as the outcome of a crisis in long-distance trade relations, mainly due to the breaking-up of the Kuṣāna, Sātavāhana and the Roman empires, and the second phase coincides with the fall of the Gupta empire (Sharma 1987). After the fall of the Gupta empire, the political situation made it difficult to collect taxes, to bring these to towns and then disburse salaries to officials and soldiers and to give gifts to the Brahmans in terms of money or cattle, and at this time land grants to the Brahmans increased to a much larger scale than before. Artisans and merchants migrated from the urban to rural areas, and "when the towns declined, the Brahmans too migrated to the countryside and thus contributed to the spread of technology" (ibid.).

In addition to this economic explanation, the Brahmanical distaste for cities and the competition with Buddhism and Jainism probably also supported the process of urban decay. It has been suggested that the Brahmanical ideology's hostility to the city "exerted a fundamental function in determining the decline of the urban and mercantile economy of the subcontinent, the struggle which coincided basically with the struggle against the Buddhists and the Jains" (Verardi 1996: 239) and that the urban decay led to the supremacy of the Brahmanical social and economic model that was based on land (Verardi 1996). The Brahmanical model became a central feature in subsequent development.

Of the four *puruṣārtha*s in the Hindu traditions, there was, it seems, a tendency to associate the attainment of *artha* and *kāma* with the city, *dharma* with the village and *mokṣa* (salvific liberation) with the wilderness. A person had to live in a village in order to realize *dharma* and leave the village or city behind and enter into the wilderness in order to attain the ultimate goal in life. However, with the growth of traditions of pilgrimage to places endowed with salvific powers, it was claimed that the cities were able to grant salvific liberation. That the institution of *tīrtha*s was important for the development of regional identities and political formations was possibly a further cause of the expansion of pilgrimage and salvific space.

Salvific space, epigraphic and archaeological evidence

While Sharma's interest was the understanding of Indian feudalism, several other Indian historians influenced by Sharma's work have applied his ideas in focused historical studies of Hindu pilgrimage traditions (Arya 2004; Nath 2001, 2009; Nandi 1979/1980, 1986). These studies agree that many places that became pilgrimage sites in the middle of the first millennium CE had an urban history before they became pilgrimage centers and that these cities had been affected by the urban decline and were then redefined as Hindu pilgrimage places for economic reasons. S. N. Arya, in his study of Hindu pilgrimage from 300 CE to 1200 CE, while admitting that there were several reasons for the development of the practice of pilgrimage, writes that "the decline of commerce and the gradual decay of urban centres seemed to have contributed in a large measure to this process" (Arya 2004: 2). He then relates pilgrimage to economic changes in India in the centuries from around the end of the third century CE, which led to agrarian expansion and urban decay. He argues that the Brahmans of the decaying towns were given villages and pieces of land for their rehabilitation and that these places were slowly recognized as *tīrtha*s, and, likewise, many of the urban settlements which declined in the Gupta and post-Gupta periods became *tīrtha*s. One economic institution that made this possible was the ritual of gifts (*dāna*). The focus in the descriptions of *tīrtha*s is the salvific rewards and these rewards are accessed by gifts to Brahmans at the pilgrimage places. In the *Mahābhārata* and the *Purāṇa*s, the ritual gifts one should give to Brahmans are a central part in the descriptions of the *tīrtha*s. The rewards of offering food to Brahmans have a prominent place in the *tīrtha* chapters. A person who feeds Brahmans will enjoy all worldly pleasures, in addition to attaining the salvific goals. Favored gifts are cows (especially the *kapilā* cow), plots of land, villages and gold. Arya is able to argue that many of the pilgrimage places were "great deserted towns of ancient India" and that "their decay and desertion were quickly followed by their proclamation as holy *tīrtha*s" (Arya 2004: 132).

A notable feature of these studies is that the inscriptions that the historians refer to, which mention the places as *tīrtha*s, seem often, but not always, to appear later than the description of the places as *tīrtha*s in the texts. There seems to be a pattern, with respect to many places, that the first epigraphic evidence of sites as *tīrtha*s is quite late, often in the fifth, sixth and seventh centuries CE. The earliest *tīrtha* chapters of the *Mahābhārata* are usually dated a few centuries earlier than the epigraphic evidence. What this means is not clear. One could speculate that this is because the *tīrtha* texts inserted in the *Mahābhārata* and the *Purāṇa*s have been dated as too early by scholars. Or it could simply mean that the tradition of mentioning *tīrtha*s in inscriptions is later than the tradition of describing them in texts. This discrepancy between the first time a place is mentioned as a *tīrtha* in inscriptions and the first time it is mentioned in the texts could probably lead to a critical evaluation of the dating of some of the textual material. One exception seems to be Puṣkara, which is mentioned as a place where one should donate 1,000 cows and appears in the Nāsik cave inscription dated by Arya to the second century CE. However, in the material Arya presents, there is a gap of 700 years until the next inscriptions, dating from the tenth and eleventh centuries, which confirm Puṣkara as a *tīrtha*. Arya does not suggest any solution to this problem in his documentation and the problem could be in the sources he utilizes. Nonetheless, he provides evidence of a number of towns that decayed and were later redefined as *tīrtha*s. One of the examples he uses for discussion is Gayā, which Faxian described as a walled city in ruins. In the *Mahābhārata* and *Rāmāyaṇa*, it is described as a *tīrtha*. With respect to the town of Ayodhyā, Arya writes: "A large number of towns which on the basis of archaeological evidences are found to be in a state of decline during the early mediaeval period were picked up for glorification as *tīrtha*s. Ayodhyā is definitely one of them" (Arya 2004: 69). Mathurā was hardly mentioned in the *Mahābhārata* and not at all in the *Rāmāyaṇa* (Goldman 1986), and the city became a Hindu pilgrimage place probably only after these texts had been completed. Mathurā is known to have been an important center of Buddhism and Jainism and the claim that it is a Hindu sacred city points to a process of transformation of older cities into Hindu salvific space. According to Arya, other towns in a state of decline in the early medieval period and thereafter that were proclaimed as *tīrtha*s, in addition to Ayodhyā and Mathurā, are: Prayāg, Puṣkara, Kauśāmbī, Kurukṣetra, Mahiṣmatī, Ekāmraka, Dvārkā, Śrāvastī and Kānyakubja (Kanauj). Kānyakubja began declining in the third century CE and afterwards passed through the three phases of decay, migration and sanctification, which are typical for this process. Migration from Kānyakubja is documented from the seventh century, and from the end of the ninth century it is confirmed as a *tīrtha* and described in the *Matsyapurāṇa* (Chapter 13) and *Varāhapurāṇa* (Chapters 157 and 158).[3]

Archaeological evidence shows that Vārāṇasī was in a state of decay in the third to fourth centuries. The earliest epigraphic reference to Vārāṇasī as a *tīrtha* is, according to Arya, in the sixth century (2004: 75). Hans Bakker confirms this view, writing that Vārāṇasī "had no special religious significance within the Brahmanical tradition (beyond a local one) before the beginning of the Christian era" (Bakker 1996: 33) and that its transformation from a commercial place to a sacred place "took place in the fourth to sixth centuries of the Christian era" (ibid.).[4] Vārāṇasī is hardly mentioned in the *tīrthayātrāparvan* of the *Mahābhārata* (two of its *tīrtha*s, the Vṛṣadhvaja and Kapilāhrada, are mentioned). That Vārāṇasī was a commercial and not a political center was probably one reason that it was transformed into a *tīrtha*. Inscriptions in the eighth to tenth centuries emphasized the duty to protect Vārāṇasī. The number of inscriptions referring to Vārāṇasī as a *tīrtha* increased in the eleventh century and at this time it had become so important that other *tīrtha*s were compared to it in order to increase their own status (Arya 2004: 77). In the *Kāśīkhaṇḍa*, the god Skanda recommends that one should hire someone as a resident in Vārāṇasī if one is not able to stay there oneself:

> *svayaṃ vastum aśakto 'pi vāsayet tīrthavāsinam,*
> *apy ekam api mūlyena sa vastuḥ phalabhāg dhruvam.*
>
> If one is unable to stay personally, one should make at least one person stay there by hiring him as a resident of the *tīrtha*. Surely, he gets the benefit of the one who reside.
>
> (2.53.95)

Arya argues that Citrakūṭa became a pilgrimage place in the Gupta period (Arya 2004: 70). Kedāranātha is mentioned in the *Mahābhārata*, but the first inscriptions are dated to the eleventh and twelfth centuries. Mathurā went into decline between the third and fourth centuries and it had a small population during the Gupta period, but the chapters of the *Purāṇa*s (*Vāyupurāṇa*, Chapter 104; *Varāhapurāṇa*, Chapters 150–178) perhaps composed in that period proclaimed it a *tīrtha* (Arya 2004: 81). Prayāg is also referred to as a *tīrtha* in inscriptions from the sixth century and this is one of the earliest inscriptions referring to *tīrtha*s (ibid.). Vidiśā (modern Besnagar) in Madhya Pradesh was already a Buddhist center at the time of Aśoka, but became a well-known Hindu *tīrtha* only after the Gupta empire. Similarly, Amarāvatī was a Buddhist township, which went into decline from the fifth century onwards and in the sixth century it is mentioned in inscriptions as a Hindu *tīrtha*. Banavāsī in Karnataka decayed from the fourth century and inscriptions from the eighth century refer to the migration of Brahmans from the place, and an inscription dated 1055 refers to the site as a *tīrtha*. Arya argues that Kurukṣetra became a *tīrtha* only in the fourth or fifth centuries CE. The earliest inscription mentioning it as a *tīrtha* is in the fifth century. Māhiṣmati went into decline, according to Arya, in the fourth century and appeared as a *tīrtha* soon after in the descriptions of the *Purāṇa*s (*Vāyupurāṇa* and *Matsyapurāṇa*) (ibid.: 112). Other inscriptions mentioned by Arya are from the ninth and eleventh centuries and show that Kurukṣetra was widely known as a *tīrtha* (ibid.: 81). The city of Nāsikya (Nāsik) suffered, according to archaeological evidence, decay after 200 CE, and after the Gupta age inscriptions provide information of migration of Brahmans from the city to donated villages, and after that inscriptions declare Nāsikya as a *tīrtha*. Bhṝukaccha was an important town up to the sixth century and then went into decline after the departure of the Brahmans. The earliest epigraphy material of the town as a *tīrtha* is found in the seventh century (ibid.: 107). R. N. Nandi concludes on the basis of the epigraphic material that:

> the places from where the brāhmaṇas migrated during this time [between the fifth and seventh centuries CE] were all-important ancient towns which the archaeologists find in a state of decay about the third–fourth centuries A.D. and which the Purāṇic writers of the early medieval period proclaimed as *tīrtha*s or holy places worth a religious journey by the *jajamana*.
>
> (Nandi 1979/1980: 80)

*Purāṇa*s and pilgrimage places

The *Purāṇa*s are the most important group of texts for the understanding of the expansion of the Hindu traditions of salvific space. The texts represent popular religion (as opposed to the religion of the elite) and are largely about salvific places and the narratives and rituals performed at these places. The purpose of much of the textual material seems to have been to promote the places and the rituals. The exaggerated rewards of the salvific places probably indicate a situation in which priests at the different places were competing for the ritual clients. Bhardwaj considered the *Purāṇa*s as an important way for the pilgrimage sites to attain their status as sacred space:

> In the process of the spread of Hinduism, partly through actual spatial expansion and partly through absorption of non-Hindu tribal populations, those areas which came to be sanctified early have, therefore, a large number of sacred places associated with the sacred streams, the coast, or the hilltops. As the process continued, more of such places could be expected to be consecrated. As observed earlier, once the major sacred points had been selected

> and became accepted as such through the religious lore and literature common to Hinduism over the country, the further addition of places of sanctity, one surmises, encountered some opposition from priests with vested interests in the established ones. . . . Often the priests had to invent or manipulate a legend and write a *sthala purāṇa* (a sacred book of legend of the place) to promote the recognition of their sacred place in the existing religious literature. . . . As the *Purāṇas,* and the *sthala purāṇas* achieved the status of being the sacred word (hence true) the place considered sacred by them would be accepted as such without question.
>
> (Bhardwaj 1973: 85–86)

The *Purāṇa* texts are also concerned with impurity (*pāpa*) and the removal of impurity – that is, purification and pilgrimage to *tīrtha*s is one way to get rid of impurity. Impurity has a number of causes and is almost omnipresent. The omnipresence of impurity means that getting rid of it is a constant concern. Since impurity is almost ubiquitous, one becomes easily contaminated with new impurities, and visits to *tīrtha*s have to be carried out again and again. To keep one's purity means to be constantly aware of the sources of impurity, and the sources are many. Rituals such as fasting, and so on, function to purify the body from the impurity suffered. P. Olivelle has noted that "it is purification not purity that is at the heart of the system" (Olivelle 2005: 247). That impurity includes both bodily impurity associated with natural processes, such as contact with others, and the breaking of social rules means that the individual is in constant need of purification. The cleansing of the body of impurity and the cleaning of the person of moral impurity (*pāpa*) are closely related. This is probably one reason for the power of the pilgrimage sites. Many pilgrimage places are associated with water and taking sacred baths is a key ritual. The purification of *pāpa* by using water combines the physical experience of the cleansing property of water with the salvific property of sacred water. The promotion texts of the pilgrimage places take it for granted that all persons need to get rid of impurity. But this does not necessarily mean that all persons are considered to have carried out morally bad acts. Impurity is not automatically linked to one's own morality. For instance, at the *śrāddha*, the priest eats what is offered to the departed and by that action he takes over some of the impurity of the departed. He can get rid of it again by ritual acts such as fasting. The blending of physical and salvific purification is well illustrated in this verse about Mathurā from the *Varāhapurāṇa*:[5] "He who goes to Mathurā on the Aṣṭamī day and spending the night as a celibate, cleaning the teeth in the morning, washing the clothes and taking the bath, circumambulates there in silence, gets all his sins removed"[6] (158.37–38). Cleaning teeth, washing clothes and taking a bath is presented here as prerequisites and methods for the removal of *pāpa*.

The text adds that even the touch of a person who has purified himself and circumambulated the site accomplishes all that is desired (*Varāhapurāṇa* 158.39), and this points to another function of pilgrimage. Pilgrimage makes a person purer than others who have not performed the pilgrimage. A social element of the purification process of pilgrimage, therefore, may be that it possibly gives the person a higher social status, which is a function of the person's purity. On the other hand, compared to the early Vedic tradition, the pilgrimage tradition represented a more open and inclusive tradition. It was accessible to all, regardless of their impurity. The pilgrimage tradition functioned to spread the ideas and religious practices of Brahmans who wanted to include as many as possible as their ritual clients. Persons from all *varṇa*s, both genders and all *āśrama*s can attain the salvific rewards from bathing at the *tīrtha*s.

Several historians have argued that the descriptions in the early *Purāṇa*s produced around the third and fourth centuries CE about the onset of the *kali*-age are about the crisis in the economy that led to urban decay and the feudalization of the society (Nandi 1979/1980, 1986; Sharma 1987). This is a possible interpretation, but not the only interpretation of the idea of the *kali*-age. Other interpretations relate the idea to a crisis in the Vedic religion following the Buddhist critique of the Vedic sacrifice, as well as to foreign invasions and a crisis in kingship. These interpretations do not, of course, exclude each other. Related to the first interpretation might be the idea that, in the *kali*-age, everything is more impure and that, therefore, everyone, without really having performed any morally impure acts, nevertheless needs to be purified from moral impurity. What is interesting with the interpretation of linking the *kali*-age with urban decay and feudalization is that it relates closely to the expansion of the pilgrimage traditions, as this expansion is interpreted as a response to these social processes. R. N. Nandi writes:

> A careful study of the features of the Kali age would, however, suggest that many of the developments indicated by these features actually relate to certain determining aspects of medievalism in India such as the decay of towns and the growth of a village-based subsistence economy; the regimentation and diversification of castes; the greater incidence of *varṇasaṃkara;* the denunciation of essential artisanal workers as "impure" and "untouchable"; the ruralisation of an important section of urban brāhmaṇas, social insecurity and political anarchy; the growth of popular religion based on temple-centric cults, *bhakti* missions, etc.
>
> (Nandi 1979/1980: 71)

The concept of the *kali*-age probably helped to introduce a number of new ritual practices, such as worship of images, *dāna* and pilgrimage that needed to compete with the Śramaṇa traditions of Buddhism and Jainism (Nath 2009: 135). According to *Viṣṇudharmottarapurāṇa*, in the *kali*-age it is auspicious to construct temples and divine images (3.222.28).[7] The Brahmanical tradition was seriously threatened by the success of these religions and the change in the cultural values that they caused. The historian Vijay Nath evaluates the situation for the Brahmanical tradition as critical and the idea of the *kali*-age as crucial: "Only by justifying the restructuring of the existing rituals to suit a decadent *kali*-age could the brahmanical ideologues succeed in countering such a threat and diffusing the crisis" (Nath 2009: 135). The middle *Purāṇa*s, according to Nandi, which post-date this transitional phase, pay less attention to the disorder and have fewer verses on the *kali*-age, and in these *Purāṇa*s the treatment seems more conventional (Nandi 1979/1980: 71).[8] However, the "*kali*-age paradigm, in fact, proved to be a highly effective strategy in achieving this end, even though it was responsible for transforming Brahmanism from an elitist to a broad based syncretistic system" (Nath 2009: 135).

Nath has, in a number of publications, argued for the relationship between the agrarian expansion and the growth in the number of pilgrimage places and the expansion of the areas included in Hindu pilgrimage. She has especially used the *Purāṇa*s to document this development. *Tīrtha*s and the *tīrtha* rituals became central in the Hindu traditions from the period in which the *Purāṇa*s became a Brahmanical textual genre around the fourth century CE (Nath 2007), perhaps around the same time as the *tīrthyātrāparvan* of the *Mahābhārata* was composed. The expansion of the tradition of *tīrtha*s happened in the same period as the composition of the *Purāṇa*s, and the two processes – expansion of traditions of salvific space and expansion of the textual genre of the *Purāṇa*s – seem to have been closely related. The large increase of the number of Hindu *tīrtha*s was part of the expansion of the Purāṇic religious traditions. The number of *tīrtha*s mentioned in the *Purāṇa*s grew over time, and later *Purāṇa*s include more *tīrtha*s than the earlier ones (Nandi 1979/1980: 104). The expansion of pilgrimage and *tīrtha*s parallels the expansion of the genre of *Purāṇa*s. Descriptions of *tīrtha*s constitute a major part of the *Purāṇa*s, and the composition of many of them might very well be related to the promotion of sacred places. The promotion of pilgrimage and sacred places is, as we saw in the previous chapter, part of the response by Brahmans to the economic situation in which sacrifice was severely criticized and fewer and fewer people gave donations for its performance, and in which the number of Brahmans was increasing. Competition with the Buddhists and other religious groups for *dāna* was an important reason for the success of the innovations. The sacrificial priest looked down upon the priests who performed ritual work with, and received their income from, images of deities. It is, in other words, tempting to see the expansion of pilgrimage as a response to a social and economic situation.

The presentation of the *tīrtha*s in the *Purāṇa*s is connected to the rituals and economic income of the Brahmans. The encouragement to give gifts (*dāna*) such as cows, gold and land to the Brahmans is pervasive in the texts on pilgrimage in the *Purāṇa*s, but there are also verses that warn the Brahmans not to accept gifts. These verses perhaps express the view of the Vedic priests who considered the new type of priests, who were occupied with statues and *tīrtha*s, as a danger to religion. R. N. Nandi writes:

> The Purāṇic *dāna* rites, which also included the ritual of *tīrthayātrā*, seem to represent a conscious and systematic attempt to collect essential subsistence from the unwilling *jajmana* by imposing on him the obligation to obtain immunity from *pātaka* and its effects which would overpower him even without an apparent cause, for the very nature of the Kali age is stated to be an automatic decrease in the quantum of *puṇya* and a corresponding increase in

> the quantum of *pātaka*. In the Kali age, the surest means of acquiring *puṇya* and destroying *pātaka* is to give gifts (*dāna*) to brāhmaṇas . . . The compulsion to make the unwilling clients pay adequately to their brāhmaṇa soul-helpers can be seen from the fact that *dāna* and *tīrthayātrā* begin to appear as important rituals only from the third centuries A. D.
>
> (Nandi 1979/1980: 100)

The *tīrthayātrā* ritual made people come from afar to give donations to Brahmans. It was a very effective way to collect economic values, and this important economic function explains in itself perhaps the enormous geographical expansion of the ritual. Nandi thinks that the expansion of the *dāna* ritual confirms the growing awareness of the Brahmans that the agricultural surplus was their main source of livelihood. Most of the rituals can also involve gifts of food. The impurity (*pāpa*) from which one needs to be purified is common and applies to everyone. In the *kali*-age, impurity is also the general state and, therefore, everyone is in need of the moral purification available at the *tīrthas*. Nandi also argues that the other groups were declared impure in order to make them unfit to receive gifts, so the gifts could be monopolized by the Brahmans. This is an interesting argument, but Nandi probably goes too far in claiming the whole *tīrtha* system as an economic conspiracy. He is, however, correct in emphasizing that the *tīrthayātrā* has an economical side and that the phenomenon cannot be fully understood without analyzing this aspect. He argues that, due to the waning of income from the *saṃskāra* rituals because of the decline of towns, the concept of *tīrtha* represented "an attempt to revive the prospects of gift-exchange" (Nandi 1979/1980: 104). Nandi in fact views the origin of pilgrimage as providing "some alternative ritual base of subsistence to the *jajmani* Brahmans, who lived in the decaying towns and depended on dynastic patronage" (ibid.). The *tīrtha* rituals are closely connected to the rituals of purification and thus the ideology of impurity. Vijay Nath puts it bluntly:

> Thus the concept of sin and the various ritual modes of expiation prescribed in the form of innumerable Dharmaśāstric rulings was posited and supported through a ritualism that aimed at creating lucrative source of income for the brāhmaṇas. . . . Significantly, the efficacy of all such ritual performances according to the lawgivers depended on the brāhmaṇas being the main beneficiaries of gifts of food and variety of other items offered on the occasion.
>
> (Nath 2009: 132)

The role of giving food to Brahmans is illustrated in one of the narratives about Vārāṇasī. The story of the foundation of Vārāṇasī in *Matsyapurāṇa* (Chapter 85) includes a story of Vyāsa, who lived by begging and experienced starvation because no householders would give food to Brahmans. When he did not see any reason why the residents of the city would not give him food, he cursed the city and its people to ruin. R. N. Nandi notes that this chapter in the *Matsyapurāṇa* is dated from between 700 and 1000 CE – a period during which the city was in a state of desertion (Nandi 1979/1980: 106). According to Nandi, the meaning of this strange story about Vārāṇasī seems to be simply to illustrate the negative consequences of not giving food to Brahmans. Nandi sees the establishment of the *gṛhya* rituals as a way of dealing with the loss of income from the *yajña* ritual. When the towns decayed, the income from the *gṛhya* rituals was also not sufficient, and the rituals of *dāna* and *tīrtha*s were introduced.

Nandi's economic arguments also relate to the conflict between the traditionalist priests and the temple priests, which was discussed in Chapter 3. The negative statements about the *devalaka,* argues Nandi, shows that there was a competition between the traditionalist (*śrotriya*) and the temple priests (*devalaka*) for ritual clients. Nandi writes:

> The emergence of the temple priests as serious contenders of the *jajmani* gifts during the early medieval period brought into sharp focus the conflict between the Vedic-educated intellectual Brahmans and the unintellectual practitioners of different folk-cults, the former trying to brand the latter as transgressors of Vedic discipline and priestly conduct and the latter trying to pick up some intellectual cover by organizing bhakti missions and neo-intellectual monastic orders and also preparing elaborate texts in support of the cult and philosophy. . . . For the orthodox fire-ritualists, the stakes were fairly high, since it was on their assured clientele the *devalakas* were making encroachments by inducing prosperous householders to pay liberally for the construction of temples and maintenance of temple based cults.
>
> (Nandi 1979/1980: 115)

The *devalaka*s were condemned in the *smṛti* literature and in the *smṛti* chapters in the *Purāṇa*s. Statements such as the one in the *Nāradapurāṇa* in the chapter on *śrādddha* that a *devalaka* ("a professional worshipper of images") is among those excluded from the *śrāddha* (1.28.11–18) shows that the traditionalist priest and the *devaklaka*s were competing for the same clientele. A noted tendency is that the client base of the *devalaka* priests is continuously broadened. The *devalaka*s were criticized for performing rituals for *śūdra*s and many of the new forms of religion related to *bhakti*, such as festivals and singing of songs in the vernaculars, did perhaps also have the function of expanding the client base of the Brahmans. Some of the Brahmanical texts present a very strong condemnation of this new religious culture and, in the *Nāradīyapurāṇa*, it is stated that anyone who lived off the earnings of the *devālaya* (temple) would be condemned to hell for a *kalpa* and then endure 100 successive rebirths as a Cāṇḍāla (Nandi 1979/1980: 116). The expansion of pilgrimage places can be understood as part of the general expansion to increase the number of religious clients for the *devalaka* priests. However, the temple, once established, soon became also a Vedic institution – that is, it has been argued that the *gṛhya* rituals were the patterns for key temple rituals and institutions (Willis 2009).

In the *Purāṇa*s, the treatment of *tīrtha*s is often in connection with rituals that involve *dāna* to Brahmans. The emphasis is on the salvific rewards, and most striking is the sheer number of places listed. In the *Matsyapurāṇa*, a number of tribal gods and goddesses are mentioned. After descriptions of *śrāddha* in Chapters 16–21, Chapter 22 details descriptions of sacred sites, the *tīrtha*s, places to perform *śrāddha* – that is, *tīrtha*s dear to *pitṛ*s. The chapter is called *Śrāddhamāhātmya* and a number of places are mentioned: Gayā, Prayāga, Daśāśvamedha, Gaṅgādvāra, Nandā, Lalitā, Mayāpurī, Mitrapada, Kedāra, Gaṅgāsāgara, Brahmasara, Naimiṣa, Gaṅgodbheda, Varāhakṣetra, Ikṣumati tīrtha and Kurukṣetra; the rivers Sarayū, Irāvatī, Devikā, Kālā, Chandrabhāgā, Dṛṣavatī, Veṇumatī and Vetravatī; and the places Jambūmārga, Nīlakuṇḍa, Rudrasarovara, Mānsarovara, Mandākaini, Acchodā, Vipāśā, Sarasvatī, Vaṃśobheda, Harodbheda, Gaṅgodbheda, Bhadreśvara, Viṣṇupada and Narmadādvāra. Offering *piṇḍa*s at these places, the text says, is equal to offering *piṇḍa*s in Gayā, a statement pointing to the competition between the different sites for ritual clients. The mere thought of these places offers rewards, much more than when one performs *śrāddha*s there. Further places are mentioned where it is beneficial to perform *śrāddha* and give gifts (*dāna*). The places that are *pāpahara* ("release one from sins") are so sacred that by merely having *darśan* of the places one is freed from moral impurity (*darśanād api caitāni sadyah pāpaharāṇi-vai*). Merely remembering these places washes away all moral impurity (*smaraṇād api pāpāni naśyanti śatadhā dvijāḥ*). Then, after the treatment of the ritual process of taking a sacred bath in order to attain heaven, comes the treatment of major pilgrimage places (Chapters 102–112). There cannot, states the text, be purity of mind without taking a sacred bath (*snāna*) (102.1). After a detailed description of the bath, the procedure and the mantras to be recited, the text starts describing Prayāg as a *tīrtha* where this ritual can be performed (103–112). There are many other places that drive away all moral impurity (*sarvapāpahara*); there are too many to describe, over hundreds of years, so the narrator describes one of them, Prayāg (104.5–6). The descriptions also include the rivers Gaṅgā and Yamunā. The moral impurity (*pāpa*) disappears the moment one enters Prayāg and even the perpetrators of evil deeds (*duṣkṛtakarma*) attain salvific liberation (*labhate tu paramāṃ gatim* [104.12–13]).

What is most striking about these descriptions of *tīrtha*s in *Matsyapurāṇa*, except for the salvific rewards being offered, is probably the number of *tīrtha*s mentioned. More than 100 are referred to in the *Śrāddhamāhātmya* chapter. It illustrates that, when the salvific space of *tīrtha*s had been accepted, their number grew enormously. In principle, it seems, any location could become a *tīrtha*. Any place where the ritual of *śrāddha* is performed is a *tīrtha*, any site where sacred baths are carried out is a *tīrtha* and any place where there is a temple can, in theory, become a *tīrtha*.

The Purāṇic conception of salvific space marks quite a remarkable change compared to earlier views. In the Purāṇic tradition, visiting many of these places peripheral to the Brahmanical culture was a source not of antagonism but of salvation and fulfillment of all wishes. This was a significant reversal of attitude. There are several reasons for this dramatically altered view of space, but a more important reason was probably the need for the Brahmans to increase their ritual clientele in order to maximize income. A main function of the *Purāṇa*s was to expand the influence and sources of income of the Brahman priests (Hazra 1940). While Vedic traditions had been restrictive and emphasized segregation, the *Purāṇa*s were more inclusive and open. In geographical terms, the *Purāṇa*s presented a very large number of salvific places. With the diminishing role of the sacrifice, the Vedic gods also became less important.

The composition of the *Purāṇa*s has been understood as an attempt to revitalize the Brahmanical social order, which had been undermined by the widespread popularity of Buddhism. The Brahmanical tradition needed to make their *tīrtha* tradition a popular institution in order to compete for the *dāna*. Some places of Hindu pilgrimage probably started as Buddhist sites of pilgrimage (Entwistle 1987). Places such as Gayā, Vārāṇasī and Mathurā are all close to important Buddhist pilgrimage places and one possible reason for their origin as Hindu pilgrimage places is as imitations of Buddhist pilgrimage.

The length of the *tīrtha* sections of the *Mahābhārata* and the *Purāṇa*s reflects the fast growing number of *tīrtha*s. A characteristic of the Purāṇic descriptions of the institution of sacred place and pilgrimage is the massive growth in their size (Nath 2007). In the *Mahābhārata*, Pulastya is mentioned as the first who promoted pilgrimage as a religious practice (*Mahābhārata* 3.80–83). Why there was a need to attach the institutionalization of pilgrimage to Pulastya is unclear. Here, it is presented as a secret circulating among the *ṛṣis*. To claim something as secret can be a rhetorical means to claim ancient origin for a new tradition: it was not known because it was kept secret (for a different interpretation, see pp. 92–93, 111). In several *Purāṇa*s, this tradition from the *Mahābhārata* is followed and Pulastya, in conversation with one or more of the Pāṇḍava brothers, promoted new pilgrimage places.

Expansion of *tīrtha*s, which is typical of the *Purāṇa*s, was a way for the Brahmanical tradition to spread and conquer new areas. Brahmans who left the cities incorporated places of religious importance to non-Vedic traditions into the Brahmanical sacred geography. V. Nath argues that "developments connected with the rise of new *tīrtha*s made it relatively easy for the aggrandizing cultural agents to acquire tribal land in the name of upcoming centres of pilgrimage" (Nath 2001: 134). New *tīrtha*s could develop into urban areas and become regional pilgrimage centers and such *tīrtha*s were probably important in developing regional identities. Nath writes that "the most significant change that came about in the importance of priests in the age of the Purāṇas was related to the ever-widening spatial horizons," and concludes that with "brahmanical cultural influence fast penetrating into peripheral ones, the demand for the services of brāhmaṇas was no longer confined to the heartland" (Nath 2009: 128).

The migration of Brahmans to other parts of the country was, according to Nath, due to land grants. "But having once settled down in those outlying areas, the recipients, on account of their ever-multiplying numbers, could not have desisted seeking fresh clientele from amongst the local population" (ibid.). Nath mentions the creation of new sections of Brahmans from amongst the indigenous priestly class as one important consequence of this geographical expansion. Nath sees a close relationship between the expansion of *Purāṇas* and *tīrthas* and emphasizes their role as instruments of acculturation – that is, the geographical expansion of Hindu traditions from the central areas. A large number of ritual practices were performed at the *tīrthas* and the descriptions of the rituals of pilgrimage in the *Purāṇas* are perhaps based on these rituals. In the *Purāṇas*, the journey to the pilgrimage place hardly receives any attention. The focus is on the place, and one reason for this is probably because it was at these places the Brahman priests were situated. It was important to attract pilgrims to the sites and to have them perform rituals there. Hindu pilgrimage traditions as described in the *Purāṇas* are *tīrtha*-oriented, not travel-oriented. The texts are written to promote the salvific power of the places. Little value is ascribed to the journey as such. The numbers of rituals to be performed are mainly carried out at the *tīrtha* itself. The quantity of Purāṇic material dealing with *tīrthas* is enormous and reflects the tribal and folk religious traditions that were utilized to mobilize around the *tīrtha* traditions. A number of tribal or local deities were included in the *Purāṇas*. V. Nath thinks that "the integration of tribal deities into the *tīrtha* tradition was achieved largely through their induction in the Purāṇic pantheon" (Nath 2009: 187). The enormous number of *tīrthas* made peripheral regions sacred and included them in the Brahmanical tradition. A number of folk religious motifs are found in the *tīrtha* narratives. The *Nāradapurāṇa* mentions 400 principal *tīrthas* on the banks of Narmadā, *Brahmapurāṇa* refers to a large number of *tīrthas* along the Godāvarī and the *Skandapurāṇa* mentions 68 *tīrthas* at Hātakeśvara in Saurashtra, and so on (ibid.: 174). Purāṇic myths and geographical expansion of *tīrthas* strengthened each other: "The *tīrtha* tradition was thus largely fed and sustained by a kaleidoscopic and constantly swelling Purāṇic lore, kept alive by oral transmission in the form of *kathā*. Sans the Purāṇas, it would have lacked all substance, base and direction" (Nath 2009: 175).

The *Purāṇas* have, to a large degree, been oral traditions performed by bards who recited from memory, with some degree of freedom in how they wanted to shape the material. The audience of the *Sthalapurāṇas* and *Māhātmyas* of place were pilgrims at the *tīrthas*. The reciters of the *Sthalapurāṇas* and *Māhātmyas* performed at the *tīrthas*, possibly at the festivals when an especially larger number of persons had gathered, and the length of the *Sthalapurāṇas* and *Māhātmyas* was probably decided by the ability to attract an audience for many days in a row. Local narratives were included in larger narratives and these reciters functioned to disseminate the Hindu traditions. Several researchers on Hindu pilgrimage agree that the *tīrthas*, in remote tribal belts, can function to integrate the surrounding areas into the cultural mainstream and that they provide the political powers with religious legitimacy (Morinis 1984; Nath 2009). The Hindu concepts of impurity and purity are implied in the pilgrimage rituals, and the establishment of numerous *tīrthas* in new areas undoubtedly helped to spread this ideology, and thus also the religious practices: the idea of the ritual purity of Brahmans and the social system based on these ideas. It has also been suggested that declaring a place a *tīrtha* was a form of land grabbing and that pilgrimage places were closely associated with power, especially with the construction of monumental temples at the sites (Agrawala 1963; Nath 2009).

Regional kingdoms, cities and pilgrimage

Expansion of *tīrtha*s was associated with the growth of feudal kingships in the regional areas between 1000 and 1200, the "heyday of political feudalism" (Sharma 1965). The literature of the *tīrtha*s typically displays regional biases: *Matsyapurāṇa* for the banks of the Narmadā river, the *Brahmapurāṇa* for the eastern part of Orissa, *Mārkaṇḍeyapurāṇa* for the Vindhya region, *Garuḍapurāṇa* for the Mithilā region, *Bhāgavatapurāṇa* for the Deccan, and so on (Nath 2009). The feudal kingship organized regional centers of pilgrimage within their kingdom. They supported large-scale settlements of Brahmans, who served as priests in the temples and promoted a Hinduized type of worship in wider areas, leading to more pilgrimage places. This strengthened pilgrimage towns and also led to establishments of new pilgrimage towns. The German historian Herman Kulke has argued that the feudal kingdoms in this period, in the absence of bureaucracy, used ritual means to counterbalance the centrifugal forces that threatened the kingdoms (Kulke 1978). He argues that the aim was achieved by the means of three elements that all relate to pilgrimage: first, royal patronage of the places of pilgrimage of great importance within their kingdoms; second, systematic and large-scale settlements of Brahmans; and third, construction of new imperial temples (ibid.: 132). Kulke argues that the history of Hindu places of pilgrimage "is inextricably linked with the *bhakti* faith" and that it was because of *bhakti* that "all-Indian Brahmin Hinduism . . . came down to villages and rural centres and, *vice versa*, various autochthonous deities in a long and gradual process of Hinduization were included in the pantheon of bhakti Hinduism" (ibid.). It was through folk religion, he argues, that *tīrtha* became a main part of popular religion because pilgrimage and the rituals at the *tīrtha*s were despised by the high caste-Brahmins/Vedic Brahmins. Kulke quotes a verse from *Mahābhārata* (*Śāntiparvan* 76. trans. Vol. 8, p. 173) in support, which says that Brahmans who perform services for a fee are regarded as Cāṇḍālas among Brahmans:

> They that are employed in courts of justice for summoning people, they that perform worship for others for a fee, they that perform the sacrifices of Vaiśyas and Śūdras, they that officiate in sacrifices on behalf of a whole village and they that make voyages on the ocean – these five are regarded as Cāṇḍalas among Brāhmaṇas.

Kulke notes that a feature of the worship of gods at the centers of pilgrimage is the royalization of the rituals and that this royalization was connected to the legitimation of royal power. The *tīrtha*s "became centres of a multicentred royal network" (1978: 133), which united larger areas. The *tīrtha*s owned property scattered over large territories and the pilgrims who visited the *tīrtha*s likewise returned to all parts of the kingdom.

Kulke also notes that land grants to Brahmans in the early period were donated to individuals or small groups in quite remote places and the purpose of this was inner colonization in the early nuclear areas (ibid.). Towards the end of the first millennium CE, land was granted also to large groups of Brahmans; sometimes many hundreds were systematically settled. Kulke argues that the Brahmans functioned as administrative and ideological specialists and that their traditional ideology of contentedness and worldly abstinence made them able to counteract the centrifugal forces.

The rise of the regional kingdoms coincides with what has been called a third period of urbanization, which had begun in the early medieval period, in the tenth and eleventh centuries, and gained momentum by the fourteenth century (see Chattopadhyaya 1994; Sharma 1987). The presence of a large temple or a great number of shrines could make the place an important pilgrimage destination and this contributed to urbanization. Chattopadhyaya has suggested that the majority of the urban centers in this period corresponded to different tiers of regional powers. Kulke argues that the building of the new gigantic temples coincides with the heyday of feudalism in India. He gives the examples of Kandariya-Mahādeva temple in Khajuraho (1002 CE), Bṛhadīśvara temple in Tañjaur (1012 CE), Udayeśvara temple in Udayapur (1059–1080 CE), Liṅgarāja temple in Bhuvaneśvar (ca. 1060 CE), Jagannāth temple in Purī (1035 CE) and Koṇārk temple (1250 CE). All these new, gigantic temples became centers of pilgrimage. With the large number of services required and pilgrims visiting, a major temple could not exist without an urban context, and most often "temples appear to be in towns whose origins can be dated from the time when the major construction of the temple structure occurred" (Stein 1982: 454). A city was considered incomplete without a temple. B. Stein contends that the city and the temple completed each other, in the sense that a city required a place deity to protect the people of the city, that the city developed as a result of the construction of a temple and that caste, sect and political elements of the rural area were represented in a paradigmatic form in the city (Stein 1982). Major South Indian temple cities include Cidambaram, Madurai, Kāñcī, Kumbhakoṇam, Thañjaur, Tirumala, Tiruvaṇṇamalai (see Figure 4.1) and Śrīraṅgam. Many of these cities originated at sacred spots next to rivers or mountains and, referring to South India, George Michell argues that "the simultaneous growth of pilgrimage and trade is an outstanding feature of urban life in the region" (Michell 1993:13). The cities of Cidambaram, Madurai, Tiruvaṇṇamalai and Śrīraṅgam each have one dominating temple.

Later expansions

It is not the purpose here to describe the further history of the Hindu pilgrimage traditions, which is intricate, complex and shifting and covers a large number of regions and localities, with their own complex political and economic histories. The general tendency, however, is further expansion and growth of the pilgrimage traditions. For example, Gayā probably gained the importance it has today in the thirteenth and fourteenth centuries (Yang 1998). Pilgrimage became the main ritual of Hinduism, although periods of war and destruction also had great consequences for the sacred centers, pilgrimage places and pilgrimage travel. Many temples and images were destroyed and travel was unsafe. "Perhaps no aspect of Hinduism," writes P. Granoff, "was as greatly affected by political shifts in mediaeval India as the cult of sacred objects and pilgrimage sites" (1992: 550). B. Saraswati has suggested that one of the great differences between the pilgrimage places in South India and North India is that in South India it is the temple that is sacred and the object of pilgrimage, while in North India it is the *kṣetra* that is sacred and that the destruction of temples in North India, thus, did not destroy the sacredness of the places (Saraswati 1985). Descriptions of how sites retain their sacredness even though there are no sacred objects there are found in *Māhātmya*s, and such descriptions might be responses to destruction of temples. In the *Sābhramatīmāhātmya*, Śiva tells Pārvatī: "There is no doubt that this place belongs to me, O Daughter of the Mountain, though there is no *liṅga* of mine here" (91); "But the wise should know that the place itself is to be regarded as my *liṅga*. And everywhere there one should offer flowers and incense, and all kinds of offerings" (110; Granoff 1992:551–552).

The most powerful *liṅga*s in the *kali*-age are the *liṅga*s that are hidden, the text states. P. Granoff has suggested that the narrative motif found in the *Purāṇa*s of hidden (*gupta*) *tīrtha*s that are rediscovered relates to periods after war and the destruction of pilgrimage temples or periods when temples or images have been concealed to thwart their destruction (Granoff 1992). The situation in India varied greatly and periods of destruction were followed by periods of rebuilding. New temples were erected after periods of repression and destruction.

A new significant transformation of many important pilgrimage places happened in the fifteenth and sixteenth centuries in North India. In this period, several

Figure 4.1 The temple city of Tiruvaṇṇamalai seen from the mountain of Aruṇācalam

Photo: Knut A. Jacobsen

pilgrimage places were heavily influenced by the *bhakti* movement, especially Vṛndāvan and Ayodhyā as the centers of the worship of Kṛṣṇa and Rāma, respectively (Entwistle 1987; van der Veer 1988). Pilgrimage to these places focused on living at the place in which Kṛṣṇa and Rāma had dwelled. Salvific space here meant being present at places where closeness to the divine could be experienced.

An extraordinary growth in pilgrimage traffic developed over the last two centuries, an increase that happened well before the population growth of the twentieth century (Yang 1998). Pax Britannica made travel easier. During the period 1780 to 1820, the number of pilgrims visiting Allāhābad (Prayāg), Gayā and Vārāṇasī trebled (Bayly 1983). A large number of Brahmans make their livelihood from pilgrimage: *pujārī*s (priests) perform the ritual in temples, *paṇḍā*s organize pilgrimage, *ghāṭiyā*s take responsibility for bathers, *karmakāṇḍa*s perform rituals and *mahāpatra*s perform rituals related to death.[9] In cities like Ayodhyā, Vārāṇasī, Prayāg or Gayā, this amounts to a large number of people; much of the economy of the sacred places has depended on the pilgrims. C.A. Bayly has argued that, around 1810, there were more than 40,000 Brahmans living on charity in Vārāṇasī city alone (Bayly 1983). This accounted for 17–20 percent of the population. Another economic dimension of pilgrimage places is the annual fairs or *melā*s, which often coincide with the arrival of large groups of pilgrims. The fairs can last for a day or for many weeks (such as the *kumbhamelā*s). A.A. Yang argues that pilgrimage places often developed from fairs and marketplaces (Yang 1998). The pilgrim population had a major influence on the organization of the economy through markets, bazaars and fairs, and provided a significant extra income for rulers who collected pilgrim dues (Bayly 1983).

The neutrality of British colonial power with regards to religious issues favored the consolidation of Hinduism, and mass pilgrimage to many places started only with the economic, political and technological changes of the British. The pilgrim tax was abolished in 1833, but even before this abolition the number of pilgrims had grown. Pilgrimage had now become a status ritual that spread from aristocratic families to the recently ennobled zamindars and to the emerging business and service class (Entwistle 1987). From the late eighteenth century, aristocrats and merchants began to restore the old *ghāṭ*s in cities such as Mathurā, Vṛndāvan, Ayodhyā and Vārāṇasī, and many new ones were built throughout the nineteenth and twentieth centuries (ibid.). Improvements in the transportation system, population growth, economic growth and strengthening of religious identities, together with the merging of pilgrimage traditions with tourism in the twentieth century, produced a peak in pilgrimage that has continued into the twenty-first century.

One reason for the peak in pilgrimage travel is that the sacred and secular institutions share the same interest in the growth of pilgrims. The pilgrimage site Bakreśvar (a *śaktipīṭha*) in West Bengal was studied by Buddhadeb Chaudhuri in the 1970s, and he questioned how the idea of its sacredness is transmitted in order to attract pilgrims (Chaudhuri 1981). The main temple in Bakreśvar is a Śiva temple devoted to Śiva as Bakranāth and another important attraction is its hot springs, which are believed to have healing powers. A feature of Bakreśvar that Chaudhuri investigated was the increase in the number of pilgrims in the recent past. How was it, therefore, that while there was a secularization of society, the number of pilgrims nevertheless continued to grow? Bakreśvar gives several reasons. The Sanskrit school attracted students from a wider area and they "have played an important role in propagating the cult of Siva of Bakreshwar" (Chaudhuri 1981: 49). The Brahman priests have usually had a *jajmānī* relationship to pilgrim families, and members of these families have moved to a wide area and have propagated the sacredness of the place. The priests have also used modern ways of communication associated with tourism to attract pilgrims, such as distribution of pamphlets and postcards describing the sacredness of the region and the extraordinary powers of the hot springs in the area to cure diseases. *Sādhu*s wander and spread the word about sacredness, as well as the food and gifts offered to them at the places of pilgrimage. Other persons who also have material benefits from the pilgrims, such as shop owners, propagate the place's sacredness. "The local shop-owners," writes Chaudhuri, "are always very interested to propagate the sacred myth of Bakreshwar out of their own economic interests as it would help to draw a steady flow of visitors" (ibid.: 50). The annual fair in fact attracts shop owners as far away as Kolkata and also beyond the state of West Bengal to set up shops. Chaudhuri counted 606 shop owners in the annual fair of 1974, with around 20,000–25,000 pilgrims. Chaudhuri also notes that modern media, such as newspapers and radio, improved transport systems and tourism have also contributed to spreading the religion of Śiva at Bakreśvar. The Brahmans distributed pamphlets at the site about the sacred stories of the place. It is also notable that the sacredness of the place was advertised in newspapers in Kolkata by the Tourist Department of West Bengal (a phenomenon of increasing importance in India in general). All these activities reflect economic interests. Lastly, Chaudhuri mentions that politicians would exploit the sacredness of the place and organize many meetings there, especially at election times. Also, non-political movements organized meetings at the place. Reports in the media of political and other meetings mentioned the stories and sacredness of the place and so indirectly promoted the holiness of the site.

Chaudhuri has documented processes that can be observed at many other places in India. Sacred and secular institutions share the same interest in the growth of pilgrim numbers. Even the beggars, notes Chaudhuri, "have abiding interest in the perpetuation of the sacred myth of Bakreshwar which would attract more and more visitors to the sacred area and fetch them more money" (ibid.: 52). He concludes that the most distinctive feature of Bakreśvar was not the dominance of Śiva worship, but "the presence of numerous ritual styles, sects, faiths, temples and shrines" (ibid.: 86). This plurality also functions to attract people, and the economic incentive here is to offer as varied products as possible and to include everyone. The more varied the religious traditions, the more people will come and contribute to the economy. Chaudhuri notes that the commercially oriented attitude of the Brahman families is quite conspicuous: "The economic implications are often more emphasized, sacred contents are becoming less meaningful" (ibid.: 91).

The phenomenon of Hindu salvific space at pilgrimage places has throughout history aimed to attract as many devotees as possible and to promote the belief that all the goals of religion are easily attainable for all. The point of Hindu salvific space at pilgrimage places is to include everyone. No-one is excluded; even the worst sinner can easily attain *mokṣa* just by taking advantage of the salvific power of the pilgrimage place. One important reason for this attitude seems to be economic; the point is to attract as many pilgrims as possible. The web page advertising the 2013 *kumbhamelā* in Prayāg reads like a commercial: "This is the only time and place in the world where you can unburden your sins and achieve 'Nirvana' from the vicious cycle of birth and rebirth."[10] The same web page states: "Kumbh Mela is not just a mere festivity like Diwali and Holi," but "this event gives them a golden opportunity to liberate themselves from the miseries and sufferings of life. It enables them to take a holy dip in the sacred water and wash away all the sins they have committed in the past." It is easy, and nothing other than contact with the water is needed: "taking a holy dip in water paves the way for attainment of Moksha." Here, the Hindu idea of salvific space is expressed in the exemplary way.The salvific power has been made available by the falling down to earth of a drop of the drink of immortality of the gods from a pot, *kumbha*, at the *triveṇī*, where the rivers Yamunā, Gaṅgā and Sarasvatī meet, and is available in a particular potent way at the time of the *kumbhamelā*. The increasing number of pilgrims to the Prayāg *kumbhamelā*s indicates that the idea of salvific space and pilgrimage is thriving in contemporary Hinduism. The economic value of pilgrimage is so great that its popularity in Hindu traditions is partly because of the economic importance it has for the groups who can profit from it. Its economic value can be compared to the modern tourist industry, with which it has many similarities. The exaggerated claims repeatedly found in most *tīrtha* texts read like advertisements aimed at convincing people to buy products.

5 Narratives and doctrines of salvific space: the example of sage Kapila

Pilgrimage places associated with sages and ascetics are often linked to the goal of salvific liberation, especially places associated with those sages and ascetics who are believed to have realized the goal of *mokṣa*. Such sites, therefore, illustrate well some important aspects of the idea of salvific space. The salvific power of the sages is still believed to be present at the pilgrimage places and the stories of the sages point to the religious attainment available at the site. The presence of ascetics at pilgrimage sites is a reminder to the pilgrims that *mokṣa* is the ultimate goal of life for many Hindu traditions and that the lifestyle of a *saṃnyāsin* is the supreme means to fulfilling this goal. According to the ideology of the four *āśrama*s, the last stage of life should ideally be as a *saṃnyāsin*. Renunciation leads to holiness. Many ascetics move from pilgrimage place to pilgrimage place and their presence at the sites is an important part of what makes the places holy. Ascetics' organizations have established monasteries at many pilgrimage sites to provide for the ascetics and to maintain a presence. Some of the pilgrimage places associated with ascetics are linked to the attainment of *mokṣa* or a better rebirth. It is believed that it is particularly important for old people to travel on a pilgrimage because they are aware that death is approaching and that washing away moral impurity (*pāpa*) and gaining religious merit (*puṇya*) is of crucial significance since moral impurity and merit relates especially to death and one's status in the afterlife. Other pilgrimages may be oriented around seeking to be in the presence of the divine, the fulfillment of *vrata*s in order to keep a promise for having received assistance from divinities, attaining success in business (or thanking the god for such success), and many other goals. However, the pilgrimage places of sages associated with the philosophies of salvific liberation tend to focus on the salvational goal. In this chapter, I will present the pilgrimage places associated with the founder of the Sāṃkhya system of religious thought, the sage Kapila.[1] I have tried to identify all the pilgrimage places in India associated with him and most of the references to him in the Hindu texts. For the major gods, such a task would perhaps not be possible, but since there is a limited number of pilgrimage places associated with Kapila and a limited number of references to him in the Hindu texts, a complete overview is possible. The sites and stories connected to him illustrate some of the important patterns of salvific space. These places are associated with *mokṣa*, renunciation and salvific power, but also reveal the various strategies used by the promoters of the pilgrimage places to attract pilgrims and the pragmatic nature of pilgrimage traditions.

When investigating the pilgrimage places associated with the sage Kapila, in order to study the place of the sage in the history of religions of India and in contemporary Hinduism (see Jacobsen 2008a), I observed that being salvific or salvational was an important quality of the places associated with Kapila. I realized that the concept of salvific space had value for describing Hindu pilgrimage sites in general. Salvific space focuses on the rewards of visiting the places, on the pragmatic dimension of pilgrimage and especially its relationship to salvational goals. Descriptions of pilgrimage places in the Hindu texts center primarily on the rewards and very little attention is given to the journey. Salvific space rather than salvific travel was highlighted. Pilgrims travel to pilgrimage places for many reasons, but the basic belief is that the pilgrimage places have the power to solve the problems presented to them by the pilgrims. The different salvific rewards offered by the pilgrimage sites, such as the reward of healing a disease, the improved afterlife status of relatives, moral purification, and so on, are not opposed to each other. Such rewards are promoted by the sacred narratives of the location, told by the ritual performers and others who secure an income from the places, or are found in texts associated with the places. Sage Kapila is known as the founder of the Sāṃkhya system of philosophy, a prestigious Hindu framework of religious thought that focuses on salvific liberation, which in this system is often called *kaivalya*. He is also associated with salvific liberation. Kapila, according to the narratives and traditions, was a renunciant and a powerful ascetic. The places he is supposed to have stayed at became filled with salvific power and this power has continued to supply the pilgrims with salvific rewards. This is a common pattern of many of the places associated with Kapila. The stories of the locations associated with him focus on the attainment of salvific liberation.

Several of the places linked to Kapila are important sites for performing the ritual of *śrāddha*. There is, in general, a close relationship between the ritual of *śrāddha*, pilgrimage and *tīrtha*s. Even in the *Dharmaśāstra*s, a body of literature that mostly does not propagate pilgrimage, *tīrtha*s are sometimes mentioned as places recommended for the performance of the *śrāddha* ritual. *Śrāddha* is performed for the dead to secure their existence in heaven or to grant them *mokṣa*, salvific liberation. Contradictory conceptions of death and the afterlife exist in the Hindu traditions. The ideas of karma and reincarnation assume a more or less immediate rebirth; the rituals for the dead, the *śrāddha*, assume that the dead will spend a year on their way to the world of the ancestors to gradually gain an ancestor body. The *śrāddha* functions to feed the dead so that the year-long journey to the world of the ancestors is successful and ensures that the dead do not linger as ghosts (*bhūta*) but move on. The fear of ghosts has perhaps been more important than the fear of hell in Hindu religious life (Jacobsen 2009c), although the fear of hell is also a motivation for going on pilgrimage and washing away moral impurity. The rituals around death focus on the successful transfer of the dead. Successful transfer, in many Hindus' understanding means *mokṣa*, which may denote the end of rebirth and union with the divine, but is often understood to mean a rebirth in heaven, or can even signify rebirth into a wealthy family. In the promotion texts of the pilgrimage places, these goals are often combined: the person, when they die, is moved on a divine vehicle to heaven and, after enjoying themselves there, they will be reborn in a beautiful body into a wealthy family and when they die they will attain salvific liberation.

The most important of the pilgrimage places associated with Kapila for the *śrāddha* ritual are the pilgrimage sites of Sidhpur in Gujarat, which has the status of being the main Hindu place for performing *śrāddha* for mothers, and Gaṅgā Sāgar in Bengal, which is an important place due to its association with the river Gaṅgā's salvific power, as well as being mentioned in the narrative of how the river came to earth. The reason Sidhpur is the main place for the performance of *śrāddha* for mothers is that Kapila instructed his mother Devahūti at this place in the teaching of the Sāṃkhya system of religious thought and she attained *mokṣa* there. What Gayā is for performance of rituals for dead fathers, Sidhpur is for dead mothers (see section "Sidhpur in Gujarat" below). Sons, therefore, go on pilgrimage to Sidhpur to perform *śrāddha* for their mothers and these pilgrims come from large parts of India. Both the narratives and the rituals of Sidhpur and Gaṅgā Sāgar are about salvational goals.

Pilgrimage, Kapila and sacred narratives

Many sacred narratives about Kapila, some more important than others, are found in Hindu texts: the *Mahābhārata*, the *Rāmāyaṇa* and the *Purāṇa*s, as well as in several *Māhātmya*s of places. However, the sacred narratives about Kapila exist not only in the texts; they are alive in the holy landscapes in India today. Kapila is associated with sacred narratives that are linked to India's geography. Thus, the sacred narratives of Kapila are located in space, not only in texts; the stories took place at particular locations and they are kept alive at these places by ritual performances and pilgrimage activities. Some of the pilgrimage centers base their sacredness on a few well-known episodes in the life of Kapila, well-known in the sense that they are renowned in the Epics and the *Purāṇa*s. These places have pan-Indian significance. Other sites of Kapila worship draw pilgrims from only the regional or local areas. Local traditions tell about *tapas* performed by Kapila and about the miracles that later happened there because of the permanent presence of his power. The stories are generally related to salvific liberation.

Several of the pilgrimage places of Kapila in India today draw huge numbers of pilgrims, especially to the annual festivals. The salvific power attributed to these places is believed to have originated with Kapila's presence, sometimes associated with special events, and the fact that Kapila was the founder of the famous Sāṃkhya system of religious thought adds to the power of the sites. Since the teaching of Sāṃkhya is about the realization of salvific liberation, the places focus on this goal. The association with Sāṃkhya also adds an intellectual and ascetic quality to several of the locations. Some features of the philosophy of Kapila are presented in the *Māhātmya* texts of the places. A few persons associated with the places, such as Brahman priests or *saṃnyāsin*s often have some basic knowledge of the Sāṃkhya philosophy. However, the pilgrims travel there not to learn about the Sāṃkhya system of religious thought, but to draw upon the salvific power of the sites, which they hope to benefit from by being present at the places. They also hope to have *darśan* of Kapila and the sacred site, and perform several rituals, especially *pūjā* and *darśan*, ritual bathing and the *śrāddha* rituals.

Pilgrims come to the sites associated with Kapila in order to draw upon the salvific power created by his presence, but most do not come to worship Kapila, although they usually visit the temples to have *darśan* of him. There are mostly ascetics present at the Kapila sites, which also form a connection to Kapila's salvific power. This is further heightened by the fact that some of the *āśrama*s that have been established at these locations bear the names taken from the philosophical or narrative traditions of Kapila, such as Kardamāśrama, Kapilāśrama or Sāṃkhyayogāśrama. The salvific power of many of these centers of pilgrimage is based on the belief that Kapila once practiced asceticism at the place and, since Kapila is known to have discovered and revealed a way to *mokṣa*, the sacred places associated with Kapila are considered to have strong salvific powers. At some places, stories describe particular events that endowed the places with salvific power.

The sacred sites of Kapila are often part of greater sacred complexes. The specific places in which Kapila is said to have stayed are named as Kapilatīrtha, Kapilāśrama, Kapilāhrada, Kapilasaṅgama or Kapiladhārā, but these names are not always the names of the sacred complexes. Several of these locations are of pan-Indian significance: Gaṅgā Sāgara, the place where the river Gaṅgā enters the Indian Ocean; Tirupati in Andhra Pradesh at the foot of the mountain that leads to Tirumala and the temple of Veṅkaṭeśvara, which is the place in India that receives the greatest number of pilgrims annually; Kolāyat in Rajasthan in the desert close to the border of Pakistan, where a lake contains the salvific and healing power of Kapila; Amarkaṇṭaka in Madya Pradesh, where the Narmadā river begins; Vārāṇasī, the important pan-Indian pilgrimage center, situated where the rivers Varaṇā and Assī merge with the river Gaṅgā and where Gaṅgā turns north and pilgrims can greet the sunrise in the east on the west side of the river; and Sidhpur in Gujarat where Kapila is worshipped as the savior of his own mother and where salvific power for mothers in particular is believed to exist. Traditions claim that Kapila enjoyed the natural beauty of many of these places and therefore selected them as places for his *tapas*.

However, many of the places associated with the sage Kapila might have been connected to him by narrators who promote the pilgrimage places by utilizing the resemblance of the word *kapilā,* which is used both for rivers and cows, to the sage's name Kapila. The narrators try to draw as much holiness as they can to the places because the function of the stories is to promote the salvific power of the site in order to attract as many pilgrims as possible. In the "Story of the origin of the river Kapilā," told in the *Skandapurāṇa* (5.3.21) about the river Kapilā, a tributary to the river Narmadā, it is stated that more than 100 crores (one crore is ten million) of sages, after performing penance there, attained salvific liberation and became free from rebirth and never returned to *samṣāra*. The text states: "Since the noble-souled Kapila performed penance there, a meritorious Tīrtha has sprung up there. It was resorted to formerly by the sages following Kapila; it has been praised by the name Kapilā. It is destructive of all sins" (*Skandapurāṇa* 5.3.21.58b–60; translation G. V. Tagare). Another possibility is of course that the river was named after *kapilā* because of the red-brown color of its water, and that the place and the name of the river came first and the association with the sage Kapila afterwards. It can be proved for other places that the name Kapilā (in the sense of "the red-brown cow") existed before the association of the sage Kapila (see section "Kapilatīrtha in Tirupati and the Kapila Places Associated with Cows" below). It is probably also the case with rivers. In the same chapter of the *Skandapurāṇa*, we do indeed receive this explanation as to why the river is given the name Kapilā:

> Formerly, O king, the daughter of Dakṣa sported about in the waters of Narmadā with great joy along with the Trident bearing one (Śiva). (71) After rising up suddenly from the water she changed her clothes. The wet clothes of the goddess were sportingly squeezed and pressed by the attendants. (72) When the clothes were being squeezed dry, drops of coloured water resembling the rainbow fell down. Hence the great river named Kapilā issued forth. (73–74a) The tawny-coloured water issuing from the clothes got mixed with the unguents. Due to the *kapila* colour the river became Kapilā by name too (74b).
>
> (Translation G. V. Tagare, slightly modified)

However, the point here is that, because of the resemblance with the name *kapilā*, the sites named after a *kapilā* river or *kapilā* cow often do become associated with the sage Kapila. The association of the sage Kapila with the salvational goals helps to promote the place as salvific space and adds significance. A link with the previous presence of a famous sage (*ṛṣi*) is one of the main foundations for the establishment of salvific sites. It is tempting to also understand this as an element of a historical process of making pilgrimage sites part of the Brahmanical tradition. Kapila is a Brahmanical sage associated with Viṣṇu and the Hindu philosophical *śāstra*s. By connecting the locations to the sage Kapila, the places become incorporated into a larger narrative. It is perhaps of significance that the major Kapila places, such as Sidhpur, Kolāyat and Gaṅgā Sāgar, are found in the peripheries. Some of the minor places devoted today to sage Kapila that are found in the geographical areas where the early Vedic tradition flourished, such as in Kāmpil in western Uttar Pradesh and Kolyād in Jind district in Haryana, witnessed another transformation. Kapila was also the name of one or more *yakṣa*s, who were protectors or gatekeepers, and these *yakṣa*s with the name Kapila were later connected to the sage Kapila and their identity changed. This illustrates the way Hindu traditions created salvific space and pilgrimage traditions from older traditions that connected divinity to specific sites.

Some of these pilgrimage places are well known, while others have received little or no attention in research literature. Two of the most interesting of the sacred places associated with Kapila are Sidhpur in Gujarat and Gaṅgā Sāgar in Bengal. They are connected to sacred narratives found in the *Mahābhārata*, the *Rāmāyaṇa* and the *Purāṇa*s, and the rituals performed there are closely linked to the sacred narratives about Kapila and the salvific power and activities that are associated with him. The sacred sites of Sidhpur and Gaṅgā Sāgar demonstrate the close link between narratives, rituals, sites and salvific power in the sacred geography of Kapila and, in general, in the pilgrimage traditions of Hinduism.

Sidhpur in Gujarat

The city of Sidhpur (also called Siddhapura, Siddhapada or Siddhakṣetra, and prior to 1200 its name was Śrīsthal[2]) lies in Gujarat, close to Pāṭaṇ and between Pālanpur and Mahesāṇā on the Delhi–Ahmedābād railway. It is a significant local and regional pilgrimage center and one of the most important places in the sacred geography of Kapila, being particularly auspicious and popular for the performance of *śrāddha* rituals for dead mothers.

Sidhpur is to female ancestors what Gayā, especially, but perhaps also Prayāg or Vārāṇasī are to males, so in order to perform *gayāśrāddha* to the mother and female ancestors, many Hindus go to Sidhpur (see Figure 5.1). This is not only a fact in the *tīrtha* promotion texts of Sidhpur, but an empirical reality as well. The fact that Kapila gave *mokṣa* to his mother is quite astonishing in the patriarchal culture of India and the contrast to Paraśurāma, who killed his mother and who is also worshipped here, and perhaps symbolizes male guilt, is striking. In addition to its significance for understanding salvific space, it makes Sidhpur a place of

Figure 5.1 *Śrāddha* in the city Sidhpur, where *gayāśrāddha* is performed to the mother

Photo: Knut A. Jacobsen

unique interest for the study of gender in patriarchal India. The story of Kapila's mother, Devahūti, and her asceticism also became a model for female asceticism and therefore fundamental in several institutions with female ascetics. Sidhpur perhaps compensates, so to speak, in a small way for the excesses of the dominant patriarchal practice and ideology. Sidhpur is a place in which men honor their mothers and repent the suffering caused to them by a repressive society.[3]

The *gayāśrāddha* is performed at the Kapilāśrama, Kapila's *āśrama*, a place of meditation situated two miles west of Sidhpur. The significance of Sidhpur to the sacred geography of Kapila derives from the belief that it was the place where he was born and where he gave the Sāṃkhya teaching to his mother Devahūti.[4] A well in Sidhpur contains, supposedly, the water from the tears Devahūti shed when she was experiencing the elation of having attained *mokṣa*.

At the pilgrimage center Kapilāśrama, there are temples to many different gods, but the main ritual is linked to only one of the temples. In this temple are statues of Kapila, his mother Devahūti, his father Kardama and Viṣṇu, of whom Kapila is considered as an *avatāra*. This temple is next to Bindusarovar ("pond of tears"), which is one of three sacred waters here; the others are a well called Jñānavāpikā ("the well of knowledge") and a tank called Alpasarovara ("small pond"). The Sanskrit text *Siddhapura Māhātmya*, a text of 114 verses of an unknown date, identifies the location at which Kapila taught the truth of Sāṃkhya to his mother as the water tank Bindusaras or Bindusarovar in Sidhpur.[5] The pond is also mentioned in the *Bhāgavatapurāṇa*, which is the foundation text for the narrative of the child Kapila and his teaching of his mother. According to the *Bhāgavatapurāṇa*, the water tank is Viṣṇu's tears of compassion (3.21.38); according to the oral tradition of Sidhpur that is related to the pilgrims, the water in the Bindusarovar is Devahūti's tears of happiness at having realized *mokṣa*. *Siddhapura Māhātmya* claims that, on experiencing the highest state, pure teardrops flowed from Devahūti's eyes (20).

The *Siddhapura Māhātmya* is structured as a conversation between Kapila and his mother, Devahūti. The drawing on the first page of the printed edition depicts the child Kapila in conversation with Kardama and Devahūti. The manuscript presents Kapila's teaching and Devahūti's realization of *mokṣa*, but is a pilgrimage text that focuses on Sidhpur, the river Sarasvatī and surrounding *tīrtha*s. The author first pays homage to the gods and his own teachers (1–5), then mentions some teachers of Sāṃkhya (6) and lastly describes Kapila:

> *kapilo vipulas teṣu sāmkhyācāryo mahāmuniḥ*
> *kevalam vāsudevāmśo devahūtyām ajījanat*

> Kapila the great sage, the teacher of Sāṃkhya, who was well known among them and who was exclusively a part of Kṛṣṇa, was born of Devahūti.

According to the *Siddhapura Māhātmya*, Kapila was on a pilgrimage to the various sacred places when he came to the *siddhāśrama* next to the water tank Bindusarovar. On arrival in Sidhpur, Kapila started to perform *tapas* and reached "the highest state" (8–9). His mother, Devahūti, then came to Kapila and told him that he should marry, since this was considered right according to the *śāstras*. Kapila answered that the only purpose of his birth was to give *mokṣa* to the mother (15) and that there cannot be liberation without knowledge. This knowledge requires that the notion of "mine" with respect to the body in particular be relinquished (18). Upon hearing that, Devahūti attained the highest state (19) and, thereupon, pure teardrops flowed from her eyes (20). After having attained *mokṣa*, she stated:

> *vande bindusarovaram ca kapilam sāmkhyādhipam yoginam siddham siddhapadaṃ puraṃ sukṛtināṃ kaivalyamokṣapradam,*
>
> *gaṅgā yatra sarasvatī priyatamā prācī jagatpāvinī māta mātṛgayā sadā vahati yā pāpāpahā puṇyadā* (21).
>
> I offer my namaskār to the pond Bindusarovar; to the perfect yogin Kapila, the leader of Sāṃkhya; to the city called Siddhapada which is the city of learned people and which grants *mokṣa* in the form of *kaivalya*, in which city Gaṅgā Sarasvatī, always flows, dearest Pracī – which is instrumental in purifying the whole universe, the mother Mātṛgayā, and which is the killer of sins and granter of merit.
>
> *sāmkhyācāryamahāmuniḥ kṛtayuge svādhyātmaniṣṭhārataḥ prakhyātaḥ kapilo hi kardamasutaḥ siddhaś ca siddhāśrame,*
>
> *tīrtham bindusarovaraṃ ca sumahadvijñānadīpojjvalaṃ kṣetraṃ mātṛgayeti siddham iti yatkhyātam trilokeṣv api* (22).
>
> In the *kṛtayuga,* Kapila – who was the teacher of the Sāṃkhya philosophy and a great sage – was constantly with complete confidence engaged in his own philosophy for realising *ātman*. He was known as the son of Kardama and a perfect person. In that place leading to perfection, there is a sacred place named Bindu Sarovar – where there shines a lamp in the form of extremely great knowledge; a place which is well known as leading to perfection named Mātṛgayā.

The sage Kapila, the teacher of *mokṣa*, and the geographical place are brought together and create salvific space. It is at the site where Devahūti attained *mokṣa* that *śrāddha* or *piṇḍadāna*, the ritual of offering *piṇḍa*s (riceballs) to dead mothers, should take place. The *śrāddha* ritual has the same function as the transference of merit (*puṇya*) to the dead in Buddhism, and it is a means to salvation, according to Hinduism. Through the *śrāddha* ritual, the dead can be ensured a better rebirth on earth, the attainment of heaven or even *mokṣa*. After claiming that the Mātṛgayā is a means to *mokṣa* – that is, a salvific space – the *Siddhapura Māhātmya* states: "In the great ocean of *samsāra* innumerable women have been my mothers, since I have had many previous births in different classes of beings"

(24). This remarkable statement means that all women should be treated like one's own mother! The focus on women and salvation is also a dominant theme in the story of Kapila in the *Bhāgavatapurāṇa*. When describing renunciation, the text promotes a negative view of the body, which also implies a recommendation for female renunciation. The fact that Kapila teaches renunciation to his mother makes the text a prescription for female asceticism. "A woman is the *māyā* created by God," and one should look upon her as one's death, "like a deep pit covered by grass," says the text (*Bhāgavatapurāṇa* 3.31.40). But similarly, a woman who wants salvific liberation should look at the man who thinks he is her husband as *māyā* because, just as the song of the hunter is death to a deer, likewise, a husband, children and home are *māyā* to a woman (*Bhāgavatapurāṇa.* 3.31.42). Kapila's mother, Devahūti, became a renunciant, meditated on the form of Viṣṇu, and, by means of devotion, powerful renunciation and knowledge, she attained purity of mind, transcended the *jīva*, neglected the body and became filthy, like a fire covered with smoke. She was so deeply absorbed in Vāsudeva that she was not conscious of her physical form. Continuing in this way, she attained *brahman*, the state called *nirvāṇa* at the place Siddhapada, and her body was, according to the *Bhāgavatapurāṇa*, transformed into a river (3.33.24–37). In the Hindu traditions, rivers are thought to be female divinities in water form; that is, rivers are the goddesses' bodies. Bathing in a river thus means immersing oneself in a goddess in water form. The water's ability to remove moral impurity is connected to this idea; the body is cleansed by divine water that also has the ability to wash away more than ordinary dirt. The story shows the close connection between a sacred site, salvific power and *mokṣa* in the stories about Kapila and his teaching.

The *śrāddha* or *piṇḍadāna* ritual in Sidhpur has five parts. Previously, it also included bathing in the river Sarasvatī, but this river dries up for long periods because dams have been constructed upstream. A hundred years ago, the riverbank was crowded with *āśrama*s; today, most of the buildings are empty and derelict. It illustrates the fact that sacred sites are always changing and that changes in the natural surroundings may have a great impact on the sacred sites. Such changes might have the consequence that pilgrims cease to visit the place. Given the economic importance of pilgrimage to the local economies, locals may try to renew the sacredness of the sites. A modern cremation facility called Mokṣadān, which uses water from tube wells for cooling and fountains, was opened next to the riverbank in the late 1990s. The ritual bathing that previously took place on the banks of the Sarasvatī has been moved to Kapilāśrama. This has shortened the ritual from the original two days, to only one day. The ritual involves the cutting of hair, bathing in the Bindusarovar, the sacrifice of 16 *piṇḍa*s, watering the papal tree with water from the Bindusarovar, *darśan* in the Kapil Mandir and payment to the Brahmans.

With each of the 16 *piṇḍa*s (rice balls), a different Sanskrit *śloka* in the simple *anuṣṭubh* meter is repeated. This collection of *śloka*s, called *Mātṛṣodaśī*, expresses the son's sorrow and remorse for the different types of pain and suffering he may have inflicted on his mother. The verses seem to demonstrate feelings of guilt, an indication that one function of the pilgrimage to Sidhpur is to relieve the son of such feelings. For each *piṇḍa* that is offered, the son asks to alleviate a particular hardship his mother suffered as a result of performing the duty of reproduction. This includes the pain a mother feels as a result of the suffering experienced by not giving birth to a son, the physical pain of pregnancy, the suffering of birth when the baby is wrongly placed in the uterus, the disgusting taste of the medicines she had to take, the mothers that die in childbirth, the pain experienced during her son's childhood and finally the pain of fear the mother feels at the door of death.[6] The sixteenth verse states:

yasmin kale mṛtā mātā gatis tasyā na vidyate
tasya niṣkramaṇārthāya mātṛpiṇḍaṃ dadāmy aham

> For the mothers that have died now, and for those that have no liberation, for the alleviation [of their punishments], I offer this *piṇḍa* to my mother.

According to some sources,[7] the famous story of Paraśurāma is the foundation story of the *mātṛgayāśrāddha* ritual in Sidhpur. Paraśurāma cut off the head of his own mother, Reṇukā, on his father's command. In this interpretation, the ritual serves to atone for the matricide. Taking a dip in the Bindusarovar and using its water in the *śrāddha* ritual cleansed Paraśurāma of his guilt for killing his own mother. However, Paraśurāma is not mentioned in the *Siddhapura Māhātmya.* Moreover, the story simply states that the water of the Bindusarovar has this salvific function, but does not explain why. It is the story of Kapila that currently provides the explanation of the salvific power of the site: The power of Kapilāśrama in Sidhpur, the reason the *gayāśrāddha* takes place here, is due to the fact that Kapila performed *tapas* and gave a teaching to his mother that led her to salvific liberation at this place. Next to the Alpasarovar in Sidhpur is a statue of Paraśurāma, which serves as a reminder to visitors of the sacred narrative of him and Reṇukā, although there is no daily ritual worship of the statue. *Pūjā* is performed to the *mūrtis* of Kapila, Kardama, Devahūti and Viṣṇu in the Kapilāśrama and numerous other gods at the many temples of this pilgrimage place.[8]

The figure of Paraśurāma personifies feelings of guilt regarding the mother and the power of the place to purify moral impurity (*pāpa*). In this context, the Kapila story has various functions. Kapila exemplifies the son's wish and ability to grant salvific liberation to his mother. While Paraśurāma was able to dwell on his own guilt, Kapila was able to save another person, his own mother. In the *mātṛgayāśrāddha* ritual, the son is able to both expatiate guilt, as demonstrated in the story of Paraśurāma, and grant *mokṣa* to his mother, as shown in the story of Kapila. Paraśurāma and Kapila represent the two sides of pilgrimage, getting rid of impurity (*pāpa*) and obtainment of merit (*puṇya*). Thus, while the verses recited in the *piṇḍadāna* ritual express feelings of guilt, the stated purpose of the ritual is to grant salvific liberation to the mother. The son is made to feel like Paraśurāma and achieves the same goal as Kapila. A parallel to the Kapila story, but in which a son grants salvific liberation to his father, is the story of Gayā. In Gayā, Rāma offered *gayāśrāddha* to save his father, Daśaratha. In the same way as Rāma saved his father by performing *śrāddha*, Kapila saved his mother by offering her the Sāṃkhya teaching of salvific liberation. He becomes a paradigm, not by teaching philosophy to the mother, but on a more general level by providing her with the Sāṃkhya teaching that became the tool by which the mother was able to attain salvific liberation. The means by which a son can save his mother is through the pilgrimage to Sidhpur and the performance of *śrāddha* and *piṇḍadāna*.

Thus, the story of Kapila offering *mokṣa* to his mother has become paradigmatic for those wishing to help their mothers in their afterlife to attain *mokṣa* or any other salvific goal. Therefore, persons come to the pilgrimage site of Sidhpur from all over India to accomplish what Kapila once achieved. For a son, the appearance of his mother in a dream might be interpreted as a reason to go to Sidhpur even many years after his mother's death.[9] Some are told to go to Sidhpur on pilgrimage by spiritual advisors, Muslim or Hindu, in order to cure a sick member of the family. The disease, they are told, is caused by the dead mother's inability to attain *mokṣa*. Psychological problems are also sometimes interpreted as being caused by the mother, who in this way communicates that she is stuck in the world between this and the next, and is in need of ritual help to attain *mokṣa*. The Sidhpur *Māhātmya* describes several pilgrimage places in the area with salvific power.

Kapilāśram is a peaceful and calm salvific site. Sidhpur is a place of remarkable architecture and Brahmans, the latter of which dominates the Kapilāśram with their presence and their rituals. However, affluent Muslim Bohra traders also made Sidhpur their home and the city's moderate wealth is due to trade. Another source of Sidhpur's prosperity is the growth of isabgol, which is used as fiber in food supplements.

The salvific site of Sidhpur illustrates the close connection between the sacred narratives about a sage or sacred persons and the rituals performed at the pilgrimage centers. This is a significant feature of the sacred places devoted to Kapila. The stories serve to make the promises of the pilgrimage centers credible. The promise is that the sites themselves have the power to remove moral impurity and grant *mokṣa* when the correct rituals are performed. Since Kapila was a provider of *mokṣa*, his presence has given salvific power to the site and, because the mother attained *mokṣa* here by the help of her son, it is possible for other sons to attain the same for their mothers. The idea of salvific space captures this important aspect of the pilgrimage place of Sidhpur.

The Gaṅgā Sāgar

The other pilgrimage place that illustrates the close association between the philosophy of salvific liberation and salvific space is the Gāṅgā Sāgar. The role of Kapila in the famous Gaṅgā Sāgar event is celebrated every year in a Kapila festival during Makara Saṃkrānti on the island of Sāgar, south of Kolkata (Calcutta), which is one of the islands at the place where the river Gaṅgā joins the ocean. This is the location where Kapila is believed to have built a hermitage, practiced meditation and caused the event that resulted in the river Gāṅgā coming to earth.

In the texts describing the Gaṅgā Sāgar Melā, Kapila is presented as the founder of the Sāṃkhya system (*Kapila sāṃkhyadarśan ke praṇetā*) (Bhaṭṭācārya 1986) and many of those who worship the Gaṅgā Sāgar Kapila probably assume that this Kapila is synonymous with the Sāṃkhya sage.[10] The main temple on Sāgar Island is a Kapila temple and the participants in the festival do their best to pay homage to him here. The Gaṅgā Sāgar festival is one of the greatest bathing festivals in India and certainly the greatest in West Bengal. The festival attracts more than half a million people every year, mainly from Bengal. Ascetics from throughout India come for the *melā*.

A significant role is attributed to Kapila in the sacred narrative relating how the river Gaṅgā came to earth. When the sacrificial horse of King Sagara was stolen, his sons went looking for the horse and almost destroyed the earth. They arrived at the place in which Kapila was performing *tapas* and found the horse tied to a tree next to him. Assuming the sage Kapila to be the horse thief, they became angry with him. Kapila then killed the sons of Sagara with a fire or a deadly sound that emanated from his own body. The relatives of the sons of Sagara were told that, since the sage Kapila had caused their deaths, the sons would not attain heaven if ordinary water was used in the *śrāddha* ritual. Only water from the river Gaṅgā was pure enough to convey the sons of Sagara to heaven. Kapila was thus responsible for starting the chain of events that brought the river Gaṅgā to earth.

Gaṅgā Sāgar is associated with salvational goals for several reasons: because Kapila performed *tapas* here and was a teacher of *mokṣaśāstra* (on how to attain *mokṣa*), and because the sons of Sagara attained *mokṣa* from this place. The water is thought to be extraordinarily pure because the *śrāddha* ritual performed using the water at this site could bring salvation to the sons of Sagara. The place is, therefore, associated specifically with the purifying role of water, the ritual of bathing and *mokṣa*.

Since Kapila had a central role in the Gaṅgā myth and since the location at Gaṅgā Sāgar is accepted as the place where the burning of the sons of King Sagara took place, as well as the place where they were purified from moral impurity and ascended to heaven, Sāgar Island is a sacred site for Kapila worship. In the main temple of the Gaṅgā Sāgara, in the Kapil Mandir, there are three *mūrti*s next to each other. Kapila is seated in the middle in the *padmāsana* (lotus position). To the right of Kapila is a *mūrti* of Gaṅgā sitting on a crocodile with a small statue of Bhagīratha on her lap; to the left is the *mūrti* of King Sagara. The statues are painted bright red.

As the temple is situated in a flat, sandy area close to the ocean, it has been destroyed regularly by storms. In a report from 100 years ago, a number of facts were recorded (O'Malley 1914: 256). It was reported that the *mūrti* was a shapeless block of stone that had been painted red. It was kept in Kolkata (Calcutta) for most of the year and taken to Gaṅgā Sāgar a couple of weeks before the festival. Some years before this report, the temple had been washed away. Since a new temple had not yet been built, the *mūrti* was placed in a temporary temple on a platform of sand four feet high. A bamboo railing in front of the *mūrti* protected it from the crowds, who filed past it from early morning to late evening (ibid.).

According to an article in a Bengali newspaper dated 4 February 1837, the first temple at the Gaṅgā Sāgar was constructed in 417/437 CE. It was claimed that, at that time, the Guru Sampradāya of Jaipur state installed the idol of Kapila in the temple (ibid.). The current temple at Gaṅgā Sāgar dates from 1974 and is controlled by monks belonging to one of the *akhāṛās* of the Rāmānandī order with its center in Ayodhyā.[11] They arrive in Gaṅgā Sāgar a few days before the festival and afterwards they return to Ayodhyā with the proceeds collected in the temple (Bhaṭṭācārya 1986). This is considered payment for the temple's protection. Kapila is a fierce ascetic at Gaṅgā Sāgar and his nature thus harmonizes with the ideals of the warrior ascetics.

Kapila is the main deity of the Makara Saṃkrānti festival at Gaṅgā Sāgar. Many pilgrims attend the festival for three days. On the first day, they bathe in the ocean, shave their heads, offer *piṇḍa*s (rice balls) to the ancestors and take *darśan* in the Kapil mandir. The ritual bath and *darśan* are repeated on the following days. *Piṇḍa*s are offered only by those who have recently experienced the loss of a parent. The reason for offering *piṇḍa*s at the Gaṅgā Sāgara is obviously related to the story of the descent to earth of the river Gaṅgā: Kapila said that the relatives of the sons of Sagara should perform *śrāddha* with water from the Gaṅgā at the Gaṅgā Sāgar in order to transport them to heaven. Thus, since the sons of Sagara could be saved if their descendants performed *śrāddha* there, *mokṣa* should be available to everyone performing rituals at the place. H. H. Wilson provided an interesting description of the rituals at Gaṅgā Sāgar 150 years ago:

> In front of the temple was a banyan tree, beneath which were images of Rāma and Hanumān. The pilgrims commonly wrote their names on the walls of the temple, with a short prayer to Kapila, or suspended a piece of earth or brick to a bough of the tree, with some solicitations, asked for health, or affluence, or offspring, and promised, if their prayers are granted, to make a gift to some divinity.[12]

This shows the pragmatic nature of pilgrimage to salvific sites. It is noteworthy that people wrote prayers to Kapila for children, health and material wealth. This indicates the popularity and multi-functionality of this pilgrimage center. At the time Wilson was writing, 100, 000 persons, according to his estimations, attended the festival. Today, more than 500, 000 people participate in the annual event.

The pilgrimage to Gaṅgā Sāgar was once considered very dangerous because the river had a large crocodile population and the surrounding jungle contained many tigers. The Hindi saying "*Sab tīrth bar bar, Gaṅgā Sāgar ek bar*" ("To all *tīrtha*s many times, to Gaṅgā Sāgar only once") was understood to mean that the trip was so dangerous and hazardous that the pilgrims could not be expected to return home alive. When they left their homes, the pilgrims would bid farewell to their families and friends, not expecting to see them again. Nowadays, the trip is not dangerous and the meaning of the saying has therefore changed. Now it is understood to mean that one has to go to all the *tīrtha*s several times, but Gaṅgā Sāgar is so full of salvific power that it is enough to visit the site only once.

There are many *āśrama*s of ascetics at the Gaṅgā Sāgar. The belief that Kapila once performed *tapas* at this place has influenced the names of the *āśrama*s. Many of them have names connected to Kapila and Sāṃkhya; signs at the entrances read Kapil Samkhya Yoga Ashram and Kapil Kudīr Sāṃkhya Yoga Āśrama.

An interesting twist in this narrative is found in the story of the *tīrtha* Kapileśvara on the northern bank of Narmadā, a place known to be "particularly destructive of sins" (*Skandapurāṇa*, *Āvyantya-khaṇḍa* and *Revā-khaṇḍa*, Chapter 175). When Kapila had killed the sons of Sagara, he became very distressed because he realized he had incurred sin. As an ascetic, he recognized it was improper to have destroyed thousands of humans. He thought: "A thing done cannot be undone. I shall, therefore, go to the Kapila Tīrtha that is destructive of all sins and get rid of my sins." Thereafter, he settled on the banks of Narmadā and performed penance and worshipped Śiva. The text then states that one who takes a bath at this place obtains the merit of gifting 1, 000 cows. Here, the salvific place has become the supreme power, and even the sage Kapila has to go on pilgrimage to a Kapila pilgrimage place to purify himself!

Kolāyat

The narratives and rituals associated with the pilgrimage site Kolāyat, another pilgrimage place linked to Kapila and thought to be named after him, is illustrative of salvific power as the key element in the promotion of sacred sites. The town of Kolāyat, close to Bīkaner in Rajasthan, is said to take its name from Kapila. The name Kolāyat is possibly derived from the Sanskrit Kapilāyatana, meaning "the place (*āyatana*) of Kapila." According to the tradition of Kolāyat, Kapila discovered the natural beauty of this place while traveling in a north-easterly direction and chose it as a place to perform *tapas*. Since Kapila selected it as a favorite place, it was called Kapilāyatan. The place is also called the Kapila *kṣetra*, meaning "the sacred area of Kapila." The sacred lake in Kolāyat is called Kapilsarovar, "the lake of Kapila" (see Figure 5.2).

After Kapila had performed *tapas* here and caused the place to possess salvific power, according to the Kolāyat tradition, people forgot about worshipping the gods because of the salvific power of the site, and the gods became jealous of that place. Instead of undergoing the hardships of *tapas* and sacrifice or undertaking long journeys to places of pilgrimage, such as to Ayodhyā and Vārāṇasī, people would attain salvific liberation the easy way, by just taking a dip in the holy lake at Kapilāyatana. Because of this situation, the gods contemplated hiding this salvific place from humanity and moving themselves to Kolāyat, states the *Śrī Kapila Māhātmya Kolāyatjī*. However, the text continues, the god Skanda felt sorry for humanity and brought this salvific place to light for the benefit of all, so that everyone could easily obtain *mokṣa* in this dark *kali*-age (see also Sehgal 1972: 117).

According to the pilgrimage tradition of Kolāyat, one can attain *mokṣa* by bathing in the sacred lake. The lake is probably the main reason that Kolāyat, which is situated in a very dry area, developed as a pilgrimage place. Kolāyat belongs

Figure 5.2 Kapilsarovar, "the lake of Kapila" endowed with salvific power at Kolāyat

Photo: Knut A. Jacobsen

to the group of *tīrtha*s developed into pilgrimage places partly or mainly because of some extraordinary features associated with water, but the narrative of the site states that it was because Kapila visited there. The lake is the center of an oasis surrounded by desert. Kolāyat then probably developed its pilgrimage traditions by adding narratives about the real or fictional presence of the ascetic Kapila that made one potential meaning of the name Kolāyat possible. The lake itself is cherished by the promotion texts of Kolāyat for its salvific powers: "The Kolāyat lake with its mystic tradition has a magical effect on the minds of the simple people and they reveal it in singing songs in its praise, deep in religious ecstasy" (Sehgal 1972: 117).

Next to the lake is the temple of Kapila. The fact that the *pujārī* of this temple cannot be a *gṛhasthā* (a householder) is said to indicate that some of Kapila's sanctity is still present in Kolāyat. Close to the temple lies what is claimed to be Kapila's Samādhisthāna (one of several in India). The main festival in Kolāyat is at Kārttik Pūrṇimā, when storytellers sing and tell stories about Kapila, and people take sacred baths in the lake and take *darśan* of Kapila in the Kapil Mandir; lighted lamps made of flour are set afloat in rows in the tank.

Several stories about the salvific powers of Kolāyat are told in the *Śrī Kapila Māhātmya Kolāyatjī*. This short text (ten pages) in Hindi is sold during the festival. In addition, stories about Kapila are performed at the annual festival at Kārttik Pūrṇimā. Professional storytellers (*kathāvācaka*s) sing and narrate the local stories about Kapila.[13]

The text *Śrī Kapila Māhātmya Kolāyatjī* is construed as a conversation between Agastya and the god Skanda, who is the narrator. In the text, Skanda reveals the salvific power of Kolāyat through stories. Kolāyat is described as better than all the other *tīrtha*s and the site is said to give salvation to all those who do penance there. Such statements are common to a large number of promotion texts of *tīrtha*s and point to the quality of salvific space as the central feature in the presentation of the places and in the belief system connected to the places. According to the *Māhātmya* text, Kolāyat is the gem of all pilgrimage centers, although in the *kali*-age few people know about the greatness of this *tīrtha*. This, the text says, is because most people are occupied with the accumulation of wealth. Kolāyat is also called Kapiltīrth and Kapilāśram. The text claims that the site itself is able to grant *mokṣa*, but only the gods (*devatās*) know this and that is why they have kept it a secret. Salvific power, in other words, is presented as a force that the gods believe endangers their own powers.

The text narrates how Kapila, after having passed his teachings to his mother, traveled northwards. There he found an area with trees full of creepers and beautiful birds. Because of the beauty of the place, he stayed to perform *tapas*. The text states that Kapila was seated there like a *mūrti*, resembling the statue of Kapila in the temple. A second *mūrti* emerged from Kapila, who then left his gross material body in the form of the *mūrti* of Kolāyat, and moved north-eastwards with his subtle material body. Part of Kapila, in other words, remained in Kolāyat in his gross material body, which actually became the *mūrti*. These events, the text claims, happened in the *satyayuga*. Since then, persons from all the *lokas* who came to the site would be granted salvation. However, in the *kaliyuga*, the power of this place was kept a secret until the god Skanda revealed it. Significantly, at this site, one can gain salvation without knowledge of ultimate reality, the text states. Knowledge, memory or vision of this place is all that is required to gain salvation! This is the case not only for humans, but also for wild animals. Kolāyat is one of those places that grants the salvational goal even to animals that are merely present at the place. They are also included in the working of the salvific power. It is especially auspicious to bathe at the festival of Kārttik Pūrṇimā. Salvation in this context means going to Vaikuṇṭha, the heaven of Viṣṇu. Having heard this, Agastya praised Skanda, confirming that Kapilāśram is the best of all *tīrtha*s.

In the rest of the text, Skanda narrates several stories to illustrate the salvific power of the pilgrimage place of Kolāyat. The first story describes six sisters who bathed in the Kapilsarovar every day for three years. Because of their daily baths in the sacred lake, they gained memory of their previous lives, as well as salvation. According to the storyteller (*kathāvācakas*) who published the cassette *Śrī Kapila Mahimā Śrī Kolāyatjī*, the six sisters worshipped Kapila, who, satisfied with their devotion, showed himself to them and promised to grant them a wish. Their wish was to stay together forever. Thereafter, these six girls were known as the six *Kṛttikās* (the Pleiades), and they are still present as stars in the sky, the text states. Because of the power of Kapila, they will shine in heaven until the end of the *kalpa* and continuously remind us of the greatness achieved by bathing at any *tīrtha*.

The second story is about a *saṃnyāsin*, who, together with his dog, circumambulated the Kapilsarovar at the Kārttik Pūrṇimā festival. Some people disliked the dog doing this, and they tried to put a stop to it by beating the dog and chasing it away. Oblivious to this, the dog continued its circumambulation. People then tried to convince the *saṃnyāsin* to take the dog away from the site. A discussion arose and the crowd was divided into two camps of opinion; some were in favor of letting the dog proceed and others were against it. While the discussion was going on, the *saṃnyāsin* and the dog completed the circumambulation. The dog then went down to the lake, drank some water and sat there with its eyes closed. People looked on in amazement at this, the text claims. Suddenly, the dog died and at that very moment a flying vehicle arrived. The dog then turned into a human and proceeded to the world of the gods (*devaloka*). At this, all the people who had been against the dog's endeavor felt ashamed, and those who were in favor of its efforts started to chant the name of Kapila. The text concludes: "As the result of the sacredness of this place, the dog gained salvation and proceeded towards heaven." This dog is also identified with a star (near the polar star). The story illustrates that the salvific power of the place includes everyone, even animals.

The third story is about a man who was blind. When he was given some lentils from Kolāyat, he suddenly gained knowledge of his previous life. He realized that he had been a deer living in the Kolāyat area. Whilst living there, his head had become stuck in a tree while he was rubbing against it to gain relief from itching. Unable to free itself, the deer died. Animals ate him and when the rain came, his skeleton was washed away and reached Kapilsarovar. His head, however, was still stuck in the tree. Because his moral impurities were washed away in the pure water of the Kapilsarovar, he was reborn into a rich *vaiśya* family, the text informs us. He then asked the people in the village to go to Kolāyat and find the head and throw it into the Kapilsarovar. As soon as the head entered the water, the man's eyesight returned to normal. The text states that all the people involved, therefore, began to chant the name of Kapila with hearts full of respect. The *vaiśya* then went to live in Kolāyat. The storyteller closes this tale by confirming that, even though one visits all the other *tīrtha*s, the work is not complete unless one visits Kolāyat; and if one goes to Kolāyat, the reward (*puṇya*) will be as great as if one had visited all the other *tīrtha*s combined. In other words, the salvific power of Kolāyat is as potent as the power of all the other *tīrtha*s. This story also illustrates the site's capability to cure diseases and the salvific power of this sacred water.

The last story is about a man who died in Kolāyat. The messenger of Yama, Citragupta, captured him with his noose and delivered him to Yama. Yama asked Citragupta how many good deeds the man had done in this life. Citragupta answered that he had done no good deeds, but had died in Kolāyat. Then Yama said: "If he died in the land of Kapila (*kapil-bhūmi*), all his moral impurities were washed away. Allow him therefore to be born in a sacred house." The man was born into a wealthy family and, living in Kapilāyatan, he ultimately attained *mokṣa*. The salvific power of the place Kolāyat is so strong that it washes away all moral impurities and finally grants *mokṣa*. These stories illustrate the fundamental idea of salvific space.

The stories belong to a local pilgrimage tradition, but the pattern is typical of the Kapila centers of pilgrimage in general and to a large section of Hindu pilgrimage narratives. It is Kapila's presence at some point of time at the site that has established the salvific power of the places; a salvific power that can be tapped by visiting the site. It is present particularly in Lake Kapilsarovar. Not only humans but animals as well benefit from this salvific power.

These stories from Kolāyat illustrate a central theme in Hinduism and pilgrimage – the notion that the salvific power of place often transcends the power of gods; that is, places may replace gods as salvific powers. Although the Hindu tradition is a god-centered religion, the personal gods are often surpassed. This is the case not only in the intellectual tradition of the *Upaniṣads* and traditions of Indian philosophy, in which *brahman* transcends the personal gods, and in the ritual philosophy of the Pūrvamīmāṃsā, in which the ritual acts transcend the gods, but also in popular traditions, such as those associated with pilgrimage, and the rituals and power of place. This tension between personal gods and salvific power is present in the text *Kolāyat Māhātmya,* as well as at the pilgrimage place. The gods know that, when salvific power is easily accessible, their power becomes unimportant to humans and humans discard them. According to the *Kolāyat Māhātmya*, the gods considered the salvific power of Kolāyat a threat, and out of jealousy they attempted to keep Kolāyat secret. However, the salvific power of the place is now available to all, according to the promotion texts of Kolāyat.

Kapilatīrtha in Tirupati and the Kapila places associated with cows

The pilgrimage centers associated with Kapila that we have discussed so far are related to specific episodes in his life. A number of Hindu *tīrtha*s are linked to cows and some of these to the brown cow (in contemporary Hinduism, many identify the *kapilā* cow with the white cow), the *kapilā dhenu*. Several such pilgrimage places are mentioned in the *Mahābhārata* and the *Purāṇa*s. Typical references to this group of Kapila pilgrimage sites are exemplified in the following verses from the *Purāṇa*s.

> *tato gaccheta rājendra kapilātīrtham uttamam,*
> *tatra snātvā naro rājan gosahasraphalaṃ labhet.*

> King! Thereafter one shall go to the excellent Kapilātīrtha. King! A man bathing there will obtain the fruit [equal to giving] of a thousand cows (*gosahasraphalaṃ*).
>
> (*Kūrmapurāṇa* 2.41.93)[14]

> One who gives away a milk cow (*kapilā*) after bathing at Kapilātīrtha receives the benefit [equal to] having given away the whole world in charity (*sampūrṇapṛthivīṃ dattvā*). The sacred place Narmadeśa is unparalleled.
>
> (*Matsyapurāṇa* 191.71–72)

> I shall now tell you about the most important Kapilā *dhenu* (brown cow), the giver of which attains the world of Viṣṇu. . . . All the pilgrimage places in the world are contained in the head and neck of the brown cow, as ordained by Brahmā. Circumambulating such a cow is equivalent to circumambulating the whole earth.
>
> (*Varāhapurāṇa* 111.1, 111.3 and 111.5)

The *kapilādāna*, the gift of a *kapilā* cow, is described in *Revākhaṇḍa* of the *Āvyatyakhaṇḍa* of the *Skandapurāṇa* (5.3, Chapter 119). Gifting a *kapilā* cow at the Kapilā *tīrtha* after taking a bath and listening to the divine narrative from a Brahman enables one to attain a number of benefits because, of all the *dāna*s, the *kapilādāna* is the most exceptional. "Even Brahmā had recourse to it formerly in the assembly of sages and Devas," the text says. The cow should be given immediately after it has calved, probably because it then gives milk and is most valuable.

> O king, sins, verbal, mental and physical, committed formerly in the course of seven births, perish by the gift of a *kapilā*.
>
> Gifts of plots of land, cash, food grains, elephants, horses, gold, etc., do not deserve even a sixteenth fraction of *kapilādāna*.
>
> A man who takes his holy bath there and makes the gift of a *kapilā* cow, goes to Viṣṇu's city on death after being sung about by groups of celestial damsels.
>
> He sports about for a long time in Svarga (heaven) for as many thousand years as there are hairs on the body of that cow as well as that of the calf.
>
> After descending down in due course, he is born as a human being into a large family full of wealth and food grain.
>
> He will be well versed in the Vedic lore, an expert in all the scriptures. Free from ailments and grief etc., he lives for a hundred years.
>
> (*Skandapurāṇa* 5.3, Chapter 119)

The *Mahābhārata* (*Āraṇyakaparvan* 83.47) refers to a Kapilā *tīrtha* and states that, if one bathes and offers ablutions to the ancestors and gods here, one gains merit equivalent to thousands of *kapilā* cows. In these examples of Kapilā *tīrtha*s, cows are central, not the sage Kapila. There are many Kapilā *tīrtha*s that are not linked to Kapila the sage, but some of these *tīrtha*s have become connected to him. The similarity of the name Kapila and the word *kapilā* and the fact that they are both easily connected to salvific space and sacredness seems to have probably caused this blending of the two. The purpose may have been to increase the attractiveness of the place and the greatness of its salvific power.

A Kapilatīrtha associated with cows is mentioned in the text with the interesting name *Kapilapurāṇa.*[15] This text, bearing the name Kapila, does not contain any of the teachings of Kapila. Instead, it is mainly concerned with places of pilgrimage, although only one Kapilatīrtha is mentioned, the Kapilatīrtha at Virajā *kṣetra* located on the river Vaitaraṇī. The text states that, if one takes a bath at this Kapilatīrtha on the fourteenth day of the *pitṛpakṣa*, both Pārvatī and Śiva are pleased and one attains the fruit equal to the giving of a *kapilā* cow and goes to Goloka (*Kapilapurāṇa*, 7.23–26). This example reveals a possible origin of this group of *tīrthas*. The *kapilā* cow has probably given its name to these sites, and sometime later some of them became associated with the sage Kapila.

The most important pilgrimage center that connects Kapila to a cow or cows is probably Kapilatīrtha in Tirupati, Andhra Pradesh. Other than the Vatican, no pilgrimage site receives as many visitors annually as the Veṅkaṭeśvara temple at Tirumala. Kapilatīrtha is situated at the base of the Tirumala hill where the road to Tirumala starts ascending. This *tīrtha* marks the lower border of the sacred area of the Tirumala hill (Rao 1952: 158). The main attraction of the Kapilatīrtha is a beautiful waterfall, at the base of which a water tank and a temple complex have been built. When going on a pilgrimage to Tirumala, it is common to stop at the Kapilatīrtha and bathe under the waterfall. This is said to cleanse one from moral impurity and give religious merit (see Figure 5.3).

The temple of the Kapilatīrtha, which is next to the water tank, houses a *liṅga*. This *liṅga* manifested itself, according to the temple's foundation narrative, because of Kapila's worship of Śiva. After the *liṅga* had manifested itself, a cow

Figure 5.3 Pilgrims bathing under the waterfall in Tirupati

Photo: Knut A. Jacobsen

used to come every day to stand over the *liṅga*. Milk then flowed from its udders down onto the *liṅga*. This type of story of how a *liṅga* is discovered is quite common. On the wall next to the *svayambhūliṅga* in the Kapileśvara mandir, there is now a painting of this scene, with Kapila sitting next to it. This image has been reproduced in the flowerbeds in the beautiful park outside of the temple. According to another foundation myth, Śiva requested that he be allowed to stay on the Tirumala hill. The god Viṣṇu then allotted him a place on the banks of the Kapilatīrtha where the *liṅga* now is worshipped. In an inscription dating from between 1011 and 1044, there is a reference to a Kapileśvara temple known as the Kapilatīrtha (Rao 1952: 124–125). The sage Kapila is not usually called Kapileśvara, but the reference could possibly be to this sage. Another inscription states that the tank was provided with stone steps all around in 1531 (ibid.: 107). A nineteenth-century description of the temple mentions that a wooden cow, a calf and Kapila Mahāmuni were placed on top of a three-foot-high anthill in the temple (Ramesan 1999: 531). By then, Kapila had certainly taken on the role he has today at this *tīrtha*.

The reason for visiting the Kapilatīrtha is to take advantage of the waterfall's purifying function. Only a minority of the visitors are able to identify Kapila and to explain the painting of him.[16] In fact, when asked to identify Kapila, many answered Kapaleśvara and explained it as a name of Śiva.[17]

In the case of the Kapiladhārā in Vārānasī, it may be possible to prove that the word *kapilā* and the name of the sage Kapila have been confused, at least if the Kapiladhārā in the *Skandapurāṇa* is a reference to the Kapiladhārā found in Vārāṇasī today. Kapiladhārā in Vārāṇasī and the Kapilatīrtha in Tirupati have some common features. Next to the main temple of Kapiladhārā in Vārāṇasī, which has a *liṅga*, is a smaller shrine with a *mūrti* of Kapila. In the *Skandapurāṇa* (4.2.63), the origin of Kapiladhārā in Vārāṇasī is told: Five divine cows named Sunandā, Sumanā, Suśīlā, Surabhi and Kapilā came to Vārāṇasī from Goloka. "Due to the caressing glance of Śiva their udders flowed." According to the text, this milk created a second ocean of milk. Śiva named the pool Kapilāhrada, and declared that if devotees offered riceballs with great faith as *śrāddha* offerings, the ancestors would be pleased. Devotees should offer *śrāddha* here when the new moon falls on a Monday. At the time of the *śrāddha*, Brahmans are also to be fed and the gift of an auspicious red-brown (*kapilā*) cow is to be offered to the ancestors. The text celebrates the Kapiladhārā as the best place for the performance of *śrāddha*. This *tīrtha* is full of milk in the *kṛtayuga*, honey in the *tretā*, ghee in the *dvāpara* and water in the *kaliyuga*.

The sage Kapila is not mentioned in the text in this episode. The site seems to take its name from the order that devotees offer an auspicious red-brown (*kapilā*) cow there. Today, there is a *mūrti* of Kapila situated there and bathing in the pool is compared to bathing at the pilgrimage place of Gaṅgā Sāgar. The story of the Kapiladhārā in Vārāṇasī illustrates the difficulty of relating Kapila pilgrimage centers to the historical presence of a figure named Kapila, and it illustrates the pragmatic approach to salvific space.

The legendary origin of the sacred place Tarakeśvar in Bengal describes a similar story, except that the story about cows was not subsequently associated with the sage Kapila, and this illustrates that, in other cases, the sage Kapila was probably added. The myth describes how the god of a place called Taraknāth was hidden under a forest. The king's cows used this forest for grazing and, in the forest, there was a raised stone upon which the women used to grind their rice. This constant grinding had made a depression in the stone. One day, a cowherd noticed the mysterious behavior of one of his cows named Kapilā. She was a milk cow, but suddenly stopped giving milk. The cowherd saw that she went into the forest with full udders and returned from the forest after a while with empty udders. The cowherd then followed the cow into the forest, where he found to his surprise that the cow discharged its milk spontaneously onto the stone used for grinding. The cowherd reported this to the king, who in a dream was told by the god Śiva (Taraknāth) to build a temple at that place (Chakrabarti 1984). The notion that a *kapilā* cow will find a *svayambhū liṅga* is a motif repeated in several narratives of sacred sites. Some of these places were later associated with the sage Kapila, most probably because the similarity of the words created an opportunity for the association or it was simply the result of a confusion. Kapilā seems to also have been a common name given to cows.[18]

Other Kapila pilgrimage sites

In addition to the places already mentioned, there are a number of other pilgrimage places associated with Kapila in India, at which there are temples of Kapila and, at some locations, *melā*s or festivals celebrate the salvific power made available by Kapila at these sites.

Several temples associated with the worship of Kapila are found in Vārāṇasī. In addition to the Kapiladhārā mentioned previously, there is a Kapileśa ("Lord Kapila") *liṅga.* Kapila is said to have established the Kapileśa *liṅga* and it is believed that even monkeys can achieve liberation if they visit this particular *liṅga.*[19] In Gayā in Bihar, there is a temple and monastery called Kapiladhārā. The temple is built on top of a small cave that is called Kapila's Cave (Kapil *guphā*) because Kapila is believed to have meditated in it. At this Kapiladhārā, there is also a *samādhisthāna* that the monks and nuns currently staying in Kapiladhārā believe to be Kapila's.[20] The origin of the place is, however, uncertain.

There are pilgrimage places associated with Kapila located along the Narmadā river, perhaps because one of its tributaries is named Kapilā. At Amarkaṇṭak, where the Narmadā river begins and which is an important pilgrimage site, especially for people in Orissa and Madhya Pradesh, there is a beautiful waterfall called Kapiladhārā. As with many other Kapila sites, this is a place of natural beauty where there are *āśrama*s of ascetics. The place in Amarkaṇṭak in which Kapila is said to have stayed is close to the waterfall and is marked by a Kapila mandir. Kapileśvara-Tīrtha is at Kolyād, where the rivers Airaṇḍī and Narmadā meet.[21] On the northern side of the Narmadā, close to Śūlpāni, is Kapilatīrtha with the Kapileśvar Mandir.[22] At Bharuc, there is also a temple of Kapila on the beach where the Narmadā enters the ocean.

There is yet another sacred site of Kapila located at the Kapiladhārā close to Bhanvargaḍh, on the border between Rajasthan and Uttar Pradesh. A yearly *melā* is held there at the Kārttik Pūrṇimā, which attracts people from the surrounding villages and *sādhus*. There is also a Kapila temple in Janakpur in Nepal. The Kapila temple located in Kolyād in Narvana in Jīnd district, Haryana is advertised in Kolāyat, Rajasthan, by a singer (*kathāvācakas*), in order to attract devotees of Kapila to come to this place during their melā. There might also be an economic interest in connecting these two pilgrimage centers that have similar names.

Yakṣas and Kapila

The Hindu pilgrimage tradition has been influenced by beliefs associated with the pre-Vedic *yakṣa*s and *yakṣinī*s, divine beings identified with owning and guarding specific territory. The *yakṣa*s and *yakṣinī*s were also worshipped as guardians at pilgrimage sites after the places had become identified with narratives of Hindu gods. However, some *yakṣa*s were transformed into Hindu divinities and sages. Several places associated with Kapila are probably examples of this transformation. A few of the sites today connected to sage Kapila are located in the geographical areas where the early Vedic tradition flourished, such as in Kāmpil in western Uttar Pradesh and Kolyād in Jīnd district, in Haryana. Most of the Kapila pilgrimage places are outside of the areas of the settlements of the early Vedic tradition, but in this area Kapila was a name of one or more *yakṣa*s who were worshipped as protectors. That these *yakṣa*s were called Kapila made it possible later to connect them to the sage Kapila. In this way, their identity was changed. This transformation illustrates the process described in the previous chapters of how the Hindu ideas of salvific space and pilgrimage traditions were influenced by earlier traditions that connected divinity to specific sites. There is a tradition in the city Kāmpil in Uttar Pradesh that the city was named Kāmpil after Kapila because he performed *tapas* there. The Sanskrit text *Kāmpilyamāhātmya* (compiled in the twentieth century) claims that Kapila performed *tapas* in Kāmpil at the Kapilāśrama before he went to Gaṅga Sāgar and that, since then, Kāmpil has been the foremost of *tīrtha*s (*Kāmpilyamāhātmya* 2.15–18). In addition, the current inhabitants of this city also believe that the city was named after the sage Kapila (Filippi and Marcolongo 1999: 72). However, the city was probably named after a *yakṣa* called Kapila, who was later confused with the sage Kapila. The worship of Kapila in Kāmpil takes place at a temple that the inhabitants of the city believe is the *samādhi* of the sage Kapila. The temple contains a small Śivaliṅga and this was dedicated to the *yakṣa* Kapila, and this Kapila was later identified as the sage Kapila (ibid.). The Kapila temple located in Kolyād in Narvana in Jīnd district, Haryana probably also represents the transformation of a *yakṣa* called Kapila into the sage Kapila. Kolyād in Jind district is part of the larger Kurukṣetra district. That *yakṣa*s were worshipped as guardians at the pilgrimage place Kurukṣetra, even after the places had become identified with narratives of Hindu gods, is well known. It is mentioned in the *Mahābhārata* that the *yakṣa* Macakruka, thought to own a lake at the border of Kurukṣetra, was the gatekeeper of the area and should be saluted when entering the region (*Mahābhārata* 3.81.7, 3.81.178). Kurukṣetra was guarded by four *yakṣas*, one in each corner and two of these were Macakruka and Kapila. In the *Mahābhārata*, the *yakṣa*s were *kṣetrapāla*s and guardians of grounds and pools that must be worshipped by the pilgrims (Sutherland 1991: 121–122). The worship of them, therefore, was bound to places. The transformation of the *yakṣa* Kapila into the sage Kapila explains perhaps the presence of worship of Kapila in these old areas of settlement of the early Vedic tradition.

Salvific power and sacred time

The largest numbers of pilgrims arrive at these salvific sites associated with Kapila for the annual *melā*s, pilgrimage festivals. These *melā*s or festivals celebrating Kapila are held on Kārttika Pūrṇimā and Makarara Samkrānti. Kārttika Pūrṇimā and Makarara Samkrānta are the greatest annual bathing days in Hinduism in general and do not seem to be connected to any specific events in the mythology of Kapila. Kārttik (October–November) is the main festival month in Hinduism and Kārttik Pūrṇimā, as well as Makarara Samkrānti, are considered particularly auspicious days for taking sacred baths to wash away moral impurity. Kārttik Pūrṇimā marks the end of the *cāturmāsa*, the four months in which the *saṃnyāsin*s perform penance. Kārttik Pūrṇimā is also often associated with the ancestors. That the majority of the Kapila places have their main festivals at Kārttik Pūrṇima may be just because it is a main festival day generally in Hinduism. This is the case with Sidhpur, Kolāyat and Kapiladhārā, near Bhanvargaḍh. There is a connection between Kapila, the ancestors and the *śrāddha* rituals reflected in the timing of the festivals. But even though the rituals both in Sidhpur and Gaṅgā Sāgar are focused on the ancestors and *śrāddha* rituals, their main festivals are held on different days – during Kārttika Pūrṇimā in Sidhpur and during Makara Samkrānti at Gaṅgā Sāgar. More importantly, however, is how the places change character during the festivals. At Gaṅgā Sāgar, around 500,000 people arrive for the annual festival at the time of Makara Samkrānti. The large crowds going to a single place to take sacred baths at the same time functions to confirm the truth of the salvific power of the site. That the sacred site is in demand confirms its power. With hundreds of thousands of persons coming to take advantage of the salvific power, how can that power be doubted?

Conclusion

The salvific sites associated with Kapila are influenced by his personality. Kapila was a sage who taught a system of religious thought and who attained *mokṣa*. He was not a powerful god who defeated demons or other evil forces. The power of the places is thought to be due to his salvific attainment and the salvific power ascribed to the places is because of his previous presence. The sites illustrate that salvific power is believed to be a quality of the places themselves.

Most of the main temples or shrines devoted to Kapila in India today are at pilgrimage centers. There is considerable traffic to these centers associated with the ancient sage Kapila, especially during the yearly festivals that often draw a huge number of people. At these sites, Kapila is known to be the founder of Sāṃkhya, but is also celebrated for having performed other deeds. Each of these centers celebrates the particular deed or deeds of Kapila that took place there. The power of these places is believed to have originated with Kapila's presence at some time in history and each site is associated with sacred narratives about what he did there. Hindus go on pilgrimages to these places for several reasons, the most common being to take advantage of the power of the sites, especially participating in ritual bathing and performing the *śrāddha* ritual. Worship of Kapila in the Kapila temples is part of the ritual, but is not the most important part. Since Kapila is best known for having discovered and revealed a way to *mokṣa*, his very presence has infused the places with salvific power. Some of these centers are pan-Indian centers of pilgrimage, while others are regional and some merely local.

Several of the Kapila pilgrimage locations are in settings of natural beauty. There is a prevailing notion among the *saṃnyāsin*s who worship Kapila that he was fond of beautiful nature.[23] This might be because yoga, according to some of the Hindu traditions, is to be performed in places pleasing to the mind (*Śvetāśvatara Upaniṣad* 2.10). The places associated with Kapila attract *saṃnyāsin*s, and *āśrama*s and *maṭh*s have been established there. All the sacred places of Kapila are associated with water in the form of waterfalls, rivers or streams, or lakes or tanks. This might be because the sacred bath is such a large part of the Hindu pilgrimage culture. In the case of Kapila, several reasons can also be specified. First, Kapila is associated with the coming to earth of the river Gaṅgā. He is the person who informed Sagara's relatives that only the water of Gaṅgā was pure enough to save the souls of the sons of Sagara. According to the sacred narratives, therefore, he fully understood the salvific power of the water of the Gaṇgā. Second, Kapila is associated with *mokṣa*, and water is considered to have the purifying quality of releasing humans from moral impurity. In the *Māhātmya*s of the sites associated with Kapila, the purifying quality of water is emphasized. The salvific attainments associated with these places were achievable because Kapila had performed *tapas* there, but it is bathing in the water or circumambulating the sacred tank that is the immediate source of purity.

The fact that Kapila is considered the founder of Sāṃkhya, a *mokṣaśāstra*, associates him with release from rebirth. Among Hindus, the religious motive for going on a pilgrimage is generally concerned either with gaining favors in this life or with earning religious merit – that is, to be cleansed of moral impurities (Bhardwaj 1973: 148–162). Visiting a pilgrimage place is all that is required to attain salvific goals, according to the texts that promote the sites. Since Kapila is known to have given salvific knowledge to humanity, the sites of Kapila worship focus on purification and the *Māhātmya*s of the places also tell of curing of diseases due to the salvific power of the sites. At some places of pilgrimage to Kapila, *śrāddha* and *piṇḍa* are performed. Although Bhardwaj, in his discussion of the purposes of pilgrimage, categorizes *śrāddha* and *piṇḍa* as lifecycle rituals, the function of *śrāddha* and *piṇḍa* is to ensure salvific goals. Thus, they harmonize with the main purpose of the Kapila pilgrimage – the visiting of salvific space.

While the places associated with Kapila share the common feature of *tīrtha*s in the Hindu tradition – links with natural beauty, water and *tapas* – they are also associated with particular narratives. The close connection between the sacred narratives and the rituals performed at the pilgrimage center is a significant feature of the sacred places. At every place of pilgrimage to Kapila, there are stories about him that explain the sacredness of the place. Thus, in contemporary India, the sacred narratives about Kapila found in the *Mahābhārata*, *Rāmāyaṇa* and the *Purāṇa*s take place at specific sites. These narratives belong as much to the geography of Hindu India as to the sacred narratives and rituals of the Hindu tradition. The place where Kapila was born, the place where he gave the sacred knowledge of ultimate reality to his mother, the different places where he performed *tapas* and the place where he killed the sons of King Sagara are all part of India's pilgrimage geography. The promise of the Kapila places of pilgrimage is that the sites themselves have salvific power, and the figure of Kapila and the sacred narratives serve to lend credibility to this promise.

6 The structure of Hindu salvific space: a pluralistic pilgrimage tradition or why there is no Mecca of Hinduism

A typical feature of Hindu pilgrimage sites is that they are connected to other places. In the narratives, pilgrimage sites are thought to travel to other pilgrimage places, they are hierarchized in accordance with the strength of their ability to remove impurity – that is, their salvific power – there is a competition between places and pilgrimage sites can be replicated at other pilgrimage places. This chapter examines connections and aspects of the structure of the Hindu geography of salvific space. Salvific space in India constitutes sacred geographies that include thousands of pilgrimage sites. The Hindu sacred geography is extensive, but in India it is not the only one. There are Buddhist, Jain, Sikh, Muslim and Christian and also different tribal sacred geographies. These are associated with different sacred narratives and doctrines, but, nevertheless, often overlapping sacred geographies. Examples of such overlapping sacred geographies are the shared Hindu and Jain pilgrimage sites of Mount Girnār in Gujarat and Mount Ābū (Arbuda) in Rajasthan, the Hindu and Buddhist site Bodhgayā in Bihar and many Hindu and Muslim shared sacred sites, such as the Hindu and Muslim shrine of Vāvar on the Śabarimala pilgrimage in Kerala. Shared often means contested. A number of shared Hindu and Muslim shrines have been in processes of transformation over the last decades; some have emerged as centers of contestation and some have been transformed into Hindu places (Sikand 2003). Power of place often mirrors the identity of the societal powers. Political developments may cause changes to the sites, and changes in the demography influence the flow of pilgrims as well. When the religious group that uses or patronizes a pilgrimage place stops visiting it for different reasons, the pilgrimage tradition connected to the place may cease to exist. The history of South Asia abounds with examples. Old pilgrimage places may also be revitalized and new pilgrimage traditions created. Pilgrimage places and traditions are dynamic and changing.

Hinduism is not a homogeneous religious tradition; it is a pluralistic tradition without a center or a central authority or text. Diversity, multiplicity and plurality are key words for describing the mosaic of Hindu religious traditions (Jacobsen 2009a). Diversity, multiplicity and plurality also characterize the geography of salvific space, which can also best be considered as a mosaic. Many structures and patterns are found within the mosaic of Hindu sacred geography, but no dominating single center. Openness to the greatest possible plurality is often a good way to approach religion in South Asia, and this is also the case with Hindu sacred geography. The textual traditions of *Purāṇa*s and *Māhātmya*s expanded Hindu salvific space to include large areas of South Asia. The mosaic of Hindu salvific space was shaped to a large degree by this geographical expansion of the Brahmanical traditions, and many of the divine powers worshipped at the pilgrimage places were in this process identified with the major gods and sages of Hinduism.

While diversity, multiplicity and plurality without a single center describe the geography of Hindu salvific space, the pilgrimage priests and the promotion texts at many Hindu places of pilgrimage claim that their place is the single most powerful sacred center for all Hindus, all pilgrimage places, and perhaps the center of the world as well. Their site is the place at which all the other *tīrtha*s come together, and so visiting their pilgrimage site is equal to having visited all the *tīrtha*s. All the salvific rivers are said to be present in a single pool or single bathing place so that bathing there is equal to having taken baths in all the pools or rivers; or their site is the place where all the other *tīrtha*s go on pilgrimage to purify themselves from the moral impurity they have accumulated from the pilgrims taking baths there. During the month of *māgh*, it is claimed by the promotion narratives of Prayāg that all *tīrtha*s come to Prayāg to take sacred baths. Therefore, in the month of *māgh*, everyone should go to Prayāg. It is also implied in this claim that it is of no use to go on pilgrimage to any other place in the month of *māgh*, since the salvific powers of all the other *tīrtha*s are absent from their places because they are in Prayāg at this time. However, the promotion narratives of Ayodhyā claim that Prayāg needs to go to Ayodhyā to purify itself, making Ayodhyā an even more powerful site than Prayāg. The texts promoting Vārāṇasī claim Ayodhyā has no salvific power. There are seven salvific cities and Ayodhyā is indeed one of them, but the salvific power has left Ayodhyā and all the other cities, except Vārāṇasī. And so on. Personification of the salvific powers of place and the sites' ability to travel, which are two remarkable features of Hindu salvific space, make such unusual narratives of geographical places possible. Even priests and *Māhātmya* texts at minor local pilgrimage places make claims that their place is the most powerful salvific site and is the center of the world. *Tīrtha*s are not equal; they are often ranked in hierarchies and there are competing hierarchies. Some *tīrtha*s are obviously more important than others. That there are narratives about the journeys of all the *tīrtha*s to other places – for example, that all *tīrtha*s travel to Kurukṣetra during the solar eclipses – shows that the concept of a single supreme pilgrimage place is there, but that there nevertheless is no agreement about such a place. There are many competing sites and narratives.

The hierarchies of *tīrthas*

A characteristic feature of the promotion texts and narratives of *tīrtha*s is that every place, when described, is celebrated as the supreme salvific space and better than all others. Often, a *Māhātmya* text will repeatedly state that there is no better *tīrtha* than the one being described. Even at small pilgrimage places, *paṇḍit*s, *pujārī*s or pilgrimage priests (*paṇḍā*s) may claim that their particular place is the world's most important site, that it is the center of the universe. In an interview with a *paṇḍā* in the small but beautiful ancient pilgrimage place Miśrik (Misrikh) in Uttar Pradesh in February 2008, I was told that Miśrik is the center of the world and therefore the world's foremost *tīrtha*. This is supported by the sacred narratives, which say that all the waters of all the *tīrtha*s are present in the pool at Miśrik and therefore bathing in the pool is like being purified by bathing in all the *tīrtha*s. In the *Māhātmya*s quoted in *Tīrthavivecanakāṇḍa*, even the less significant places dealt with collectively at the end of the text, such as Kokāmukha, are praised as the best: "There is no pilgrimage place (*kṣetra*) superior to Kokāmukha, no more auspicious region, no more meritorious sacred bathe, and no place dearer [to Viṣṇu] than Kokāmukha" (*nā 'sti kokāmukhāt kṣetraṃ nā 'sti kokāmukhāc chubham, nā 'sti kokāmukhāt snānaṃ nā 'sti kokāmukhāt priyam*).[1]

One common way to create a hierarchy of *tīrtha*s and to claim superiority of one site is to compare the reward offered to pilgrims with that at other sites. In the *Māhātmya* of Naimiṣāraṇya or Naimiṣa (Nimsār), it is claimed that walking for eight miles along the Gaṅgā gives a reward equal to the *aśvamedha* sacrifice; the same result is attained by walking four miles in Vārāṇasī or two miles in Kurukṣetra, but by walking in Naimiṣāraṇya one attains the reward of an *aśvamedha* sacrifice for every step. In such comparisons, several places are listed and, for the comparison to have rhetoric power, the other places have to be those considered most important at the time of writing. The hierarchy of salvific sites, according to this statement, is first Naimiṣāraṇya, then Kurukṣetra, Vārāṇasī and the Gaṅgā last. *Matsyapurāṇa* (186.11) says that the river Yamunā purifies a person after bathing for seven days, the river Sarasvatī for three days, the river Gaṅgā after bathing once, but Narmadā purifies after the mere sight of it (thus making the hierarchy Narmadā, Gaṅgā, Sarasvatī and Yamunā last). *Vanaparvan* (82.20) of the *Mahābhārata* states that Naimiṣāraṇya is the best *tīrtha* on earth and Puṣkara the best in the atmosphere, but that Kurukṣetra is the best in all the three worlds. Another way to state superiority is to create a hierarchy of where sins committed at a sacred place are destroyed. Committing a sinful act at a sacred place is worse than committing the same act anywhere else.

> *anyakṣetraṃ kṛtaṃ pāpaṃ prayāge tu vinaśyati,*
> *prayāge hi kṛtaṃ pāpaṃ gaṅgākṣetre vinaśyati*
> *gaṅgākṣetre kṛtaṃ pāpaṃ kāśīṃ prāpya vinaśyati*
> *kāśīkṣetre kṛtaṃ pāpaṃ kurukṣetre vinaśyati*
> *kurukṣetre kṛtaṃ pāpaṃ pṛthūkṣetre vinaśyati*
> *pṛthūkṣetre kṛtaṃ pāpaṃ vajralepo bhaviṣyati*
>
> A sin committed at another place gets destroyed in Prayāg, a sin committed in Prayāg gets destroyed in the Gaṅgā region, a sin committed in the Gaṅgā region gets destroyed in Kāśī, a sin committed in Kāśī gets destroyed in Kurukṣetra, a sin committed in Kurukṣetra gets destroyed in Pṛtūdaka, but a sin committed in Pṛtūdaka becomes infallible.[2]

Pṛtūdaka (modern name Pehowa, situated in Kurukṣetra district) is thus the supreme pilgrimage place. The distance to heaven from the different *tīrtha*s is another way to form a hierarchy. *Pṛtūdaka Māhātmya* states that heaven is one *yojana* from Gayā, half a *yojana* from Prayāg, one *krośa* from Haradvāra (Hardvār), but only one cubit (*hastamātra*) from Pṛtūdaka.[3] In a verse from *Mahābhārata*, the place Pṛtūdaka is stated to be more sacred than all other *tīrthas* combined:

> *Puṇyam āhuḥ kurukṣetraṃ kurukṣetrāt sarasvatīm*
> *Sarasvatyāś ca tīrthāni tīrthebhyaś a pṛthūdakam*

> People say that Kurukṣetra is meritorious (*puṇya*), that the Sarasvatī is better than Kurukṣetra, and that Prayāg[4] is better than the Sarasvatī, but Pṛtūdaka is more meritorious than all the *tīrthas*.
>
> (*Mahābhārata* 3.81.125)

The reduplication or replication of *tīrtha*s can also be a way to hierarchize and claim superiority. In the *Brahmapurāṇa*, the claim is made that the north Indian river named Gaṅgā, here called Bhāgīrathī Gaṅgā, is just one of many channels of the real and much larger river Gaṅgā. To the north of the Vindhya mountains, Gaṅgā is called Bhāgīrathī, to the south of the Vindhyas, it is called Gautamī, and among the many channels of Gaṅgā, Gautamī is said to be the most outstanding (*Brahmapurāṇa, Gautamīmāhātmya*, 7.37–38). Every sacred river is a Gaṅgā. A. Feldhaus has made the case that replication is typical, especially in the Maharashtrian geographical imagination (Feldhaus 2003). D. Eck maintains that it is a general feature of Hindu conception of sacred space (Eck 1998). The holy places in Maharashtra (and the Deccan) are often connected to distant places in North India, especially in the Gangetic Valley, and A. Feldhaus holds that this rhetoric expresses Maharashtra's distance from, as well as inferiority to, areas in the central region of northern India. Reduplication is a way to accept simultaneously the superiority of other sites and claim superiority of one's own sites. Feldhaus gives many examples of this tendency of replication. The sacred places in Maharashtra are systematically connected to the sacred places in the north. Confluences along a river are claimed to be Prayāg and holy places along a river are said to be Kurukṣetra (Feldhaus 2003: 159). Many places in the Deccan are called southern Kāśī (Vārāṇasī). Uttarkāśī (Kāśī of the north) is in Uttarakhand in the Himālaya and this town is also, like Vārāṇasī, situated along the Gaṅgā, between the rivers Assī and Varaṇā, and has a Maṇikārṇikā *ghāṭ* as well, similar to Vārāṇasī. It does not only illustrate hierarchy, but this reduplication of the most important *tīrtha*s can also be seen as examples of the *tīrtha*s traveling, in this instance to where people can make their power more easily available so that they do not have to travel very far. Implied in this is that a visit to the local *tīrtha*s can also substitute for a visit to other regions. There is no reason to travel far when the same salvific power of place is present at the local site. The reduplication is presented also as a form of compassion for the poor. Many people cannot afford to travel on pilgrimage to places far away, but they can nevertheless visit the replicated *tīrtha*s at the local pilgrimage sites. Replication is also a way to attract pilgrims to the local shrines. It means that devotees can worship on a daily basis a god whose center is far away.

There is no agreement among Hindus or in the Hindu texts about any single pilgrimage site, river or sacred mountain being superior to all others. Research on pilgrims' opinions about which pilgrimage sites they consider the most important shows great diversity. Badrīnāth, Purī, Prayāg (Allāhābad), Tirupati and Hardvār generally finish high up on the list (Acharya 1997; Bhardwaj 1973). A regional center would probably be considered the most important factor when people from a single region are questioned. Most persons on a particular pilgrimage, if asked, would probably answer that the place they are heading to or visiting is the most significant. This parallels the way the *Purāṇa*s and the *Māhātmya*s texts handle the sites. Each place described in the texts is claimed to have supreme purificatory and salvific powers and it is often quite apparent that the places tried to outbid each other with respect to the great rewards they offered. There is an element of henotheism in the presentation of the Hindu sacred places in the *Purāṇa*s and the *Māhātmya*s. Each place that is described and paid homage to in the texts is celebrated as the most powerful and best of all sacred places and the most important pilgrimage site. This general tendency of what can be called the henotheism of salvific sites – that each site which is in focus is treated as the foremost site, while also accepting the existence of salvific power at the other sites – needs to be taken into account when evaluating the claims made about individual sacred places that they are the most important of all. The pilgrims, and sometimes authors on particular pilgrimage sites as well, also adopt this attitude of celebrating the place they are at as the supreme pilgrimage place.

Figure 6.1 Nimsār (Naimiṣa, Naimiṣāraṇya) as the center of the world. Walking around in a circle in the pool gives the merit of having circumambulated the whole earth

Photo: Knut A. Jacobsen

Many places, such as Vārāṇasī, Miśrik, Nimsār (Naimiṣāraṇya) (see Figure 6.1), Kumbhakoṇam and so on, claim to be the center of the world; however, each site is promoted as the center of the world only by some and not all persons. In Lakṣmīdhara's *Tīrthavivecanakāṇḍa*, Vārāṇasī is given the superior position, and read as a general textual statement this would imply that Vārāṇasī was accepted as the superior pilgrimage site at that time. Lakṣmīdhara describes several hundred *tīrtha*s, mostly *liṅga*s, in the city, which shows that by this time Vārāṇasī was a major pilgrimage place for Śaivas. Several of the medieval *Dharmanibandha*s on pilgrimage, such as the *Tristhalīsetu* of Nārāyaṇa Bhaṭṭa, favor Vārāṇasī by paying most attention to it, but other *nibandha*s prefer other cities. However, the authors of both *Tīrthavivecanakāṇḍa* and *Tristhalīsetu* were living in Vārāṇasī and this probably also influenced their presentations. Lakṣmīdhara was part of the government of Vārāṇasī at the time of writing, and one purpose of the text seems to have been to promote Vārāṇasī as the foremost pilgrimage site. The editor of the printed Sanskrit edition of the *Tīrthavivecanakāṇḍa*, K. V. Rangaswami Aiyangar, comments in the Introduction to the book that it is Kurukṣetra, which is given a much shorter chapter in the book, that is the superior sacred place of Hinduism. This probably illustrates the editor's own preference, or perhaps his judgment is based on an evaluation of the textual traditions that flourished in the period before Vārāṇasī became one of the foremost pilgrimage places. The *Tīrthacintāmaṇi* of Vācaspatimiśra (fifteenth century), another of the main *Dharmanibandha*s on *tīrtha*s, devotes half of more than 350 pages of text to the site Puruṣottama (the sacred area of Jagannāth) (modern Purī), while the city of Vārāṇasī is given just a few pages. Texts like these reflect the preferences of the authors and perhaps also of their patrons.

S. M. Bhardwaj's important study of Hindu pilgrimage from 1973 investigated the different levels of interconnections between the Hindu pilgrimage places and the circulation patterns of pilgrims. Based on interviews with pilgrims in the Himālayas, Bhardwaj attempted to create a scientific ranking of the Hindu pilgrimage sites. One measure he used was the distance the pilgrims had traveled to reach a place. The further the pilgrims were willing to travel, the more important the pilgrimage place was assumed to be – that is, the longer the distance, the higher the ranking. In Bhardwaj's study, Badrīnāth is ranked highest and Hardvār comes next. A criticism of this way of ranking pilgrimage places is that the ranking will be greatly influenced by the area in which the interviews are conducted. Another problem is that some sacred sites are situated further from the densely populated areas, such as the places in the Himālayas (Badrīnāth, Kedārnāth, Gaṅgotrī, Yamunotrī, Amarnāth, Vaiṣṇodevī, and so on), and in order to reach them, most people have to travel long distances. This method of ranking favors places that are isolated. However, Bhardwaj supports the view that there is a "lack of a single clear system in Hindu religious traditions establishing the rank order of sacred places" and that this "is mirrored in the varied perceptions by pilgrims about the holiest places in India today." And he adds: "The ranks are not clearly defined for the entire country, resulting in a diffuse perception of what is the holiest place" (Bhardwaj 1973: 115). He thinks, however, that there is a tendency that high caste people select well-known places because they are more familiar with the textual traditions of Hinduism, while low caste people select local sacred places in addition to the better known ones.

The pilgrimage places the individual Hindu considers most important obviously depends on which god or goddess they worship or consider the most significant (their *iṣṭadevatā*, *kuladevatā* and so on). Hinduism is a pluralistic tradition with many *sampradāya*s. Vaiṣṇavas, Śaivas and Śāktas have their own sacred geographies. These geographies are not exclusive but nevertheless influence preferences. For worshippers of Kṛṣṇa, the area Braj in Uttar Pradesh, which includes Mathurā, the birthplace of Kṛṣṇa, and Vṛndāvan, the area where Kṛṣṇa grew up, and which is associated with many of the central events in his life on earth, and the main pilgrimage places such as the hill Govardhana and the Jagannāth temple in Purī, Orisssa, are obviously more important than Vārāṇasī, which is a main Śaiva pilgrimage place, or Kāmākhyā in Assam, which is one of the major Śākta pilgrimage places. For worshippers of Rāma, the cities of Ayodhyā, Citrakūṭa and Janakpur, with their numerous *tīrtha*s connected to the sacred narratives of Rāma and Sītā, are especially important pilgrimage sites. For the Tamil Śaivas, Cidambaram, Madurai and Tiruvaṇṇamalai, in Tamil Nadu, are most important pilgrimage places, while for Tamil Vaiṣṇavas, Tirumala and Śrīraṅgam, center of the Śrīvaiṣṇava tradition, are important pilgrimage places. Vaiṣṇavas, Śaivas and Śāktas in Bengal have their own pilgrimage centers, and Vaiṣṇavas, Śaivas and Śāktas in Gujarat have theirs, and so on. However, pilgrimage places often have shrines of Vaiṣṇava, Śaiva and Śākta divinities. In North India especially, where pilgrimage places are *kṣetra*s, large areas with many individual *tīrtha*s, each *kṣetra* contains temples for worship of a large number of gods and sages. A Śaiva pilgrimage place such as Ujjain (Ujjayinī, Avantī), one of the 12 *jyotirliṅga* centers and one of the *kumbhamelā* sites, also has pilgrimage places of Vaiṣṇava and Śakta divinities. Ujjain has one of the *śaktipīṭha*s, one of the most sacred places for the worshippers of Śakti and an important site associated with Kṛṣṇa since the hermitage of Sāndīpani, the teacher of Kṛṣṇa, is believed to have been in Ujjain. The pool near the temple contains all the sacred rivers because Kṛṣṇa had called on them so that his guru Sāndīpani would not have to travel on pilgrimage, thus making a visit there equal to having visited all the sacred rivers. The Śaiva city of Vārāṇasī has numerous Vaiṣṇava and Śākta shrines and temples. In South India, where the goal of pilgrimage travel is often single temples, the temples may contain shrines of many deities. The Śivanaṭarāja temple in Cidambaram has a shrine of Viṣṇu next to the main shrine of Naṭarāja, and so on. But pilgrims are often not exclusive and many places also attract pilgrims regardless of which gods they worship. As tourism became an important aspect of pilgrimage, such inclinations probably also became less important. A magnificent temple may attract pilgrims regardless of individual preferences. As is well known, a number of different gods and goddesses are placed on the *pūjā* table of many Hindus. Also, the gods and goddesses of Hinduism partake in the same narratives and sites are, therefore, often not exclusive. Rāmēśvaram in South India is one of the *jyotirliṅga*s, but the *liṅga* was established by Rāma to atone for the sin of killing Rāvaṇa. The festivals celebrate different gods and goddesses and pilgrimage places often organize annual *melā*s in connection with them. Different gods are worshipped on different days of the week and these also influence the pattern. Hanumān is worshipped especially on Tuesdays and Saturdays and the most important Hanumān temples attract a high number of pilgrims on these days. Nowadays, pilgrims visit particularly on Saturdays since people are likely to have free time to travel during the weekend. Śani, the planet Saturn, one of the Navagrahas, is associated with Saturday, and, in case of need, pilgrimage to his temples is also performed on Saturdays. Śiva is easier pleased on Mondays and pilgrims consider this when planning visits. However, festivals are the main days for pilgrimage. People on pilgrimage tours organized by travel agencies as week-long or more bus trips often cover the most important pilgrimage places – that is, a tour of the famous sites in a particular geographical area of India. These tours operate throughout the whole country.

Why Vārāṇasī is not the Mecca of Hinduism

In Hinduism, there are many religious traditions (*sampradāya*s) and none of them stand above all the others, but is there, nevertheless, among the plurality of Hindu sacred sites, one place that is more sacred than the rest that could be considered the Mecca of Hinduism? Al-Biruni (973–1048), who observed India and wrote the celebrated *Kitab fi tahqiq ma li'l-hind* (or *Ta'riqh al-hind*) on Indian philosophy and culture for Muslims wishing to learn about religion, science and literature in India, indeed compared Vārāṇasī to Mecca, but mainly because Vārāṇasī was a place like Mecca at that time where, according to Al-Biruni, persons would go to live at the end of their lives (see Sachau 1910, Bind II: 146).[5] By "Mecca," I mean here a pilgrimage place that every person belonging to a religion should visit as part of the attainment of that religion's salvational goal and a place that is accepted by everyone belonging to a religion as the single geographical center of the religion. The promotion texts of Vārāṇasī make such claims, but does Vārāṇasī have these two characteristics? Vārāṇasī is often presented as the holiest city and the most significant center of Hinduism. Comparing the number of academic books and studies written about Vārāṇasī as a religious center and pilgrimage place to academic publications about other Hindu pilgrimage places in India would indicate so. The number is perhaps in the hundreds and new books are published every year (some of the most important are Eck 1982; Gutschow 2006; Hertel and Humes 1993; Lannoy 1999; Parry 1994; Schilder and Callewaert 2000; Singh 1993, Sukul 1974; Vidyarthi, Jha and Saraswati 1979). The number by far surpasses those about any other Hindu pilgrimage places that have been studied, and the number of academic books and studies on Vārāṇasī as a pilgrimage place and religious center is probably larger than the books written about all the other Hindu pilgrimage places combined. This certainly says something about the recent and current attractiveness and power of the pilgrimage place of Vārāṇasī, and these academic publications have probably also influenced the situation. Does this mean that Hinduism has a sacred center after all? There are surely good reasons for the current academic love affair with Vārāṇasī but is this salvific city something like the Mecca of Hinduism or just one of many important pilgrimage places in Hinduism?

Vārāṇasī is only one of many places and represents only some of the Hindu traditions. Nevertheless, Vārāṇasī would perhaps be the most likely candidate for being assessed as a possible "Mecca" of Hinduism. In Vārāṇasī *Māhātmya*s and the pilgrimage literature celebrating Vārāṇasī, the city is presented as the holy city of Hinduism and as the sacred center of the world. Western and Indian academic writers on sacred space and pilgrimage who write about Vārāṇasī often adopt this view in their presentations of the city. It should be stressed again, however, that this is a general quality for Hindu salvific space and is nothing unique for Vārāṇasī. But what qualities does Vārāṇasī have that makes the city's claim of being the center of Hinduism and a place every Hindu should visit particularly convincing?

Many of the particularities of Vārāṇasī as a *tīrtha* are presented in the *Vārāṇasī Māhātmya*s, one of the earliest of which is the *Vārāṇasī Māhātmya* of the *Matsyapurāṇa* (eighth to ninth centuries CE?) and constitutes Chapters 180–185 of the book (the length of the Sanskrit text and the English translation is 33 printed pages).[6] The largest *Māhātmya* is the *Kāśīkhaṇḍa* of the *Skandapurāṇa*, dated to the fourteenth century, but the earliest known manuscript of a text titled *Skandapurāṇa* that contains chapters on Vārāṇasī is probably from the eighth century (Bakker 1996).[7] *Vārāṇasī Māhātmya*s are also found in the *Liṅgapurāṇa* and *Kūrmapurāṇa*.[8] The *Vārāṇasī Māhātmya* of the *Matsyapurāṇa* is representative in that many of the characteristics of the praise of Vārāṇasī as a sacred place are presented here. The praising of Vārāṇasī has nevertheless many similarities to how other places are praised in their *Māhātmya*s. The *Vārāṇasī Māhātmya* of the *Matsyapurāṇa* probably represents a different theology than the Kāśīkhaṇḍa. The text is formed as conversations between Śiva and Pārvatī, and Skanda and Pārvatī. Pārvatī is interested in learning about Vārāṇasī and its excellent qualities, and Śiva repeatedly states that it is the best *tīrtha* in the world. In the beginning of the text, Śiva praises the natural beauty of the area. The birds, the beautiful trees with creepers, the insects, the aroma of the flowers, the beautiful songs by birds and celestial beings, the roars of lions and the herds of deer are praised (180.24–46). The place is praised here for its natural beauty, not for any city-like qualities. Śiva then starts describing the salvific power of the place. He proclaims that this sacred place (*kṣetra*) of Vārāṇasī is always his most secret (*guhyatama*) place (that is, superior to all other places) and is the giver of *mokṣa* to all (*idaṃ guhyatamaṃ kṣetraṃ sadā vārāṇasī, sarveṣaṃ eva bhūtānāṃ hetur mokṣasya sarvadā* [180.46]). People who bathe in Naimiṣa, Kurukṣetra, Gaṅgādvāra (Hardvār) and Puṣkara without attaining the salvific goal will attain that goal in Vārāṇasī (180.55). *Mokṣa* is achieved by people after performing yoga for thousands of lives, but is attained in Vārāṇasī merely by dying there (180.74). Vārāṇasī is also the foremost place to attain yoga powers (*siddhi*s). Vārāṇasī is the most secret of all supreme places (*guhyānāṃ guhyam uttamam* [181.13]). He who never leaves Vārāṇasī attains *mokṣa*, and animals dying in Varanasi also attain *mokṣa* (181.23–25). Śiva mentions other sites that are also sacred and where he is present, but concludes that these other sites "always remain at the feet" of

Vārāṇasī – that is, they are subordinate to Vārāṇasī. Skanda then takes over the conversation to praise Vārāṇasī. *Avimukta* (a name for Vārāṇasī usually understood to mean "never abandoned by Śiva") excels over all other sacred places (*guhyānām paramaṃ guhyam*) and there are no places more sacred than Vārāṇasī. He who lives permanently in Vārāṇasī attains *mokṣa*. Pārvatī then asks why Śiva favors Vārāṇasī over Himālaya, Kailāsa, Sumeru and other sacred places. Śiva replies that it is because of a river there that merges in the Gaṅgā (the river Varuṇā; Vārāṇasī is often defined as the *kṣetra* between the rivers Varuṇā [Varaṇā] and Assī). Then the text states that by merely listening to the praise of Vārāṇasī one is cleansed of all moral impurities. Here, the salvific power of the text apparently takes precedence over the site, since listening to the words of praise gains the same results as visiting the city. However, it is the power of the site, assumedly, that makes the text powerful. By going on a pilgrimage to Vārāṇasī, one is cleansed of all moral impurities (*pāpa*) (183.10–11). When creation is dissolved at the end of a cycle, Vārāṇasī is not dissolved, so it is the only eternal place in creation. In Vārāṇasī, Śiva remains with hundreds of attendants during the time of dissolution of a creation cycle (183.12). At the time of dissolution, the Devas, Gandharvas, Yakṣas, Nāgas, Rākṣasas and so on enter the mouth of Śiva at Vārāṇasī (183.13–14). Śiva proclaims that those who reside there merge with him (*mām eva praviśanti* [183.25]). As there is no male being equal to Śiva, and no female being equal to Pārvatī, there is, therefore, no sacred place (*kṣetra*) equal to Vārāṇasī and nor will there ever be (*matsamaḥpuruṣo nāsti tvatsamā nāsti yoṣitām, avimuktasamaṃ kṣetraṃ na bhūtaṃ na bhaviṣyati*). The text emphasizes the value of giving gifts of charity to Brahmans, such as cows, gold, food, sandals and flowers. A person who gives in charity a cow that provides plenty of milk, together with gold and silver, to a Brahman in Vārāṇasī liberates seven generations of their ancestors (183.39–50). Vārāṇasī is called the cremation ground (*śmaśāna*). It is the best of all pilgrimage sites, the best place, the best sacred area and the best of all cremation grounds (*uttamaṃ sarvatīrthānāṃ sthānānām uttamañ ca yat. ca kṣetrāṇām uttamañ caiva śmaśānām tathaiva ca* [184.16]). Vārāṇasī is better than all other sacred places. Whether they are located on earth or in heaven, Vārāṇasī is supreme to all. The sage Vyāsa, who, according to the *Vārāṇasī Māhātmya* of *Matsyapurāṇa*, stayed in Vārāṇasī, explained to Pārvatī that he stayed there because it was the place of Śiva and Pārvatī, because the river Gaṅgā flowed there, because of the delicious food available there and because he would achieve *mokṣa* in the end (185.35–36). The mere sight of Vārāṇasī destroys past and present moral impurities. The text ends with a call to the residents of Vārāṇasī to never leave the place because everyone ridicules them when they go elsewhere (185.42), presumably because they were foolish enough to leave the salvific space of Vārāṇasī.

That one should never leave Vārāṇasī relates to the focus on death. Whereas the cremation grounds in Indian villages are usually outside the towns and villages, since cremation grounds are impure and dangerous places, in Vārāṇasī, the cremation grounds are in the center. This shows that, religiously, the town is centered on death and salvation. More than anything else, Vārāṇasī, for the Hindus, is the city of death.[9] Vārāṇasī is Mahāśmaśāna, "the great cremation ground" (see Parry

1994). Being cremated at one of its two cremation *ghāṭ*s, the Maṇikarṇikā and the Harīścandra, is considered of great religious importance. A few old and sick people travel to Vārāṇasī wishing to end their life there. Dying in Vārāṇasī is defined as a good death. In Hinduism in general, it is Citragupta, the scribe of Yama, the god of death, who keeps the records of people's good and bad acts, but in Vārāṇasī, Bhairava is the record keeper. He is worshipped in order to be free from disease and evil influences. Bhairava is also the guardian of Vārāṇasī and anyone who wishes to die in the city must first gain his consent. On arrival in Vārāṇasī, one should first worship Bhairava to ask for permission to enter. Some sick people who have come to Vārāṇasī to die miraculously recover and then have to return to their villages without having attained a good death. Their recovery is interpreted in a negative way and is understood to mean that Bhairava, the guard of Vārāṇasī, did not allow them to enter the city to die. They will have to die in their own village and wait for their next rebirth in order to die in Vārāṇasī (which will then grant them *mokṣa*). However, there is no large-scale movement of the elderly to Vārāṇasī, which one is sometimes made to believe. Mostly, only people from localities close to Vārāṇasī stay in the *mukti-bhavan*s, homes for the sick who have come to die in the city. Their total number is not large. There is also no universally accepted tradition that the dead body (for cremation) or ashes (for immersion in the Gaṅgā) should be brought to Vārāṇasī. It is symptomatic of the plurality of traditions that the body of Maharishi Mahesh Yogi, who died in 2008, was brought by his devotees to Prayāg (Allāhābad), to the movement's Allāhābad *āśram*, and was cremated there. His *samādhisthān* is also on the banks of the confluence and the Maharishi Smārak is being constructed to be visible from Prayāg and the *kumbhamelā* grounds. The closest airport of Prayāg is east of Vārāṇasī, but even then, on arrival at the airport of Vārāṇasī, the corpse was transported by car through Vārāṇasī on the 100-kilometre journey to Prayāg. The *saṅgam* in Prayāg, the place where the rivers Yamunā and Gaṅgā flow together, was considered more appropriate for the cremation than Vārāṇasī.

Vārāṇasī is the place of Śiva, and it is promoted as the center of the universe because it is the only place that remains when the rest of the world is dissolved and it is the place from which the new creation starts. The city is said to be located on top of the trident of Śiva. In the *Māhātmya*s of Vārāṇasī, the pilgrims are encouraged to settle permanently in the city. Once they have arrived in Vārāṇasī, the pilgrims should never leave. As it is said in the *Kūrmapurāṇa*: "Realizing that salvation is very difficult to achieve and the world is very terrible, a man should strike his feet with stone and stay in Vārāṇasī" (*Kūrmapurāṇa* 1.31.35). Only fools leave Vārāṇasī because it is the geographical site of the city itself that gives salvation. Although Kāśī Viśvanāth, the god of the main temple in Vārāṇasī for pilgrims, is also worshipped at a number of temples around India, the salvific power of Vārāṇasī is nevertheless considered exclusive. You have to be present permanently in Vārāṇasī because the salvific power of Vārāṇasī that grants the individual *mokṣa* is lost once that individual leaves the city. However, the priests at the Kāl Bhairava temple offer a protection so that, wherever a person dies, it is like dying in Vārāṇasī. In this case, Citragupta will keep no record of the person's wrongdoings and Bhairava will take care of them.

It is the *kṣetra*, the geographical space, which is sacred. The emphasis is not on one specific temple or one specific *liṅga*, although some *liṅga*s are praised as particularly powerful – currently this is the Viśvanātha *liṅga* – but it is the geographical area that is the giver of *mokṣa*, it seems. Dying in Vārāṇasī is especially valuable and the encouragement to stay there and never leave follows logically from the focus on death; once one has arrived, one should stay until death. Even animals that die in Vārāṇasī attain *mokṣa* without having performed any rituals. In the descriptions of Vārāṇasī in *Tīrthavivecanakāṇḍa*, the dominating theme is the several hundred *liṅgas*. The idea that all other sacred places are present in or are reduplicated in Vārāṇasī becomes more prominent in the *Kāśīkhaṇḍa*. In these texts, there is also emphasis on staying in the city. That many other *tīrtha*s are reduplicated in Vārāṇasī also means that it is unnecessary to go on pilgrimage to other sites, since all Hindu *tīrtha*s are themselves present in the city. The ideas about dying in Vārāṇasī and the reduplication of *tīrtha*s there are probably closely related.

The *Kāśīkhaṇḍa* 1.5.12–30 argues for staying permanently in Vārāṇasī because there is no *liṅga* equal to Viśvanātha and no city equal to Kāśī. Only fools think of leaving:

> People learn from great men that Kāśī is the fruit of a mass of merits acquired in the course of many previous births. They come to it after undergoing various difficulties, still they are foolish enough to wish to go elsewhere, they are willing to court disaster (or hell) voluntarily.
>
> (*Kāśīkhaṇḍa* 1.5.14)

"A sensible man does not go elsewhere. As impossible it is for a pumpkin gourd to pass through the throat of a goat, as impossible would it be for a wise man to leave Kāśī," says *Kāśīkhaṇḍa* 1.5.15.

> Those who are liberated souls do not leave Kāśī. Kāśī eradicates all types of sins; it is inaccessible even to gods; it has the excellent supply of water through Gaṅgā; it snaps the noose of worldly existence; it is never left by Śiva and Pārvatī; it acts like an oyster shell for the development of the pearl of salvation and it is the very personification of blissful redemption.
>
> (*Kāśīkhaṇḍa* 1.5.18)

It is ignorance that makes people leave Vārāṇasī because, even during the periods of annihilation, the city is held on the tip of the trident of Śiva, says *Kāśīkhaṇḍa* (1.5.19). Kāśī is the raft of salvific liberation, so why would anyone abandon the raft? If anyone leaves Vārāṇasī and settles elsewhere he casts off salvation from his palm, says the *Kāśīkhaṇḍa* 1.5.30.

That a person loses his salvation once he moves outside of Kāśī seems to be a paradox, since the power of Kāśī has also been reduplicated at other places, implying salvific power is movable. But the person needs not only to visit but also to settle there and stay until death. Once outside, presumably, the person again starts to attract impurity.

Vārāṇasī is presented in the *Māhātmya*s as the supreme salvific site. It has numerous *tīrtha*s and the benefits from taking sacred baths at these *tīrtha*s are typically compared to the benefits of bathing at other competing pilgrimage places. A bath at the Prayāga *tīrtha* in Vārāṇasī gives ten times more benefit than going to Prayāg in the month of Māgh, ten times more benefit than taking a sacred bath in the confluence of Gāṅgā and Yamunā and ten times more benefit than what is obtained by those who give gifts at Kurukṣetra during solar eclipses (*Kāśīkhaṇḍa* 61.30–32). It illustrates the strategy of Vārāṇasī's pilgrimage traditions of reduplication of other *tīrtha*s to preserve the ideology of dying the good death in the city. The inclusion of them in Vārāṇasī probably also reflects the competition between the sites for ritual clients. Prayāg is not only present in Vārāṇasī but it is even more meritorious to bathe at that *tīrtha* in Vārāṇasī than to travel to Prayāg itself. "Avimukta excels over Prayāga, the foremost among the *tīrtha*s," says *Kāśīkhaṇḍa* 1.6.70. Not only that, but "if a person does not get salvific liberation even after reaching Kāśī, he cannot get salvation even if he visits millions of *tīrtha*s," says *Kāśīkhaṇḍa* 1.6.71.

But even if it is the style of the *Māhātmya*s that each place is celebrated as the best, the claim that Vārāṇasī is the holiest city or the most important sacred center of Hinduism – a claim that often seems to be accepted even though it is untrue – has nevertheless been supported by several arguments. First, Vārāṇasī is different from other main pilgrimage places, such as Tirumala, Badrīnāth and Kedārnāth, in that it is a large city. Badrīnāth (see Figure 6.2), Kedārnāth and Tirumala are *tīrtha*s centered on a single temple and exist mainly as pilgrimage places. Vārāṇasī

Figure 6.2 The main temple of the *tīrtha* Badrīnāth in the Himālaya

Photo: Knut A. Jacobsen

is not only a pilgrimage place, but multidimensional. The city covers a large geographical area. It is built along the river and a system of steps, called *ghāṭs*, leading from the river into the city. Tall buildings have been built along the *ghāṭs*. The length of the *ghāṭ* area along the river is currently more than eight kilometers and continues to be expanded. The size of the sacred bathing area alone makes Vārāṇasī unique. The sacredness of Vārāṇasī is connected to the river Gaṅgā, not only because of the general sacredness of the river, but also because the river Gaṅgā winds north as it enters Vārāṇasī. The whole city is situated on the western shore of the river when the sun rises on the opposite shore. No buildings have been allowed on the western side of the river because of the sunrise. The ritual greeting of the rising sun is an important daily ritual and is one geographical foundation for Vārāṇasī.

Second, Vārāṇasī is different from several other sacred cities in that it is also a prestigious center of traditional learning, especially Sanskrit, philosophy and yoga, but also music and other traditions of knowledge. Vārāṇasī has been a nursery of Hindu philosophy. Gurus have taught their students here for more than 2, 500 years and Śaṅkara is supposed to have composed his *Brahmasūtrabhāṣya* here in the eighth century. Several modern universities in the city have attempted to carry on this function of the city as a classical center of learning. Persons with linguistic skills have settled here and students have arrived from large areas of India, and in modern times also an increasing number from the rest of the world. Vārāṇasī, it is claimed, is "the cultural capital of India" (Singh and Rana 2002: 59). Whether that is true or not is a different matter; what is important here is that such claims would seldom be made about other major sacred cities such as Prayāga[10] and Mathurā.[11] Kolkata and Chennai are often called the cultural capitals of India, but these are not pilgrimage cities. This illustrates, however, that Vārāṇasī's claim of being "the cultural capital of India" is not in any way universally accepted by Hindus.[12]

A third argument that favors Vārāṇasī as the holy city of Hinduism is that Vārāṇasī is a multicultural city; people from many different parts of India have settled here and have kept their regional identities. They have settled in special neighborhoods and maintained their regional religious traditions. There are temples in many different regional styles, preserving regional traditions, and this supports the argument that Vārāṇasī is a microcosm of India.

Fourth, that the location of Vārāṇasī is both close to a perceived geographical center of India and is also in the center of the ancient civilization of the Gaṅgā Valley makes it easier to accept the claim of Vārāṇasī as the holy center of India than, for instance, Tirumala in Andhra Pradesh, which is the place that receives the highest number of pilgrims annually, but is situated in South India, or Purī in the east, Vaiṣṇodevī in the northwest or Śabarimala in the southwest, which all receive large numbers of pilgrims but are better defined as regional centers.

A fifth argument supporting Vārāṇasī's claim to be the holy city of Hinduism is that many of the most sacred places of India are reduplicated in Vārāṇasī, making it a mini sacred India. As one author sums up this reduplication:

> Kashi has all the four dhams, the seven holy cities, the eight Bhairavas, the nine Gauris, the nine Durgas, the nine grahas, the ten incarnations, the twelve jyotirlingas, the thirteen Narasimhas, the sixteen Keshavas, the fifty-six Vinayakas and the sixty-four Yoginis.
>
> (Chandramouli 1996: 48)

The author therefore concludes that Vārāṇasī is the holiest of the *tīrtha*s in which the presence of the divine grace is seen, heard and felt. Reduplication is a common strategy of salvific space in Hinduism. That all other *tīrtha*s go on pilgrimage to a site marks that site as superior, and the concept probably represents an attempt to appropriate the salvific powers of the other places. Reduplication was probably a conscious strategy for increasing Vārāṇasī's importance and sacredness, and perhaps necessary for defending its particular ideology of the necessity of staying permanently and never leaving the city. The reduplication made it possible to visit many of the other famous and powerful *tīrtha*s without ever leaving the city.

A sixth argument supporting Vārāṇasī's claim to be the center of the Hindu tradition is the argument made in the sacred texts promoting Vārāṇasī that the city is the only place that remains when the world is dissolved after a period of creation and is the place from which creation of the world starts at the beginning of a new period of creation. Vārāṇasī is the only place in the universe that is eternal. But, as mentioned already, it should be noted that other places make the same claims and have other myths to prove that they are the centers of the world.

Academic writers on Vārāṇasī use arguments like these to praise the city as the sacred center of Hinduism. Rana P. B. Singh, a contemporary writer on the sacred geography of Vārāṇasī, starts an article about the city by stating: "Vārāṇasī (Benares), known as the microcosm of India and the most sacred city of Hindu religion." Vārāṇasī is the "holiest for Hindus" (Singh and Rana 2002: 59). Another author writes, "To the believer, Kashi is the holiest of all places" (Chandramouli 1996: 26). That Vārāṇasī is a microcosm, an India in miniature, is a common claim. Vārāṇasī is "mini-India" (Singh and Rana 2002: 59). The pan-Indian sacred places are reduplicated in Vārāṇasī (ibid.; see Figure 6.3). Diana Eck writes: "Among India's *tīrtha*s, Kashi is the most widely acclaimed" (Eck 1982: 39). Kāśī embodies all *tīrtha*s (ibid.). It is like a symbol that condenses the whole into one place, and it condenses India into a great sacred circle, a geographical *maṇḍala* (ibid.: 41). "What is 'unique' about Kashi is that this city has most powerfully collected and refracted the light of India's *tīrtha*s to become the City of All India" (Eck 1981: 41). All the gods are present in Vārāṇasī; all sacred places are present there. The river Gaṅgā is sacred and Vārāṇasī is the heart and center of the Hindu universe. Vārāṇasī does not express a regional culture, but "epitomizes all that is India" (Medhasananda 2002: 1). People from all parts of India have settled in Vārāṇasī and this makes it not a regional place, but a mini-India that reflects the mosaic of the country. The claim that Vārāṇasī is the center of Hinduism is a standard claim repeated on many of the web pages about the city. Web pages claim that the venerable and ancient city of Vārāṇasī is the religious center of the world for Hindus[13] and is almost universally regarded as Hinduism's holiest spot.[14]

Figure 6.3 Prayāg *ghāṭ* in Vārāṇasī

Photo: Knut A. Jacobsen

Vārāṇasī is, however, only one of many Hindu *tīrtha*s and is not the center of the world of Hindus. That the location of Vārāṇasī is close to a geographical center of India and in the center of the ancient Indian civilization of the Gaṅgā Valley has probably made the claim of Vārāṇasī as the holy center of India more widely accepted. But Vārāṇasī, although without doubt an all-India pilgrimage place, has in fact many qualities of a regional center. The claim that Vārāṇasī does not express a regional culture is wrong. One common misperception about India is that the regions in the center are often not thought of as regions, but as the center or the "heartland" (Kudaisya 2006). The Gaṅgā Valley has status as the center. Sacred places such as Śabarimala in Kerala, Purī in Orissa, Kāmākhyā in Assam (see Figure 6.4), Tirumala in Andhra Pradesh and Paṇḍharpūr in Maharashtra are outside the central area and they are associated with the regions in which they are located and from which they cannot be disassociated. Their regional identity is too strong. In the presentations of the sacred city of Vārāṇasī, however, the emphasis is not on Vārāṇasī as a regional sacred center for the Bhojpurī-speaking area (Bhojpurī is a regional language spoken in Western Bihar, the Purvanchal area of Uttar Pradesh and the north-western parts of Jharkhand) but as the sacred center of all of India. Vārāṇasī is said to condense India into a great sacred circle and is the *bindu* of a geographical *maṇḍala*. The emphasis is not on its regional identity, but on its assumed status as the center of Hinduism. Vārāṇasī's status over the last 100 years cannot be disconnected from the status of Uttar Pradesh becoming the center or heartland of the Indian nation state. Hindi and its dialects, the language

Figure 6.4 The *śaktipīṭha* of Kāmākhyā in Assam

Photo: Knut A. Jacobsen

of this area, became the national language. The alphabet of Hindi (and Bhojpurī), *devanāgarī*, also became the alphabet in which Sanskrit texts in modern India are printed. With the creation of the Indian nation, Vārāṇasī became geographically situated in the middle as if in the center of a *maṇḍala* of India.

Vārāṇasī is often suggested as the center of Hinduism perhaps because the state of Uttar Pradesh does not have a regional identity. Uttar Pradesh has been perceived as the center of India and is typically characterized as the "heartland" of India, as India in miniature, as the Madhyadeśa and the Aryavarta, as the cradle of the Hindu–Buddhist civilization and as the heartland of the Brahmanical tradition. The idea of a heartland refers to the ancient past as well as to the recent past and the present. The "heartland" is a striking and an almost omnipresent recurring metaphor in the literature about the area that today constitutes Uttar Pradesh (Kudaisya 2006). The area was the "Brahmanical heartland," the "Gangetic heartland," the "heartland of Mughal India," the "heartland of British India," as well as the "Hindu heartland" and the "Hindi heartland." The historian K. M. Panikkar described the Gaṅgā Valley as the "principal core" of India and suggested that this is not only due to the Gaṅgā, "but the area from Gaya to Mathura, from Sangam to Hardwar, is recognized by everyone to be the holy land of Hinduism" (Panikkar 1959: 39). Uttar Pradesh is described as a kind of microcosm of India in which India is mirrored and summed up, as well as the religious and geographical center – that is, the center of Hinduism – indeed similar to how Vārāṇasī is described.

And also, the Hinduism of this area is often the model by which other forms of Hinduism are measured. Other forms of Hinduism are considered "regional variants," while the Hinduism in Uttar Pradesh is considered the normative core. The people there are described as "typical Indians." In the Indian languages, there is no singular provincial name for the people of this region. In contrast to the names of Tamils, Oriyas, Assamese, Marathis, Rajasthanis and Punjabis, there is no term for people from Uttar Pradesh. They are sometimes known as Hindustani, which means Indian. The lack of provincialism is sometimes ascribed to the fact that it was the core area of the Brahmanical civilization. During the 1920s and 1930s, when Indian nationalists attempted to define Hinduism as the core of the original national community of India, both in the Indian Congress and in movements more commonly identified as Hindu nationalists, it was the Hinduism of North India and especially its traditions in Uttar Pradesh that were seen as its content. A homogeneous Hindu tradition was imagined, with the center in the Hindu traditions of Uttar Pradesh. Its traditions were the norm, and other Hindu traditions were often understood as regional variants. The Brahmans of Vārāṇasī were the traditional embodiments of orthodoxy, and this also helped to promote Vārāṇasī as the center of Hinduism (Jacobsen 2009d, 2009e).

Vārāṇasī has precisely exemplified the idea of Uttar Pradesh as the "heartland" and "center of Hinduism" and the modern status of Uttar Pradesh as the heartland has also helped to promote Vārāṇasī as the center of Hinduism, rather than promoted its regional identity. The city is portrayed as the holy center of Hinduism, situated in Uttar Pradesh, the "heart" of India. Descriptions of Vārāṇasī are very similar to descriptions of Uttar Pradesh. Vārāṇasī is also said to be a microcosm of all of Hindu India, it is the archetypical representative of a Hindu sacred place, it contains and represents all that is Hindu and it sums up all of Hinduism, writes Diana Eck (1981). The central god of Vārāṇasī, Viśvanāth, a form of Śiva, is therefore considered not a regional god like Ayappan, Viṭṭhala or Veṅkaṭeśvara but as a god of the center. However, worshippers of Ayappan in Kerala and Tamil Nadu or worshippers of Veṅkaṭeśvara in Tamil Nadu, Andhra Pradesh or Karnataka do not look to Vārāṇasī as the holy center of their sacred world.

Vārāṇasī's claim to superiority as *the* sacred center of the whole of Hinduism has not been confirmed in research that maps the views of Hindu pilgrims. Vārāṇasī is important only to some of the vast plurality of Hindu traditions. Interviews with pilgrims at sacred places have shown that there is no consensus about a single, most sacred center among Hindus (Bhardwaj 1973). In Bhardwaj's investigation, pilgrims were asked to rank the pilgrimage sites, and Vārāṇasī was not among the highest-ranking sacred places. Bhardwaj found that no single sacred site had the status of India's most sacred place. Bhardwaj concludes that "although Vārāṇasī is often spoken of as the 'Mecca of the Hindus', our data show that such an appellation does not reflect the perception of the pilgrims."[15] Pilgrims usually favor sacred places in their own region, such as the sacred *tīrtha*s of Ayappan in Kerala, Veṅkaṭeśvara in Andhra Pradesh, Jagannāth in Orissa or Viṭṭhala in Maharashtra. Uttar Pradesh itself has many sacred centers, such as Ayodhyā, Vṛndāvan and Prayāg. Vārāṇasī is especially favored by people living there as a form of local patriotism.

As we saw in Chapter 2, pilgrimage places are personified in the narratives of the Hindu pilgrimage traditions. The pilgrimage place Prayāg, we are told, has to go to Ayodhyā to wash off all the moral impurity it receives from all the pilgrims bathing there in the confluence of Gaṅgā and Yamunā. In another narrative, Braj was considered preeminent because of the supremacy of Kṛṣṇa and its refusal to obey Prayāg, who is known as the king of *tīrtha*s (*tīrtharāja*), and as a result it is considered by many to be the foremost of all Hindu *tīrtha*s. According to the *Varāhapurāṇa*, the earth says to the god Varāha that it is difficult for people to go to all the *tīrtha*s in the world (there are an estimated 66,000 crores, i. e. 660,000,000,000), so she wants to know if there is an easy way of doing so. Varāha answers by revealing that there is an enormous number of *tīrtha*s and that ordinary people cannot go to all of them, but by circumambulation of Mathurā one attains more merit than by going to all *tīrtha*s on the seven islands on earth, as well as walking around the seven islands (*Varāhapurāṇa* 159.6; 159.13–14) themselves. There is no general view about the superiority of Vārāṇasī in stories about competitions between pilgrimage places. It is mainly in the texts written to promote Vārāṇasī that the city is considered the holy center of Hinduism.

One would have expected that, if it were the case that Vārāṇasī was the center of Hinduism, Śaṅkara, or someone later in the tradition, would have placed one of the five main *vidyāpīṭha*s there. There is one in each corner of India, and one in Kāñcīpuram. In contemporary Vārāṇasī, there is of course a number of institutions of the *daśanāmī saṃnyāsī* order and other ascetical orders. It is also noteworthy that, while Badrīnāth is included in all groups of four *dhām*s, Vārāṇasī is not included in any of them. Vārāṇasī is counted as one of the seven cities, but Vārāṇasī is only one of these sacred cities, not *the* city. The four cities that are part of the *kumbhamelā* festivals, the largest festivals in India in terms of the number of participants, are Prayāg, Hardvār, Ujjain and Nāsik. Vārāṇasī is not one of the four. The festival rotates between these cities in a 12-year cycle, but the one in Prayāg has the largest number of visitors. If it were the case that Vārāṇasī was the Mecca of Hinduism, one would have expected that Vārāṇasī would have been included as one of the *kumbhamelā* cities. But there is no Mecca of Hinduism. On the contrary, it is typical of Hinduism to organize pilgrimage places into groups such as four *dhām*s, 12 *jyotirliṅga*s and so on, and this practice in itself indicates the polycentric nature of Hinduism.

Systems of classification of *tīrthas*

The following verse quoted in many Sanskrit texts seems to consider the number of *tīrtha*s to be unlimited: "The *deśas* (localities) that are holy and therefore destroyers of sins are all mountains, all rivers, holy lakes, places of pilgrimage, the dwellings of sages, cow pens and temples of the gods" (Kane 1973: 560).

However, not all mountains, rivers, lakes and temples have become *tīrtha*s. A surprisingly large number nevertheless have. The number of *kṣetra*s and *tīrtha*s are in the tens of thousands. In the *Matsyapurāṇa*, the sage Mārkaṇḍeya says that the number of sacred places is so high that he would not be able to describe all of them even in hundreds of years (104.6). In some of the largest North Indian sacred areas (*kṣetras*), such as Vārāṇasī, Vṛndāvan, Kurukṣetra or Naimiṣa, there are hundreds of *tīrthas*. P. V. Kane (1973) provided an almost 100-page-long list of historical *tīrthas* (730–825), and in *Kalyāṇ Tīrthāṅk* (1957), more than 1,500 contemporary pilgrim destinations are described, but these lists are far from complete. That there is such a plurality of pilgrimage places and no salvific center among them that is superior to all the others perhaps created a need to organize them into groups. There is a large number of places and, to create order, the typical pattern is to classify salvific places into groups and systems. The Hindu tradition has classified sacred places in a number of ways. There is a concept of seven sacred cities (*saptapuri*) that grant *mokṣa*. A verse that mentions them reads: *kāśī kāñcī māyākhyā tv ayodhyā dvāravaty api, mathurāvantikā caitāḥ saptapuryo 'tra mokṣadā,* mentioning Mathurā, Dvārkā, Ayodhyā, Hardvār, Kāñcīpuram, Ujjain and Vārāṇasī. Sometimes, Prayāg or Gayā are included instead of Kāñcīpuram. Seven rivers, *Saptapuṇyanādī,* Gaṅgā, Yamunā, Godāvarī, Sarasvatī, Kāverī, Narmadā and Sindhu are meritorious. There are several groups of four sacred places (*cārdhāms*). The four abodes of the divine located at the four cardinal points of the subcontinent, *cārdhāms*, are Badrīnāth in the north, Purī in the east, Dvārkā in the west and Rāmēśvaram in the south. The four sacred places, *cārdhāms*, of Himālayan pilgrimage are Badrīnāth, Kedārnāth, Gaṅgotrī and Yamunotrī. The four *dhāms* of the order of renouncers founded by Śaṅkara in which monasteries or *vidyāpīṭhas* were founded are Badrīnāth in the north, Purī in the east, Śṛṅgerī in the south and Dvārkā in the west (Kāñcīpuram has been included as a fifth *vidyāpīṭha*). Twelve pilgrimage places to Śiva associated with the appearance of a *liṅga* of light, *Bārhajyotirliṅgas*, are Kedārnāth (Uttar Pradesh), Viśveśvara (Vārāṇasī, Uttar Pradesh), Vaidyanāth (Deoghar, Bihar), Mahākāla (Ujjain, Madhya Pradesh), Oṃkāreśvar (Madhya Pradesh), Somnāth (Gujarat), Nāgeśvar (Dvārkā, Gujarat), Tryambakeśvar (Maharashtra), Bhīmaśaṅkar (Maharashtra), Ghṛṣneśvar (Maharashtra), Mallikārjuna (Śrīśailam, Andhra Pradesh) and Rāmēśvaram (Tamil Nadu). The list varies, but this version is widely accepted. There are five element liṅgas, *bhūtaliṅgas*: Kāñcīpuram (earth *liṅga*), Kālahastī (water *liṅga*), Jambukeśvara (air *liṅga*), Cidambaram (space *liṅga*) and Tiruvaṇṇamalai (fire *liṅga*). There is a concept of 51 *śaktipīṭhas*, but D. C. Sircar has shown that there are different lists of *śaktipīṭhas* of various numbers (4, 7, 8, 10, 18, 42, 51 and 108). His "Index of the *pīṭhas*" lists several hundred places (Sircar 1973: 80–100). Some places take their names from famous *tīrthas*, claiming that they are the famous *tīrtha* for that region. Such places include seven Gaṅgās, *Saptagaṅgā*, Bhāgīrathī, Vṛddhagaṅgā, Kālindī, Sarasvatī, Sindhu, Kāverī and Narmadā; five Kāśīs, *Pañcakāśī*, Vārāṇasī, Guptakāśī, Uttarakāśī, Dakṣinakāśī and Śivakāśī; seven Kṣetras, *Saptakṣetra*, Kurukṣetra, Hariharkṣetra, Prabhāsakṣetra, Reṇukākṣetra, Bhṛgukṣetra, Puruṣottamakṣetra and Sūkarakṣetra; five Kedāras, *Pañcakedāra*, Kedārnāth, Madhyameśvar, Tuṅganāth, Rudranāth and Kalpeśvar; seven Badarīs, *Saptabadarī*, Badarīnārāyaṇa, Ādibadarī, Vṛddhabadarī, Bhaviṣyabadarī, Yogabadarī, Adibadarī (on the way to Kailāsa) and Nṛsiṃhabadarī;

and five sacred ponds, *Pañcasarovara*, Bindusarovar in Sidhpur, Nārāyaṇasarovara in Kucch, Pampāsarovara in Mysore, Puṣkarasarovara in Puṣkar and Mānasarovar in Tibet. There are also traditional lists of nine sacred forests, 14 Prayāgs, the 42 best places for performing the *śrāddha* ceremony, and others. It is notable that the typical pattern is to systematize the *tīrtha*s into groups and that no place is considered supreme in the groups. These systematizations and bringing together of individual *tīrtha*s are often theological constructions; they are nevertheless well recognized and often emphasized in *Māhātmya*s. Reasons for such systematizations include creation of pilgrimage routes and patterns of salvific space, as well as the integration of larger areas in the Brahmanical tradition.

Regional groups of *tīrtha*s have been constructed on the same pattern and perhaps for similar purposes. They integrate greater areas into patterns of salvific space and common pilgrimage tradition. Such patterns encourage pilgrims to visit many *tīrtha*s. The six abodes of Murukaṉ in Tamil Nadu are the most important temples of Murukaṉ in Tamil Nadu. There is a group of nine temples of the nine planets (*navagraha*s) in Tamil Nadu, which can be visited separately, but there is also a *yātrā* covering all of them. The four shrines in the Himālayas (Yamunotrī, Gaṅgotrī, Kedārnāth and Badrīnāth) are regional Himalāyan shrines and many feel they should perform a pilgrimage to all four in order for the pilgrimage to be complete. There is even a systematization of seven Himālayan rivers, Alaknandā, Dhauli Gaṅgā, Nandakinī, Bhāgīrathī, Pinder Gaṅgā, Mandakinī and Nayar; of five confluences of Gaṅgā on the way to Badrīnāth, five Prayāgs, Deva Prayāg, Rudra Prayāg, Karṇa Prayāg, Nanda Prayāg and Viṣṇu Prayāg; and of 108 Viṣṇu Divyadeśam temples, mainly in Tamil Nadu, sung about by the Āḻvārs, which were important for the creation of the Viṣṇu *tīrtha*s in Tamil Nadu.

The different *sampradāya*s have their own pilgrimage geography centered on temples, monastic institutions, history of saints, theologians and philosophers, and they often have some sites that are main pilgrimage sites. Gorakhpur is the center of the Nāth Sampradāy; Purī, Navadvīp and Vṛndāvan are the main pilgrimage places of Śrīmadhva Sampradāy; there are five *pīṭha*s of the Śaṅkarācāryas, and so on.

Systematizations of Hindu *tīrtha*s can also be made according to function and one such group based on function are *tīrtha*s associated with death, and Vārāṇasī belongs to this group. The other most important places in this group are probably Gayā, Hardvār and Sidhpur. However, it is quite notable that Vārāṇasī is only included in a few of these systematizations. Besides the five Kāśīs it is only counted as one of the *jyotirliṅga*s and one of the sacred cities. Polycentrism and decentering characterize Hinduism (Lipner 2004, 2006). The tradition of salvific space is a polycentric phenomenon which accommodates plurality.

Conclusion

Pilgrimage places often give the impression that their origins are lost in an ancient past beyond history and belong to the realm of sacred mythology. Their sacredness appears to observers as belonging to the nature of the places themselves, rather than being historically constructed in time and space. This is partly how they legitimate their sacredness and this is really part of the sacredness itself. However, sacred places have histories. These histories are not always known. In India, festivals organized at sacred places can sometimes become "ancient" within a few decades. A process of promoting Vārāṇasī as the single most important sacred center of Hinduism has been going on for some time and there are several different players: the priests of Vārāṇasī, the Vārāṇasī Tourist Department, Western tourists and scholars, mass media and the Internet. The British colonial power also played an important role in this, devising Vārāṇasī as a sort of eternal, religious city, rather than a city of historical, political and economic importance (Desai 2012; Dodson 2012). The city with the *ghāṭ*s, as it is today, was largely produced in the eighteenth and nineteenth centuries to revive the city as a pilgrimage destination (see Figure 6.5). This was no doubt an extremely successful undertaking, but needs to be understood as a historical process. Instead, scholars have uncritically adopted the view of Vārāṇasī as a timeless cosmic sacred space. Vārāṇasī has become an "orientalist commodity," "romanticized as a city sitting outside of mortal time" (Dodson 2012: 1). The *ghāṭ*s and buildings on the riverfront that have come to symbolize an ancient past as well as the timeless space of Vārāṇasī were in fact erected in the late eighteenth and nineteenth centuries (Desai 2012: 23).

> The religious landscape of Banaras was resurrected on the basis of a ritual geography specified in various *Puranas*. Shaped by the opportunities and limitations of colonial rule, this turned Banaras into a centre of revived Hindu

Figure 6.5 *Ghāṭ*s and river front of Vārāṇasī

Photo: Knut A. Jacobsen

> ritual life. A material environment of temples, ghats and ritual bathing tanks was simultaneously represented as antique in indigenous pilgrimage maps and religious literature and as evidence of the city's timelessness in orientalist paintings, texts and memoirs. Principal shrines were rebuilt, pilgrimage to various shrines and ritual bathing tanks were reinstated, the city's riverfront was built and new institutions that reinforced the Sanatan Dharma (orthodox religion) were established. . . . A religious geography that had been defined through ritual practice and texts became legible through architectural innovation.
>
> (ibid.: 24)

Daśāśvamedha *ghāṭ* and the Maṇikarṇikā *ghāṭ* were built in the late eighteenth century under the patronage of Ahilyabai Holkar (who also was the patroness of the building of a magnificent *ghāṭ* area in Maheśvar in Madhya Pradesh, which was the capital of her Malwa kingdom) as ritual public space and these *ghāṭ*s have become the quintessential picturesque representation of the "eternal" pilgrimage city of Vārāṇasī.

The growth of international tourism in India, the increased blending of tourism and pilgrimage and the global opportunities of the Internet have also recently strengthened Vārāṇasī's position as a possible future imagined holy city of Hinduism. As I mentioned earlier, the number of academic books and studies on Vārāṇasī as a pilgrimage place and religious center is probably larger than the books written on all the other Hindu pilgrimage places put together. However, as late as 1974, the famous historian of Vārāṇasī, Kuber Nath Sukul, in the "Preface" to his book *Varanasi Down the Ages*, wrote:

> No apology is needed for writing a book on Varanasi, not for writing it in English, because no full-blooded book has yet been written about this holy city. Books written by Europeans merely describe what they saw or learnt from hearsay – and even of these the last was written in 1909, and they are all out of print too.
>
> (Sukul 1974: 3)

This situation changed rapidly! In 2009, BBC World News showed a documentary in which an Indian journalist visited several places in India. In Vārāṇasī, the BBC journalist watched the evening *āratī* ritual (a lamp with burning *ghī* moved in a series of circles) at Daśāśvamedh *ghāṭ* and he philosophized on the idea that this ritual he observed had been going on for thousands of years and that Hinduism was an eternal tradition called *sanātana dharma*. I was amazed watching this because I had followed the creation of these new rituals in Vārāṇasī, which was done to adapt to the perceived wishes of tourists and pilgrims to see spectacular ritual performances on the *ghāṭ*s. These rituals at Daśāśvamedh *ghāṭ*, the Gaṅgā *āratī* that the journalist witnessed, were started only some years ago, around 1999. Several priests wearing a kind of uniform, accompanied by loud music from speakers, wave lamps with fire in honor of Gaṅgā. A prominent feature of the ritual is pilgrim tourists taking photos and videos[16] of the event. The model for the rituals was most probably the evening *āratī* in Hardvār,[17] to which the Vārāṇasī ritual is very similar. The same ritual performance was started around 2005 at Assī *ghāṭ* and also some other *ghāṭs* in Vārāṇasī. In October 2011, I observed the same evening *āratī* performance at the *ghāṭ*s in Ujjain and on the pilgrimage of circumambulating Mount Aruṇācalam in Thiruvaṇṇamalai, both clearly also modeled on the Hardvār *āratī*, so this type of *āratī* is spreading. Vārāṇasī is also regularly presented in mass media and popular culture as a city where old persons from the whole of India travel to in order to die and be cremated. Perhaps as many as 40, 000 Hindus are cremated annually in Vārāṇasī, but given that the population in India is 1, 200 million and around 80 percent of these are considered Hindus, 40, 000 is very low.[18] The population of Uttar Pradesh alone is 200 million. The persons cremated in Vārāṇasī are mostly from the city itself and from the villages in the vicinity of Vārāṇasī. These views presented in the mass media and in popular culture are examples of what has been the topic of this chapter, the analysis of the promotion of Vārāṇasī as the eternal sacred center of the global religion called Hinduism, which contradicts the polycentric character of Hinduism. Hinduism is a pluralistic tradition, a mosaic of regional traditions, and one characteristic of Hindu pilgrimage traditions is that there is no general agreement among Hindus about a single sacred center or holy city – the Mecca of the whole of Hinduism. Hinduism is polycentric and decentering and also traditions of salvific space exemplify this decentered polycentrism. The salvific places coexist in a "polycentric grid," but their power is reinforced by "a dialectical grid that draws its authority theologically from the same ultimate source" (Lipner 2006: 100). The concept of salvific power of place is shared, but Hindu salvific space nevertheless is a pluralistic phenomenon and has been subject to change, sometimes rapidly, throughout its history.

7 Contradictions and challenges

There are a number of contradictions in the teaching of pilgrimage and salvific space, and in recent years some additional problems have presented challenges to these traditions. One obvious contradiction is between the salvific power of the *tīrtha*s themselves and the merit of travel. Another is between the idea of the purity of sages or the divine omnipresence and the power of particular places. The salvific power of place – that is, the ability of the pilgrimage sites to grant the salvific goals to all, no matter what – poses a problem to the conceptions of *dharma*. Finally, recent changes in India, such as environmental degradation and conflicts around salvific space due to political mobilization, have challenged the traditions of salvific space.

The merit of travel and the salvific power of place

Pilgrimage involved a change in the conceptualization of travel and geographical space. Some areas were considered impure according to the *Dharmaśāstra* literature. "When someone travels to the land of the Kaliṅgas," says the B*audhāyanadharmasūtra*, "he commits a sin through his feet" (1.3.15). The pilgrimage tradition reversed this view by claiming that one attains merit from every step that brings one closer to a pilgrimage site. Many places that had been considered impure became sources of purity in the pilgrimage tradition. Purī is part of the area of the Kaliṅga empire but became one of the major pilgrimage places of Hinduism. It is the site of the famous Jagannāth temple and is also a Śaiva place, as well as one of the centers of the Śaṅkarācāryas. The *Tristhalīsetu* writes that those who are forbidden to travel to places are not forbidden to do so when their intention is to make a pilgrimage, and when they go to particular areas for pilgrimage they do not become impure from visiting such places, and this also "applies to the frontier countries" (*Tristhalīsetu* 125).

Travel towards salvific space is meritorious according to the pilgrimage tradition, but not all travel. "Only those feet are blessed which walk in the direction of Kāśī," says the Kāśīkhaṇḍa (1.2.110), but the *Tristhalīsetu* (167) quotes a verse saying that "one going to Gayā gets at every step the benefit of an *aśvamedha* sacrifice" (*padepade 'śvamedhasya phalaṃ syād gacchato gamām*). The two statements are contradictory, but that is because they promote specific sites. *Tristhalīsetu*, however, argues that the statement about travel to Gayā in fact applies to all pilgrimages, not only to Gayā. Nevertheless, it is quite remarkable that not much is said about pilgrim travel in the *Purāṇa*s and *Māhātmya* texts that promote salvific space. The emphasis in the texts of Hindu traditions of salvific space is not on the journey, but on the sites and their salvific power. These texts are mostly concerned with getting pilgrims to come to specific sites, and the rituals to be performed there once they have arrived at the sites.

In contemporary India, travel towards the *tīrtha* is through profane space by means of train, bus or car, and it is often the entering of the area (*kṣetra*) itself that marks the beginning of the real pilgrimage, which may then include visits to several *tīrtha*s within the sacred area. The real pilgrimage walks are the *parikrama*/*pradakṣiṇā* (circumambulation) routes of the places. Because modern transportation has made access to the pilgrimage places easy, the importance of *parikrama*s has probably increased. Some *parikrama*s might conceivably be the result of the lack of emphasis on the journey to the place. It has been stated that a shortage of *parikrama*s has in fact become a problem for some pilgrimage places in contemporary India. An author who has evaluated the site of Kurukṣetra as a contemporary religious travel destination is concerned that Kurukṣetra lacks a *parikrama* and writes that it "does not have any ritual about going through or visiting places" and, therefore, "because of very easy approachability to godly places," Kurukṣetra "fails to give psychological satisfaction to religious tourists" (Chaudhary 1998: 266). Presently, pilgrims associate Kurukṣetra mostly with solar eclipses. Many pilgrimage places, such as Citrakūṭa, Ujjain, Tiruvaṇṇamalai, Vārāṇasī and Nimsār, have circumambulation walks that are part of the pilgrimage. The *parikrama* becomes the pilgrimage travel and can last several days. Walking barefoot is considered appropriate conduct for performing the *parikrama*. Pilgrimage proper in Vārāṇasī is understood to be the travel within the sacred *kṣetra*. The six-day-long *pañcakrośa* that circumambulates the sacred *kṣetra* of Vārāṇasī is one of several circumambulation pilgrimages of the city. Circumambulation pilgrimages (*parikrama*s) within the sacred areas (*kṣetra*s), such as the *parikrama*s in Braj, Oṃkāreśvar, Nimsār, Citrakūṭ, Vārāṇasī, Tiruvaṇṇamalai and so on, are walking pilgrimages on sacred ground. They often become procession pilgrimages since the importance of sacred time means that large groups walk together simultaneously. In the *parikrama*s, the pilgrims walk on sacred ground but processions may also make the ground sacred as they move (the most famous of which is the procession pilgrimage to Alandi-Paṇḍharpūr [see Deleury 1960; Karve 1962; Mokashi 1990 for descriptions by participants], but there are also many others [see Daniel 1984; Haberman 1994; Sax 1991; Sekar 1992]).

Pilgrimage is religious journeying, travel for a religious purpose towards a place believed to have a divine presence or possess salvific power – that is, power to bless, heal and fulfill wishes. One widely held view is that, in order to have wishes fulfilled or for a penance to have the desired effect, one has to go through some difficulties to attain the fruits of a pilgrimage. Pilgrimage places that are in the mountains and demand longer treks, such as the pilgrimage to Kailās, Muktināth, Yamunotrī, Amarnāth, Kedārnāth, Vaiṣṇodevī and Śabarimala, may be considered more meritorious because of this quality of austerity. However, in all pilgrimages, the ascetic nature may be accentuated to include rituals that make forward movement more difficult, such as prostrating at each body length or, even tougher, prostrating 108 times at each body length. To keep count, the pilgrim can keep with him 108 stones, which he moves one at a time for each prostration he makes. Motivation for such ascetic practice might be to obtain help from a deity to solve a problem or to remove an affliction (Bhardwaj 1973: 172). This form of ascetic practice is rare among pilgrims, but when performed it is often done on the *parikrama*/*pradakṣiṇā* routes at the pilgrimage places, such as the Govardhana Hill and Citrakūṭa mountain *parikrama*s or on the route towards a mountain shrine.

Not much attention is paid in the *Purāṇa*s to the journey before one arrives at the *kṣetra* or pilgrimage place. It is there the pilgrimage really starts, it seems. It is said about Kurukṣetra that one should first go to the Yakṣa Rantuka, who is the gatekeeper of this *tīrtha*, and only then should he start his pilgrimage. Pilgrimage here means visiting the different sub-*tīrtha*s of Kurukṣetra.[1] Since the emphasis in the texts on salvific space is mostly on only the places, there are often just a couple of verses which describe the travel, as in this example from the *Kāśīkhaṇḍa*:

> One who is desirous of undertaking a pilgrimage should at the outset observe fast at home. He should then adore and honour Gaṇeśa, the ancestors, the Brahmans, holy men, in accordance with his ability. After taking food by way of concluding the observance of fast, he should joyously follow the regulations. After returning, he should worship the ancestors. He will then derive the benefits as mentioned.
>
> (1.6.56–57)

Nothing more is said here about the travel itself. The quote deals only with the rituals of leaving the home and returning back to the home. The *Dharmanibandha*s, which contain the longest sections on the general issues of pilgrimage of the Hindu texts on pilgrimage, also do not have much to say about the details of travel to a *tīrtha*. Of the general section on pilgrimage in the *Tristhalīsetu*, a total of 178 pages of Sanskrit text, the chapter on pilgrimage travel (*tīrthagamanavividhiḥ*) is only seven pages long. However, a lot of that chapter is once again about the rituals of leaving the village, before the actual travel starts. The text quotes some verses similar to the above verse of *Kāśīkhaṇḍa*, discusses certain verses that cover sequences and details of the rituals and concludes by suggesting the following sequence for leaving the village when going on pilgrimage: Two days before the day of the auspicious moment of the journey, one should start the observance of eating once a day and eating sacrificial food, and celibacy should be followed. On the following day, one should fast; shaving may be optionally observed. On the day after that, one should perform the obligatory acts, such as bathing to gain purity, worshipping Gaṇeśa as one's chosen deity, performing *pārvaṇaśrāddha* with ghee as the principal substance, honoring Brahmans as one is able to with clothing, ornaments, cattle, land, gold, and so on, making a declaration of a journey and putting on a pilgrim's red-colored dress. Then, at an auspicious moment, one should walk out from the village, circumambulate it and go to another village within a distance of one *krośa* (probably between three and four kilometers) and break the fast with the ghee left from the *śrāddha*. On the next day, the pilgrim should keep going.[2] After discussing some details about the time of departure and what dress to wear, the text starts discussing the return to the village. The travel itself is not considered worth mentioning.

However, one issue concerning the travel is discussed and this is the intriguing question as to whether the merit of pilgrimage is caused at all by the journey itself or is due only to the salvific power of the site. The salvific power of the sites is celebrated in the *Purāṇa*s and *Māhātmya*s as absolute and the salvific rewards are granted to those who are present at the sites, regardless of how they arrived there, so how could there possibly be additional rewards from the travel itself before one arrives at the *tīrtha*? If it were the case that the reward is only due to being present at the place, there is no reward from the journey itself. The pilgrimage then does not produce any benefit in addition to the *tīrtha*. It is the *tīrtha* that gives the benefit and not the travel. But it is stated as well that the pilgrim obtains the reward of an *aśvamedha* sacrifice for every step. However, if one acquires the reward of an *aśvamedha* sacrifice for every step, then seeking the salvific power of the *tīrtha* itself would have no meaning, the pilgrim having already earned the reward of thousands and thousands of *aśvamedha* sacrifices before having arrived at the *tīrtha*. The author of *Tristhalīsetu*, Nārāyaṇa Bhaṭṭa, presents some arguments of an opponent who favors the power of the *tīrtha* only and claims that pilgrimage travel as such has no merit, as it is only the *tīrtha* itself that gives rewards. This can be supported by the statement that if a person comes to a *tīrtha* accidentally – that is, he is not on a pilgrimage but just happened to arrive there for some other purpose – he nevertheless gets half the benefit of the *tīrtha*. This also shows that pilgrimage travel does not really matter. The opponent argues that "pilgrimage is not prescribed as a means to obtain the benefit of the *tīrtha*." But what about in the case of a pilgrimage carried out as a penance – would the benefit then be independent of the *tīrtha*? Not so, says the opponent, since there is no authority to support this statement, and it would also be an arbitrary decision. However, Nārāyaṇa Bhaṭṭa attempts to refute the argument that all the merit is due to the *tīrtha* and not at all to the pilgrimage and concludes that pilgrimage travel is always beneficial. Nārāyaṇa Bhaṭṭa believes that the saying "one going to Gayā gets at every step the benefit of an *aśvamedha* sacrifice" applies to all pilgrimages. Then again, in the chapter "Varying degrees of benefit caused by particular vehicles," he argues that those going on a pilgrimage by a vehicle acquire only the reward from the *tīrtha*, not the pilgrimage (*Tristalīsetu* 114). The chapter in *Tristalīsetu* called "Observances on a pilgrimage" and the previously mentioned chapter contain mainly arguments and citations about behavior at the *tīrtha* itself.

The discussion about the actual travel in the *Dharmanibandha*s concerns the consequences for the salvific rewards of traveling in vehicles. The benefit from a pilgrimage is, according to the these texts, reduced when traveling in a vehicle, but in the case of Prayāg, one who sets out on a pilgrimage to this site mounted on a bull will have to dwell in terrible hell and his ancestors will also receive punishment by being denied water (*Tristalīsetu* 110). When traveling in a vehicle to Prayāg, the site does not give any salvific rewards (*Tristalīsetu* 111). If one travels on a bullock cart, it is equal to killing the bull. Walking barefoot gives four times the benefit, but wearing shoes does not diminish the reward (*Tristalīsetu* 112).[3] This discussion in the *Dharmanibandha*s on *tīrtha*s probably had only a small influence on the pilgrims, and among the pilgrims today its influence seems negligible. The *Dharmanibandha*s were not able to create consistency in the folk tradition of salvific space.

Saints, *sādhu*s and the power of *tīrtha*s

Descriptions of pilgrimage travel, while mainly absent in the promotion texts of the sites, are, however, often found in the hagiographies and biographies of *sādhu*s and saints. *Sādhu*s and saints are part of what makes holy places holy. The presence of a saint or ascetics can also transform places into pilgrimage sites since they can be goals of pilgrimage. After death, the saints' *samādhi* shrines, their final resting places, may become significant pilgrimage sites. There are two types of pilgrims: lay people and *sādhu*s. The *sādhu*s are functionally distinguished from lay people at the pilgrimage places because they are patrons, while lay people are clients (Bharati 1970: 90). The permanent pilgrims in India are the *sādhu*s (see Figure 7.1). They often live on pilgrimage sites and they regularly travel to other pilgrimage places. Some spend most of their lives at these sacred centers, which attract monastic institutions. *Sādhu*s do not travel on pilgrimage for the sake of it, as they are already considered pure and their presence makes places holy. They themselves represent the salvific power of the sites. They may bring salvific power to the sites, as illustrated by the stories associated with some of the sites of sage Kapila discussed in Chapter 5, and they may also be guardians of the pilgrimage sites or temples, as in the case of the *sādhu*s of the *akhāṛā*s, the warrior ascetics who protect the sites by their presence and receive a part of the income from the *pūjā* at the pilgrimage places. Saints and *sādhu*s have often met the guru who initiated them at pilgrimage places. P. Granoff writes about biographies of saints of medieval India:

> Pilgrimage is often a central event in the biography of a holy man in mediaeval India. During the course of his journeys the saint may meet his guru and receive the transmission of the teaching, often in the form of books that are considered most authoritative and important to his teachings; he may also defeat opponents in debate and begin to gather around himself his own followers, thus initiating the religious community that will survive him and recount his deeds in the wide range of biographical texts that have come down to us. The saint may also act as an ordinary pilgrim, visiting holy sites and praying at famous temples. He may in addition create his own holy sites, by the miracles that he performs as he moves from village to village, temple to temple.
>
> (Granoff 2003: 181)

But Granoff notes that, despite this centrality of pilgrimage in religious biographies, the saint as a pilgrim often seems to be problematic in biographical texts (ibid.). It is incongruous that a holy man should be a pilgrim. Why would he be in need of the salvific power of a sacred place? Why should he travel on pilgrimage? He is already pure.

*Sādhu*s are expected to spend a part of their life on pilgrimage in the Himālayas or other sacred areas. Śaṅkara's hagiographies can be read as pilgrimage travel, but famous *sādhu*s both visit and establish pilgrimage centers. The Sanskrit text *Śaṅkaradigvijaya* answers the question of why holy persons go on pilgrimage, stating that "the sage makes a pilgrimage to help others. He does so by setting an example, and by providing them with the chance to be in his presence" (ibid.: 184). Granoff notes that many of the sages of medieval India were represented as *avatāra*s in the hagiographies and that it is even more baffling as to why *avatāra*s should need to go on pilgrimage. Why should they go on pilgrimage to

Figure 7.1 *Sādhu*s at the pilgrimage place of Gaṅgā Sāgar

Photo: Knut A. Jacobsen

have *darśan* of themselves? The pilgrimage of Caitanya (an *avatāra* of Kṛṣṇa) to Purī, the seat of Jagannāth (Kṛṣṇa), is a well-known example. Why would he need to travel to have *darśan* of himself? In the hagiography of Śaṅkaradeva, the saint of the Assamese Vaiṣṇava traditions, who is believed to be an *avatāra* of Kṛṣṇa, is questioned by his teacher when he wants to go on his first pilgrimage: "But you are God. What could you possibly want with a holy place? All the beings in the world will be released just by chanting your name" (*Śaṅkaracarita* by Rāmacaraṇa, quoted in Granoff 2003: 190). In the biographies, pilgrimage "is part of the holy man's efforts to rescue people from the cycle of rebirths" (Granoff 2003:185) – that is, it is the salvific power of the saint that is focused on. Pilgrimage is also a problem in biographies of saints who favor different methods and ways to salvation, such as yoga and recitation of the name of god. Sages belonging to traditions that reject pilgrimage still have, according to their hagiographies, traveled on pilgrimage. Granoff notes in the hagiographies that descriptions of the pilgrimage of saints become stories of the saints displaying themselves and "a spiritual journey for the onlookers" (ibid.:187). Thus, in these cases, the salvific power of the sites is surpassed and the saints themselves become sources of pilgrimage.

Tīrtha and *dharma*

S. M. Bhardwaj writes that *tīrthayātrā* "not only means the physical act of visiting the holy places but implies mental and moral discipline" and adds that "without the latter, pilgrimage in the physical sense has little significance in the Hindu tradition" (Bhardwaj 1973: 2). The emphasis on mental restraint is correct but, as a true description of the empirical situation, it is challenged by a number of factors, such as ease of travel, the touristic quality of much pilgrimage travel, the economic greediness of *paṇḍā*s at many pilgrimage places and the polluted state of some of the most important pilgrimage places and festivals. Bhardwaj asserts that pilgrimage to sacred places "is of no avail if a person does not lead a moral life" (ibid.: 3), and this view is stated repeatedly in the *Mahābhārata*, *Purāṇa*s and in the general section in the *Dharmanibandha*s on *tīrtha*s. However, the promotion texts on the individual *tīrtha*s claim the opposite to be true; that a person who has never performed a morally good act nevertheless attains the salvational goal by means of the power of the sites. There is also a tension between the attainment of ego-oriented salvific goals, such as healing and material welfare, and the transcendent and ascetical values promoted in the general idea of pilgrimage. In addition, since the divine is supposed to be everywhere, as is the salt in the water in the bucket used for teaching Śvetaketu the truth of *brahman* in the Chāndogya Upaniṣad, what is the purpose of going on pilgrimage? Does it not diminish *brahman*? Śaṅkara is supposed to have sought forgiveness on his deathbed for having spent much of his life on pilgrimages to shrines, since worshipping at holy places might indicate that *brahman* is not everywhere (Shulman 1980: 82). Furthermore, the popular view of salvific power of place and the narratives of the function of this power seem to be opposed to the idea of salvation as a gradual attainment of purity that is dependent upon the cultivation of human virtues. In the Hindu tradition, these two points of view, power and purity, also exist side by side in the pilgrimage tradition.

The idea that salvific space purifies moral impurity created a contradiction between power and purity. Purification in many Hindu traditions is, on the one hand, made extremely difficult and something that takes many life times and, on the other hand, the idea of salvific space made purification extremely easy, something achieved simply from bathing at a *tīrtha*, or even from just thinking about a *tīrtha*. It is implied in the traditions of salvific space that there is a belief in an almost omnipresent impurity from which humans continuously need to be purified and which also defines their status. Impurity has a number of effects, and its almost omnipresence causes it to influence many aspects of life. Purity and impurity have been part of some of the most central institutions in South Asia, such as the caste system and the Hindu ritual systems.[4] Impurity and purification are main concerns of the *Dharmaśāstra* literature. Penances suggested for purification in the *Dharmaśāstra* literature and the purification rituals at pilgrimage places are closely related. Bathing, shaving off hair and gifts to Brahmans are, according to the *Dharmaśāstra* literature, part of purification processes and are central in the pilgrimage tradition as well. I have argued that pilgrimage probably played an important role in the spreading of the ideology of purity and impurity of the Hindu traditions (see Chapter 4). Salvific space of pilgrimage traditions can be defined as the belief in the ability of pilgrimage sites to purify humans from impurity. Impurity has all kinds of sources and the concept encompasses personal hygiene, social relations and morality. The idea of purification by means of water includes purification not only from filthy substances (*gand*, *gandagī*), but also from all the impurity of physical life as compared to the pure (*śuddha*) self (*ātman*). The concept of impurity and the rituals of purification are part of the same conceptualization. The emphasis on the cultivation of human virtues was already present in the *tīrthayātrāparvan* in the *Mahābhārata*, and received further emphasis in the *Dharmanibandha*s, which tried to make the pilgrimage traditions compatible with a more conservative ideology of *dharma*, but the salvific power of the sites seems to contradict the idea of purity based on cultivation of human virtues. This idea of a contradiction was exemplified in Al-Biruni's perception of Vārāṇasī. He conceived of Vārāṇasī as an asylum for murderers (see p. 175). By entering the salvific space of Vārāṇasī one is immediately freed from the sin of violence, and Al-Biruni understood this to mean that one has, therefore, also escaped any punishment for the sinful act. One of the foundation stories about Vārāṇasī is indeed about being freed from the punishment caused by an act of violence. By entering Vārāṇasī, Śiva was released from the impurity caused by cutting off one of Brahmā's heads, a crime equal to Brahman murder. *Nāradapurāṇa* (Uttarabhāga 48. 15–16) describes someone coming to Kāśī:

> He may be a Brahman-slayer, a killer of cows, a defiler of his preceptor's bed or a betrayer of friends. He may be guilty of misappropriation of deposits or

> trysts or he might have practised usury . . . the man who approaches Vārāṇasī, the city of Śiva, shall have his self liberated from the strong bondage of worldly existence.
>
> Having reached the sacred place, frequented by gods and Siddhas, thanks to the power of his merit, the man shall be wellknown amongst Devas and Asuras. When dead he may attain *mokṣa*, the highest region.[5]

The power of salvific space is presented here as giving the highest salvific rewards to everyone regardless of sins committed, even those considered the worst sins, such as killing Brahmans or cows. The pilgrimage places seem to outdo each other by promising easy availability of salvific rewards. This is again exemplified by the description of Vārāṇasī: "In this holy centre the attainment of liberation is possible without any strain, more easily than in such holy centres as Prayāga which is very difficult to access" (*Nāradapurāṇa*, Uttarabhāga 48.25).[6] Similarly, "if a man or a woman, knowingly or unknowingly commits some inauspicious act through evil intellect, all that is reduced to ashes (the moment) he enters Avimukta" (*Nāradapurāṇa, Uttarabhāga* 48.33b–34).[7] This conceptualization of salvific space, that it purifies the pilgrim from crimes, is also a theme in contemporary traditions of pilgrimage, such as the *kumbhamelā*s. During the *melā*s, the local newspapers, as part of the coverage of the pilgrimage festival, also carry stories of persons who have previously performed criminal acts of violence, such as murder, but were never arrested and punished and have come to the pilgrimage site in order to be freed from the impurity of those sins by the site's salvific power.[8] The foundation stories of several pilgrimage places, not only Vārāṇasī, are indeed about atonements for murder or killing. The famous pilgrimage site of Rāmēśvaram in South India was founded by the god Rāma to atone for his killing of Rāvaṇa, according to the narratives of the site. At Sidhpur, the main ritual of *śrāddha* is performed in front of a statue of Paraśurāma, who atoned for the killing of his mother, Reṇukā. The place is a pilgrimage site for sons to atone for the pain they have caused their mothers to suffer. On the pilgrimage to Brahmagiri in Tryambak (Trimbak), where the river Gautamī Godāvarī begins, a *tīrtha* was established for persons wishing to make atonement for the sin of killing a cow. Gautama brought Gaṅgā, here called Godāvarī, to this place, to recompense for his sin of unintentionally killing a cow (he had lifted a twig to shoo away the cow, which in that moment fell dead), according to the narratives of the site. The other *ṛṣi*s accused him of *gohatyā*, killing of a cow. In order to atone for this sin, he performed *tapas* to bring the Gāṅgā to earth. At Brahmagiri, where the Gautamī Godāvarī Gaṅgā emerges, the pilgrims perform the ritual of atonement for killing a cow, which probably symbolizes for the pilgrims any sin they might have committed in this or previous lives – that is, a general purification. The narrative of the atonement for the killing of a cow promotes the salvific power of this site. The ritual, which involves placing a small metal cow in one's palm and worshipping this cow with an orange flower and sprinkling Gautamī Godāvarī Gaṅgā water from the well on the cow and the flower, accompanied by the recitation by the priest, exemplifies the meaning of this salvific power.[9] Pilgrims also come from

Figure 7.2 Pilgrims on Brahmagiri hill at Tryambak *kṣetra*

Photo: Knut A. Jacobsen

afar to perform precisely this ritual on the beautiful hill of Brahmagiri (see Figure 7.2). The narrative of murder here, as in the case of Vārāṇasī, probably functions to promote the salvific power of the site. Killing cows or murdering Brahmans are symbols of the most horrendous and polluting acts, and if someone could become purified from that act at the site, it demonstrated the power of the site to purify anyone from any impure act.

From the earliest traditions of pilgrimage, however, there seems to have been an awareness of the tension between *dharma* and *tīrtha*. This tension, displayed to some degree in the comparison between the means to salvation in the narrative of Kurukṣetra in the *Mahābhārata* and the teaching of the *Bhagavadgītā*, was discussed in Chapter 2. According to the *Mahābhārata*, the warriors who fought in the battle attained the salvific goal of heaven because of the power of the site of Kurukṣetra. As stated by the *Bhagavadgītā*, they attained the salvific goal because they performed their dharmic duties. So, according to the pilgrimage tradition, it was through the power of the site, *tīrtha*, and not the power of the performance of duty, *dharma*, that they attained heaven. The power of the site seems to contradict the teaching of *dharma* in the *Bhagavadgītā*, although in this case the warriors attained heaven according to both traditions. This tension between power of place and power of *dharma* is detectable in the *Mahābhārata* and the *Purāṇas*, but it became subject to technical analysis in the *Dharmanibandhas* on *tīrtha* in the sections on general issues (*sāmānya*). The *Dharmanibandhas* argue that the fruits of being present at a *tīrtha* depend on possession of ascetic and spiritual qualities and on following the rules of pilgrimage. Virtues are declared as secondary *tīrtha*s (*gauṇatīrtha*s). It is said that, wherever a person who has controlled his passions lives – that is, a person who exemplifies ascetic values – that place is Kurukṣetra, Naimiṣa (Nimsār) or Puṣkar. Anyone who is not able to perform pilgrimage may resort to secondary *tīrtha*s of truth, and so on. When the individual pilgrimage sites are treated, it is the ability of the pilgrimage places to grant the salvific goals to all, no matter what, that is emphasized, but in the general sections (*sāmānya*) of the *Dharmanibandha*s on *tīrtha*s, on the other hand, it is the ascetic qualities that are emphasized.

Even in the *Tīrthayātrāparvan* in the *Mahābhārata*, there is an emphasis on the ascetic values of pilgrimage as a prerequisite for attaining its fruits, but it is in the *Dharmanibandha*s that we get a systematic treatment of this issue. In the *Tīrthayātrāparvan*, the virtues are stated at the outset, before the description of the individual pilgrimage sites. This became the common pattern in the *Dharmanibandha*s. In *Māhātmya*s such as the *Kāśīkhaṇḍa*, the mental *tīrtha*s are described first and the pilgrimage sites afterwards (*mānasāny api tīrthāni satyādīni ca vai priye, etāni muktidāny eva nātra kāryā vicāraṇa* [*Kāśīkhaṇḍa* 1.6.26]). The *dharma* texts on *tīrtha*s, starting with Bhaṭṭa Lakṣmīdhara's twelfth century CE *Tīrthavivecanakāṇḍa* of the *Kṛtyakalpataru*, argue for virtues as the highest *tīrtha*s and state that the rewards of visiting *tīrtha*s are dependent on the ascetic attitude and moral virtues of the pilgrims.[10] This inclusion of the subject of *tīrtha*s into *Dharmaśāstra* literature can probably be understood as an attempt to gain control of the folk phenomenon of *tīrtha*s and its ideology, regulating the rewards and making them compatible with *dharma*. The *tīrtha*s and the pilgrimage traditions had been ignored in the *Dharmaśāstra*s, perhaps because the texts represented only some sections of the priestly traditions. However, the *nibandha* texts on *tīrtha*s represent a continuous process of the Sanskritization of pilgrimage sites.

The *Dharmanibandha*s emphasize that human virtues are *tīrtha*s, a means to the attainment of salvational goals, and that the fruits of pilgrimage in reality depend on the intention and mental attitude of the pilgrim. Some do not gain the fruits of pilgrimage from visiting *tīrtha*s, states the *Tīrthavivecanakāṇḍa*:

> *aśraddhānaḥpāpātmā nāstiko 'cchinnasaṃśayaḥ, hetuniṣṭhaś ca pañcaite na tīrthaphalabhāginaḥ*
>
> Who is without firm faith, who is of wicked mind, who does not believe in the authority of Veda, who does not get his doubts cast aside and who always depends on reasoning, these five types of people do not share the results of *tīrtha*.
>
> (*Tīrthavivecanakāṇḍa*, p. 6)

There are certain requirements for attaining the fruit of *tīrtha*s, in addition to visiting the sites:

> *akopanaś ca rājendra satyavādī dṛḍhavrataḥ, atmopamaś ca bhūteṣu sa tīrthaphalam aśnute*

That person will attain the result of *tīrtha*s who is devoid of anger, speaks the truth, who holds his vows and behaves with other beings as he does to himself.

(*Tīrthavivecanakāṇḍa*, p. 5)

One should constantly be engaged in the welfare of all beings (*sarvabhūtahita*), Lakṣmīdhara explains, and quotes from the *Mahābhārata*:

kāmaṃ krodhaṃ ca lobhaṃ ca yo jitvā tīrtham āvaset, na tena kiṃcinna prāptaṃ tīrthābhigamanād bhavet

A person who has conquered desire, anger, greed, lives in a sacred place, he can attain everything by visiting a *tīrtha.*

tīrthāni tu yathoktena vidhinā sañcaranti ye, sarvadvandvasahā dhīrāste narāḥsvargagāminaḥ

Those persons full of patience, who experience equally all pairs of opposites, who travel to *tīrtha*s according to the rules as described before, they reach heaven.

(*Tīrthavivecanakāṇḍa*, p. 6)

Lakṣmīdhara then cites well-known verses of the *Mahābhārata* on the mental *tīrtha*s (*tīrthāni mānasāni*):

śṛṇu tīrthāni gadato mānasāni mamā 'nagha, yeṣu samyaṅ naraḥ snātvā prayāti paramāṃ gatim

Sinless one, listen to me mention the mental *tīrtha*s. By bathing properly in pure mental *tīrtha*s, a person reaches the highest salvation.

(*Tīrthavivecanakāṇḍa*, p. 6)

The mental *tīrthas* are stated to be the following:

satyaṃ tīrthaṃ kṣamā tīrthaṃ tīrtham indriyāni grahaḥ
sarvabhūtadayā tīrthaṃ tīrtham ārjavam eva ca.
dānaṃ tīrthaṃ damas tīrthaṃ santoṣas tīrtham ucyate,
brahmacaryaṃ paraṃ tīrthaṃ tīrthaṃ ca priyavāditā.
jñānaṃ tīrthaṃ dhṛtis tīrthaṃ tapas tīrthaṃ udāhṛtam,
tīrthānām api tat tīrthaṃ viśuddhir manasaḥparā

Truth is a *tīrtha*, forgiveness is a *tīrtha*, control of sense organs, compassion to all living beings, and simplicity are also mental *tīrtha*s.

Making gifts is a *tīrtha*, self control is a *tīrtha*, satisfaction with what one has; celibacy is the highest *tīrtha*, speaking kindly to others is a *tīrtha*.

> Knowledge is also a *tīrtha*, patience is a *tīrtha*, practising asceticism is also a *tīrtha*; complete purity of mind is the *tīrtha* of *tīrtha*s.
>
> (*Tīrthavivecanakāṇḍa*, p. 6)

Lakṣmīdhara mentions a verse stating that a sacred bath, *snana*, is not merely a bath of plunging the body into water. Only that person who has purified the dirt from his mind and bathes with controlled sense organs becomes pure. He who is greedy, quarrelsome, merciless and too attached to worldly objects remains sinful and dirty, even if he bathes in all the *tīrtha*s. A person does not become free from dirt just by giving up physical dirt, but only becomes fully cleansed when mental dirt is relinquished. Beings that live in water and are born and die only in water do not attain heaven because the dirt of their minds is not purified. The same mental *tīrtha*s and arguments are found in *Kāśīkhaṇḍa* 1.6.28–42, before the treatment of the pilgrimage site. A typical pattern is that the mental *tīrtha*s are presented as a preface to the presentation of the pilgrimage site because they describe the expected mental virtues of the pilgrims as a prerequisite of pilgrimage. However, they are sometimes mentioned after a list of geographical places. The *Matsyapurāṇa* inserts, after mentioning the *tīrtha*s, a statement that *satya tīrtha* (always telling the truth), *dayā tīrtha* (giving) and *indriyanigraha tīrtha* (control of the senses) should be considered *tīrtha*s. They are discussed after mentioning the geographical sites because they are listed here as *tīrtha*s for those who are not able to travel on pilgrimage – that is, as an alternative to pilgrimage. By calling the virtues *tīrtha*s, it is emphasized that these virtues have the same salvific effects as the geographical sites. *Tīrtha* here seems to mean something that has salvific power.

The other main *Dharmanibandha*s on *tīrtha*s, the *Tīrthacintāmaṇi* by Vācaspartimiśra of Mithilā (fifteenth century), *Tristhalīsetu* by Nārāyaṇa Bhaṭṭa (sixteenth century) and the *Tīrthaprakāśa* chapters of *Viramitrodaya* by Mitra Miśra (seventeenth century) follow the pattern of the *Tīrthavivecanakāṇḍa*. *Tristhalīsetu*, which is traditionally considered to be the most authoritative (Salomon 1985: xiii), gives an elaborate treatment of the requirements for gaining the fruits of pilgrimage. Also, in *Tristhalīsetu*, human virtues are called *tīrtha*s, that is to say, *gauṇatīrtha*s, secondary *tīrtha*s. Nārāyaṇa Bhaṭṭa starts this section (67–76) by expanding the references to the word *tīrtha* and stating that the fields (*kṣetra*), fire (*agni*), water (*āpas*), gods (*sura*), priests (*vipra*), the cow (*go*) and the teacher (*guru*) are said to be *tīrtha*s. He continues with a quote from the *Kāśīkhaṇḍa*, saying that "there are *tīrtha*s of the mind as well such as truthfulness which also grant *mokṣa*," and lists the following mental *tīrtha*s as the real *tīrtha*s in which he encourages people to take a sacred bath: truth, forgiveness, control of the senses, compassion to all living beings, uprightness, charity, self-restraint, contentment, continence, amiability, wisdom, steadfastness and austerity in life.

After warning that the salvific power of *tīrtha*s is limited by the virtues of the pilgrims, the text *Tīrthavivecanakāṇḍa* begins describing the sacred *tīrtha*s on earth (*bhauma*) by quoting a well-known verse, and this verse signals the beginning of the treatment of geographical *tīrtha*s:

yathā śarīrasyodeśāḥ kecit puṇyatamāḥ smṛtāḥ tathā pṛthivyām udeśāḥ kecit puṇyatamāḥ smṛtāḥ

As a few areas of the body are known as most pure, similarly some places on the earth are known as the most meritorious ones.

(*Tīrthavivecanakāṇḍa*, p. 7)

In the *Dharmanibandhas*, "it is stated over and over in verses quoted from various purāṇas and smṛtis that a *tīrtha* is worthless for one who is not pure of mind" (Salomon 1985: xv) and this kind of discourse is contradictory to the promises of the individual pilgrimage sites. However, these statements can also be understood as attempts to make the pilgrimage tradition compatible with the *dharmaśāstra* tradition. The emphasis in these parts of the texts seems to make *tīrtha* depend on *dharma*. The statements try to turn the tables: In these sections of the texts, moral purity is presented as a prerequisite for gaining the rewards of the power of place, instead of the reward of purity being the automatic fruit of visiting a *tīrtha*.

The easy accessibility of the rewards of pilgrimage that is claimed in the promotion texts of the pilgrimage places is contradictory to teachings of *dharma* and asceticism. Ascetic values permeate the general sections of the texts on pilgrimage, but the theme of rewards (*phala*) becomes dominant in the parts of the texts on specific sites. Enjoyment (*bhoga*) and salvific attainment (*mokṣa*) are brought about by just being present at the site and bathing in its water, or even by just thinking of going to the site. The results are automatic and often do not seem to have anything to do with the intention of the pilgrim. It is repeatedly stated that moral impurities, even the moral impurities caused by the most serious offenses, such as murdering a Brahman (*brahmahatyā*) or killing a cow (*gohatyā*), are completely washed away by bathing at a *tīrtha* or by just thinking of going there. The celebration texts (*Māhātmyas*) of the individual *tīrthas* compete in promising the greatest reward to the visitors. The texts promise everyone easy access to the greatest rewards, to success in life and to *mokṣa* afterwards, no matter the acts that have been committed. The authors of the *Dharmanibandhas* on *tīrthas* counter this promise with the argument that, if mere physical presence were enough, all the fish in Gaṅgā would attain *mokṣa*. "A person does not become pure by getting rid of bodily impurities, but when mental impurities are abandoned" (*na śarīramalatyāgān naro bhavati nirmalaḥ mānase tu male tyakte bhavaty antaḥ sunir malaḥ*), it is said in the opening chapters of the *Kāśīkhaṇḍa* (1.6.35). However, the tradition of Vārāṇasī also says that even animals and insects that die in Vārāṇasī attain *mokṣa*! The *Kāśīkhaṇḍa* declares that salvation is far more easily attainable if one dies in Kāśī rather than through concentration (*samādhi*), controlling the sense organs, performance of sacrifice or other rituals, or by Vedic knowledge (1.44.37). The *Purāṇas* and *Māhātmyas* of place made salvific power of the site the supreme power, but the general sections of the *Dharmanibandhas*, on the other hand, attempted to put limits on the power of salvific space. They also tried to calculate and correlate exactly the fruits from pilgrimage with the different Vedic sacrifices, thus subsuming pilgrimage under Vedic knowledge. Such calculations are examples of scholastic attempts to incorporate pilgrimage into the conservative *dharma* tradition by putting limits on the salvific power of the pilgrimage sites. Such calculations probably never attracted much interest from the pilgrims.

In the analysis of pilgrimage, a distinction can perhaps be made between how a product is promoted and what the consumers of the product believe about it. The texts of the individual pilgrimage sites are primarily promotion texts. They read like advertisements. The views of the contemporary pilgrims may be different from those promoted by the texts. In addition, the pilgrims' views of the fruits of pilgrimage are always subject to change. The texts, on the other hand, bear witness to the time they were written. The anthropologist Ann Gold (1988) traveled on a bus pilgrimage with Rajasthani pilgrims in 1980 and reports that her co-pilgrims, when they were asked, expressed distrust of the powers of *tīrtha*s, but had the greatest trust in the economic transactions:

> Pilgrimage helps to loosen all kinds of bonds, but not because the waters of *tīrtha*s cleanse the results of bad deeds from men's souls; not one person among my informants evinced any trust in such reputed powers of *tīrtha* baths. Rather, pilgrimage helps because the cumulative effect of being removed from daily routines and attachments at home, of taking many powerful *darshans* of the gods, of voluntarily enduring hardships on the road, and above all of putting out money both for the sake of these experiences (the initial fare) and during them (the constant drain of rupees and paisa into the outstretched hands of *paṇḍā*s and beggars) is decidedly good for the soul. The effect is one of lightening; the returning pilgrim should be thinner and poorer. . . . Simultaneous understanding – pilgrimage is ascetic versus pilgrimage is self-indulgent; pilgrimage brings every goodness versus pilgrimage is quite fruitless – form the fundamental and essentially stable ground of belief among the peasant journeyers. . . .
>
> (Gold 1988: 263, 265)

Gold's conclusion about the simultaneous understanding of pilgrimage as fulfilling wishes and as fruitless is quite similar to the presentation in the texts on pilgrimages themselves discussed earlier. The tension is found in the contradictory view of pilgrimage between the promotion texts of the individual sites and the view of pilgrimage presented in the general section of the pilgrimage texts. It expresses the contradiction in the tradition itself, between the general view that declares that only the person who is pure will get the rewards of *tīrtha*s, and the promotion texts of the sites that promise that everyone, irrespectively, attains purity by visiting the *tīrtha*. However, Ann Gold reports from her pilgrimage that the pilgrims:

> nevertheless bathed methodically in every one [*tīrtha*] we visited no matter how unattractive or polluted the appearance of the water. . . . They were decidedly uncomfortable with the thought that one could be on this famed shore [of Prayāg] and not go in the water.
>
> (Gold 1988: 261)

This significant statement suitably illustrates the power of salvific space. As is often the case in Hinduism, orthopraxis – doing the right thing – is what matters. The pilgrimage priests have authority and can claim to know the doctrine of the fruits of pilgrimage, but lay people may not feel they can claim any authority to understand the extent of the power of salvific space. The popularity of pilgrimage in contemporary Hinduism, however, points to a profound trust in pilgrimage as a good thing, that it makes life better and that it makes it easier to deal with the anxiety of death, although pilgrims may be uncertain about the function of the sites' power of purification, an ambiguity that is present in the textual tradition of pilgrimage itself.

Tīrthas and pollution

The salvific power of the *tīrthas* (*tīrthānāṃ puṇyatā*) is due to the wondrous power of the ground and the power of the water (*prabhāvād adbhutād bhūmeḥ salilasya ca tejasā*), as well as their acceptance as powerful by the sages (*parigrahān munīnāṃ*), states the *Kāśīkhaṇḍa* 1.6.44. Some contemporary developments challenge the holiness of pilgrimage places and one of these is the tragedy of pollution at pilgrimage places by human and industrial waste, especially those sites situated along polluted rivers and in urban areas (see Figure 7.3). Regulation of rivers can transform the environment of pilgrimage places, such as the damming of the river Narmadā in Oṃkāreśvar (see Figure 7.4). Researchers interested in Hinduism and

Figure 7.3 Pollution of the river Godāvarī in Nāsik, one of the four *kumbhamelā* cities

Photo: Knut A. Jacobsen

Figure 7.4 The temple of the Oṃkāreśvar *jyotirliṅga* and the dam that has stopped the flowing of the river Narmadā at the *tīrtha*

Photo: Knut A. Jacobsen

the environment in India have tended to ask "Can Hinduism save the environment in India?" (see Alley 2002; Chapple and Tucker 2000; Haberman 2006; Nelson 1998). However that may be, the following questions are just as urgent: "Does environmental degradation threaten Hinduism?" or "Can religion of salvific space be maintained when the *tīrtha*s are becoming spoiled by pollution?" Does impurity caused by environmental pollution cause Hindus to lose faith in the purifying power of *tīrtha*s – namely, stop them performing the ritual of salvific space? In contemporary India, the ability of *tīrtha*s to remove moral impurity seems to be contradicted by unprecedented environmental pollution of some of the *tīrtha*s, especially those along rivers close to or in the vicinity of urban regions. The polluted state of many *tīrtha*s in India is due to several factors, such as tremendous population growth, urbanization, industrial production, poverty, mismanagement and corruption, and is not largely caused by religion. But it leads to a questioning of religion: How is it that a *tīrtha* site is able to purify invisible moral impurity, but is not able to handle the visible environmental pollution? Are the pilgrims who take a bath in environmentally polluted water or drink it able to maintain the belief that the water is purifying? Will the pilgrims find it meaningful or even physically possible to continue to perform the ritual bathing in or drinking of contaminated water? Can the religion of *tīrtha*s survive the environmental damage affecting pilgrimage places?

K. D. Alley (2000, 2002) and D. L. Haberman (2000, 2006) have documented how priests and devotees who take baths (or have discontinued the practice due to pollution) in the very polluted rivers Gaṅgā (in Vārāṇasī) and Yamunā (in Braj) try to make sense of a possible distinction between the dirtiness (*gandagī* [dirt, filth, stench]) of human-caused pollution and the spiritual purity (*pavitr* or *śuddh*) of the rivers. They have documented that there is a plurality of views on the issue. However, one dominant religious response is to deny any contamination, since the river as a goddess cannot be polluted. They claim that "even if sewage goes into the river, the river is still not polluted" (Haberman 2006: 133). Gaṅgā and Yamunā are never polluted or dirty because they are sacred. Alley documents this view in Vārāṇasī: "For Brāhmaṇ pilgrim priests (*purohit* or *paṇḍā*) who live and work on Daśāśvamedha in Banaras, the river Gaṅgā is a goddess who possesses the power to absorb and absolve human and worldly impurities" (Alley 2002: 71). To claim that Gaṅgā is unclean is to say that she is not an all-powerful goddess! They claim that Gaṅgā can handle all human pollution and that human pollution does not change her status as goddess. As a mother goddess, she is able to clean up all the mess that humans – her children – cause. Alley and Haberman, who are interested in Hinduism as a possible source for political action to protect the rivers against environmental destruction, note that, according to this belief, the rivers themselves as divine beings are able to solve the issue of pollution. In these cases, by focusing on transcendent realities, religion functions as a denial of the material destruction of the river. The transcendent form of the river cannot be polluted, only its material form. Alley argues that, according to such views, the purity of the river "has lapsed into a fixed transcendent state" (ibid.: 219). It should be mentioned here that, as stated by the narratives of *tīrtha*s, pilgrimage sites do in fact become contaminated from the sins left behind by humans taking baths in the water. The *tīrtha*s therefore actually need to be purified. But this is not considered a human task; the *tīrtha*s go on pilgrimage to other *tīrtha*s to be purified there. The pollution is transcendent and can only be removed by transcendent means. This is pollution from moral impurity and hence a transcendent issue. In a narrative about the pilgrimage places Ayodhyā and Prayāg, Prayāg was conceived of as black from being dirtied by all those washing off their sins at the site, and he had to travel on pilgrimage to Ayodhyā and became white again from taking a bath in the river Sarayū at Ayodhyā. Pollution of *tīrtha*s due to the moral impurity of pilgrims was considered possible, but it should be noted that, according to these stories, it is the sacred sites of other places that are thought to be impure, while the supreme site that is promoted in the narrative is the absolute and does not become impure by the impurities of those humans who bathe there, nor by the impurities of the other *tīrtha*s who come to purify themselves.

The view that holiness is not stained by environmental pollution because the power of purification is inherent at the sites is not the only view about impurity. A second point of view that supports religiously motivated social action to diminish the pollution is also found at sacred sites. According to this view, pollution is a serious problem, but it nevertheless does not affect the salvific power of the place and the purity of the place is considered untouched. Pollution touches only the worldly aspect of the place and not the transcendent. A third point of view even argues that contamination affects the river goddesses themselves and sees them as vulnerable as an "ailing mother in need of care" (Haberman 2006: 137). Haberman thinks this signals an emerging significant shift in the theology of the river Yamunā, to define the divine river as identical to its outer form and thus redefined from powerful mother to mother in serious need of help. *Sevā* (worship, service; see Jacobsen 2010) towards the river can become redefined as political action to save the river and its rituals from pollution, thinks Haberman.

As stated in the narratives of salvific sites, the sites are both immanent and transcendent, and, as we discovered, sites travel and can even be absent from their places! They have a transcendent form and the salvific power is part of the transcendent form of the site. In that sense, the salvific power is both different from and identical to the materiality of the site. The tension between the transcendent form of the site and the materiality of the site is present in the narratives of salvific space, and the contemporary environmental pollution of the sites has added a new aspect to this issue. However, K. Alley notes:

> Eulogies to Gaṅgā and worship of *gaṅgājala* are central sacred symbols in pilgrimages and in *pūjā,* but they do not describe *gaṅgājala* as a finite resource whose contours are shaped by a larger ecosystem. Moreover, religious rituals cannot be confused with civic ethics. *Pūjā* and pilgrimage, according to their pristine meanings, are not undertaken to generate social effects.
>
> (2000: 377)

Transcendent purity (*śuddhatā*) has to be distinguished from cleanliness (*svacchatā*), argues the Śaṅkarācārya of Jagannāth Purī (quoted in Alley 2000). Gaṅgā's transcendent purity cannot be compressed into her outward form. The outward form is important for the rituals and for visualization, but it is not identical to the transcendent Gaṅgā. Alley notes that the idea of the transcendent form of Gaṅgā is used to defend religion from the government's attempts to interfere. Religious purity is different from scientific purity. Alley notes that "the ideology of environmental cleanliness is potentially subversive to the ideology of purity upon which a pilgrim priest's own position of authority rests" (Alley 2000: 358). However, so is pollution, and Haberman argues that "the transcendent dimensions of the goddess are reached through the immanent dimension of the river" (Haberman 2000: 350). Haberman refers to the theologian Vallabhācārya's identification of three dimensions of the river Gaṅgā: its physical form, its spiritual form and its form as goddess. It is the spiritual form which functions as a holy pilgrimage site that washes away moral impurity. Haberman argues that the first form cannot be abandoned in order to realize the second, but it is realized by going through it and understanding that the world itself is divine (ibid.: 351). He emphasizes the theological framework of love of the divine in understanding the river, and the power of the river to make one a beloved of Kṛṣṇa. At the same time, the salvific power of the *tīrtha* Yamunā does not presuppose this mutual love, as illustrated in the stories of a pious person's decadent son who reached heaven by inadvertently bathing in the Yamunā (*Padmapurāṇa*, Chapter 30), and the cowherd women of

Braj who "achieved Kṛṣṇa as their lover by bathing in Yamunā" (Haberman 2000: 341), and in the statement that one is freed from sin and attains Viṣṇu's heaven from just bathing in Yamunā (*Varāhapurāṇa*, Chapters 150–151). But Yamunā has now become so polluted in Braj that many persons have stopped bathing in and drinking the water of the river, and the use of its salvific power is threatened. When a river becomes this dirty, many people stop performing the ritual bathing and drinking of the water. At that point, the strategy to define the river and its salvific power as transcendent and not really touched by environmental pollution might not work. Religious leaders may object to the possibility of a transcendent power becoming polluted and the salvific power of place being diminished, since the sacred site occupies "a fixed sacrality beyond space and time (*acyut*)" and therefore is "imperishable in both space and time" (Alley 2000: 380). The religious doctrine that salvific space is available at pilgrimage sites may seem paradoxical, but the material pilgrimage site is nevertheless not identical to the salvific power. Power can be accessed through a site, but the salvific power of the site transcends the site itself.

Tīrthas and conflict

The idea of salvific space has not only been challenged by environmental degradation but also by politicization and conflicts. Political conflicts over pilgrimage places have again highlighted difficult issues related to the transcendence and immanence of salvific sites – the paradox that the material pilgrimage site is not only the immanent form but also a transcendent salvific power and the question to what degree are contemporary geographical places to be identified with the salvific sites of the sacred narratives. Sacred narratives are often presented as describing events of previous *yuga*s, involving ideas that are removed from contemporary conceptions of history.

Ascribing sacredness to a place can be a method of claiming land for oneself or one's own religious tradition (see Chapters 3 and 4). Identifying the transcendent power of place with geographical sites may challenge other religious traditions. The idea of a site's transcendent power and the perception that the land of India is identical to places celebrated in Hindu myths can therefore be a source of dissension. It might conflict with the interpretation of sacred space of other religious communities or the disagreement might involve contemporary political and economic interests.

The conflict of sacred space in India that has received most attention is the place considered by many Hindus to be the birthplace of Rāma: the city of Ayodhyā. The Indian political party the Bharatiya Janata Party (BJP) rallied support around the supposed birthplace of Rāma as a strategy to mobilize a political constituency in order to win national elections. The strategy was to mobilize Hindu voters by focusing on identity issues and to create the impression that religious minority groups in India suppressed the Hindu majority. The difficulties experienced by Hindus wishing to worship at the birthplace of Rāma were used as a symbol to propagate the view that religious pluralism in India had a negative impact on the

Hindus. The mosque Babri Masjid in Ayodhyā was used to symbolize a postulated repression. Hindu nationalists argued that the Babri Masjid was built on an earlier temple that marked the birthplace of Rāma. Hindu nationalism here used traditions of pilgrimage and salvific space to mobilize Hindus politically. Procession pilgrimage that conquers space as it moves onwards (Davis 2005; Jacobsen 2008b, 2009b), the idea of the divine as weak and threatened by contemporary human impact on the pilgrimage sites, the identification of the materiality of the salvific site with the salvific power as such, and so on, were used for political purposes. The political movement managed to mobilize religious organizations and individuals, which led to the forceful destruction of the mosque on 6 December 1992. This was followed by communal riots in which several thousand people were killed, the majority of them Muslims. The High Court of Allahabad ruled on 30 September 2010 to divide the property into three equal parts – one part to Hinduism, one to Muslims and one part to the Hindu organization Nirmohi Akhāṛā.[11] The lawyers appealed the judgment, but the issue has not been solved. The conflict demonstrates that religious and political powers are concerned with places of pilgrimage and illustrates the way expansion of pilgrimage space can be a way to grab land for one's own religion.

By declaring places sacred for one religion, the sites are simultaneously claimed for that religion. Sacredness is a way of stating ownership. Hindu nationalism of the 1980s and 1990s used the Hindu ideas of sacred space as a way of political mobilization. In the case of Hindu nationalism, traditional Hindu views of sacred space became joined with nationalism and its homogeneous vision of space, people, culture and society. Their ideology of a homogeneous Hindu nation used geography and Hindu sacred spaces to affirm a Hindu essence, its Hinduness, *hindutva*. The use of procession to claim land was combined with the issue of Ayodhyā, claiming that the ground under the Babri Masjid was Hindu sacred ground, that it was space as a divinity on which the god Rāma had manifested. The court verdict of 30 September 2010 confirmed this interpretation, the peculiar Hindu view that spaces are divinities, as absolutes that even the gods must obey.

Shared sacred space is not an unusual phenomenon in South Asia and it can be a source of not only conflict but also of development of a composite culture (Sikand 2003; Jacobsen 2009d). A famous case of a *tīrtha* that is shared by several religions is the Ayyappan pilgrimage to Śabarimala. The pilgrimage combines the worship of the Muslim Vāvar at the foot of the Śabari Hill and the Hindu god Ayyappan at the top. The shrines of Vāvar and Ayyappan provide, according to one observer, "a place where all distinctions, including religious ones, are broken down" (Daniel 1984: 252). The composite culture of India has meant that many Hindus worship at Muslim sacred places, especially Sufi shrines.

Shared sacred space can be a source of conflict for several reasons: Religious liminality is in itself often a cause of intercommunal strife; a tradition that borrows from other traditions may nevertheless become intolerant; religious syncretism can be a cover for religious proselytism rather than a means to bring people from different communities together; and even if people from several different religious communities worship at the same shrine, it might not lead to a deeper awareness of others' faiths (Sikand 2003). Y. Sikand has observed that, in the Muslim *dargāh*s, Hindus revere the Muslim saints "in a purely functional sense – powerful beings endowed with considerable shakti or power, capable of granting their wishes, of providing sons to barren women or a cure to a deadly disease" (2003: 18). The Ayodhyā conflict illustrates that the shared religious traditions of the Hindu–Muslim composite culture, which was a dominant phenomenon in Indian religious culture, have lost much of their strength during the last 100 years. Y. Sikand has argued that the quest for social ascension translated into assertions of a more orthodox "Hindu" and "Muslim" identity, and "upwardly mobile sections within these communities fiercely attacked the shared religious traditions that had once characterized them" (2003: 14). This lead to transformation of sacred space, and pilgrimage places were used to confirm religious identities. The transformation of Śirḍī Sāī Bābā from a Sufi saint into an orthodox Hindu and the great expansion of the pilgrimage place of Śirḍī as a Hindu pilgrimage place is a similar case. A problem of the composite culture is that it is a practice supported by traditions, but not by doctrines. Y. Sikand argues, nevertheless, that shared religious traditions defy the preconception that religious communities are sharply divided from one another, homogeneous and neatly defined. They point instead to ways people can come to terms with multiple religious identities, they suggest the possibility of finding truth in a multiplicity of religious contexts and they represent a critique of religious hierarchies and orthodoxies, and perhaps also ways to share places of pilgrimage.

Conclusion

Religious geography and salvific space, temples and pilgrimage together constitute such a central dimension of Hinduism that it is probably correct to say that a majority of Hindus have been more oriented around sacred space than sacred books. The promotion texts of *tīrtha*s promise to grant those who perform the rituals at the *tīrtha*s almost all rewards it is possible to imagine. According to these texts, the power of salvific space does not depend on the intention of the pilgrim but includes everyone. "Just as fire burns even if touched unwillingly, so also Gaṅgā, even if it is bathed in unwillingly, removes sins," says the *Kāśīkhaṇḍa* (1.27.49). But the traditions of pilgrimage are contradictory and the *Kāśīkhaṇḍa* adds that "if those who are staying on the banks of the Gaṅgā were to praise another *tīrtha* and do not honour Gaṅgā, they will surely go to hell" (*Kāśīkhaṇḍa* 1.27.80). In the religion of *tīrtha*s as presented in this text, blasphemy towards the salvific site is punishable with hell, but performing the rituals, on the other hand, prevents this punishment. Performing the pilgrimage rituals scares away the messengers of death because "when seeing a person who regularly bathes in Gaṅgā, the servants of Yama [the god of death] flee in ten directions like deer seeing a lion" (*Kāśīkhaṇḍa* 1.27.108). Competition between the pilgrimage priests at the different sites is an important dimension of these texts, as is exemplified in the statement that "if a person erects a temple on the banks of Gaṅgā according to his capacity, he gets rewards that are ten million times greater than that of the erection of a temple at another *tīrtha*" (*Kāśīkhaṇḍa* 1.27.100), and furthermore:

> if a person on the banks of the Gaṅgā makes a gift of excellent gold weighing a *suvarṇa* to a *brāhmaṇa*, he will be endowed with all extraordinary powers (*aiśvarya*) and fly in a golden chariot decorated with gems that can go everywhere. He will be honoured in all the worlds, also those in other cosmic eggs, and experience all pleasures that delight the mind. Oh Viṣṇu, he will be adored by all until all the living beings are annihilated. Thereafter, he shall be the sole king in Jaṃbūdvīpa, very powerful and valorous. Then he will come back to Avimukta [Vārāṇasī] and attain the salvational goal (*padaṃ nirvāṇam*).
>
> (*Kāśīkhaṇḍa* 1.27. 124–127)

*Tīrtha*s promise every reward, extraordinary powers, pleasures, fame and honor, kingship and the final salvational goal. Performance of the ritual of *tīrthayātrā* is not required for the attainment of any salvational goal, but the *tīrtha* traditions declare that such performance is the means to attain whatever one wishes. The *Tīrthacintāmaṇi* contains some elaborate instructions in the resolutions (*saṃkalpa*s) the pilgrim should recite as part of certain rituals at the pilgrimage sites. The *Tīrthacintāmaṇi* is a *Dharmanibandha* on *tīrtha*s, but also a promotion text for the pilgrimage place of Purī (Puruṣottama). There is no better way to illustrate the salvific power of place than quoting one of the *saṃkalpa*s from this text, from the description of Purī. The *saṃkalpa* is lengthy, but its length is also an indication of the conceptualization of the salvific power of the site:

> Oṃ. Today, on the eleventh day of the bright half of the month of Jyaiṣṭha, with a desire to obtain the same benefit as that which arises from performing many thousands of horse sacrifices and many hundreds of coronation sacrifices, to take a divine form together with a hundred past and fifty future generations of my family, to become endowed with all good qualities and adorned with all ornaments, to be fulfilled in all my desires and, like a god, for all my afflictions to be gone, to be adorned with all good qualities, to be praised by many *apsaras*es and *gandharva*s, to be adorned with all types of gems, for my fatigue to have disappeared, to be young, enormously powerful, wise, to go to the world of Viṣṇu with a gold-coloured chariot that moves on its own shining in all directions, moves or stays still as I wish, and is hung with banners and flags, and there to be worshipped by many *gandharva*s, *apsaras*es, *siddha*s, gods, *vidyādhara*s, *nāga*s and excellent sages, bearing the conch, disc and club, rejoicing in a four-armed form, my fatigue lifted as a result of my own deeds, remaining there for a hundred eons, enjoying whatever joys and pleasures I desire, sporting with *apsaras*es, and after that to go to the abode of Brahmā which grants all desires, shines with many *siddha*s, *vidyādhara*s, gods and *kiṃnara*s, and there for ninety eons to enjoy happiness and after that to go to the world of the Rudras, which is attained by hosts of gods, gives happiness and release, is adorned by many thousands of chariots and is ornamented with many *siddha*s, *vidyādhara*s, *yakṣa*s, *daitya*s and *dānava*s, and there to enjoy happiness for a duration of eighty eons, and after that to go to Goloka,

> which is endowed with all pleasures, is attended by many gods, *siddha*s and *apsarase*s, and is filled with rejoicing, and for seventy eons there to enjoy many joys and pleasures that are unsurpassed and difficult to achieve for one in the three worlds, and after that go to the unsurpassed world of Prajāpati, which is filled with many *gandharva*s, *apsarase*s, *siddha*s, sages and *vidyādhara*s, making myself rejoice there for sixty eons, and then go to the abode of Indra, which is wondrous in many ways and is filled with many *gandharva*s, *kiṃnara*s, *siddha*s, gods, *vidyādhara*s, nāgas, *guhyaka*s, *apsarase*s and other denizens of heaven, and there to enjoy happiness of fifty eons, and after that to make myself wise in the world of the gods, which is adorned with many chariots, is hard to reach, is a place of purification, and is adorned with all the gods, and there for forty eons to enjoy many joys and pleasures that are hard to obtain, and after that to go to the exceedingly hard-to-reach world of the stars, and to enjoy there many excellent boons and pleasures as I desire for thirty eons, and after that to go to the world of the moon, and there enjoy many fine joys and pleasures for twenty eons, and after that to go to the world of the sun, which is worshipped by the gods, consists of various wonders, is meritorious, and is attended to by *gandharva*s and *apsarase*s, and to enjoy many fine joys and pleasures there for ten eons, and after that to go to the exceedingly hard-to-reach world of the *gandharva*s, and to enjoy every joy and pleasure there for one eon, and after that to come to earth as a universal king of the highest righteousness, a great hero, adorned with all good qualities, who himself performs many sacrifices with their priestly fees, and after that to go to the world of yogis which grants release, and to enjoy many excellent joys and pleasures there until the dissolution of created things, and after that to gain an excellent birth into an extraordinary, good and good-minded family of yogis, devotees of Viṣṇu, as *brāhmaṇa* master of the four Vedas, and after that to perform many sacrifices with their priestly fees, and after that to attain union with Viṣṇu, and then to obtain release . . .
>
> (*Tīrthacintāmaṇi* 1346, translation by Gold 2002: 386–388, slightly modified)

Most salvific goals in Hinduism are included here and the salvific power of the site is able to grant them to the pilgrim who performs the ritual and gives *dāna* to the Brahman who guides him.

In this book, I have analyzed only a few aspects of Hindu pilgrimage. I have focused on the concept of salvific space – that is, of space as divinity and as a source of salvific rewards. Salvific space has been an important element in the history and expansion of Hinduism. The idea of salvific space continuously changes. Pilgrimage sites are being transformed by tourism,[12] exploited by politics and challenged by environmental destruction. There is a remarkable flourishing of Hindu pilgrimage traditions in contemporary India; more people than ever before travel to *tīrtha*s. Pilgrimage has important economic dimensions; sacred space is a symbol of political power and domination, and sacred geography mirrors, to some degree, political power and economic interests. But the concept of pilgrimage places as divinities with salvific power is a fundamental religious concept. The divine can be present at many places, yet retains its full transcendent being. Presence in statues does not detract anything from the transcendent divine being. Tens of thousands of temples have been built to house the permanent presence of the divine. In the Hindu tradition, humans continue to travel to salvific space, the sites where two aspects of the divine – divine immanence and divine transcendence – have merged.

Notes

1 Concepts and sources

1 For a detailed academic account of bus pilgrimage, see Gold (1988).
2 For the consequences of the development of the railway system in India on pilgrimage, see Kerr (2001).
3 For examples of newly created pilgrimage routes by the Hindu diaspora in the United States, see Bhardwaj (1990: 211–228) and Bhardwaj (1991: 81–97), and in Norway, see Jacobsen (2004).
4 This builds on Durkheim's division of things into either sacred or profane. See Eliade (1961: 20–67) for a fanciful use of these concepts in analyzing religion and space.
5 Quoted from *Nāradapurāṇa, Uttarabhāga* 48.48. Translation G. V. Tagare. The *Nāradapurāṇa* is a compilation of texts from different periods. It contains several *Māhātmya*s that belong to the latest part of the book, which has been dated to the sixteenth or seventeenth centuries, or as "comparatively late" (Rocher 1986: 203).
6 Quoted from *Nāradapurāṇa, Uttarabhāga*, 48.39. Translation G. V. Tagare. Avimukta is a name of Vārāṇasī and means "never deserted (by Śiva)."
7 *Nāradapurāṇa, Uttarabhāga*, 48.49.
8 *Nāradapurāṇa, Uttarabhāga*, 48.51–52. Translation G. V. Tagare (slightly modified).
9 For an example of this interpretation, see *Nāradapurāṇa* 2.29.
10 The *Purāṇa*s were composed over a long period, from the early centuries CE to the recent centuries; exact dating of the material is problematic. The printed editions contain material from different periods. The material included in the texts has changed over time. Manuscripts carrying the same name might contain very different material (Bakker 2004). For information on how various scholars have dated the material in the different *Purāṇa*s, see Rocher (1986).
11 *Śrāddha,* a ritual performed for the dead, assumes that the dead will spend a year on the way to the world of the ancestors to gradually gain an ancestor body. One function of the *śrāddha* is to feed the dead so that the one year's travel to the world of the ancestors is successful and to make sure that the dead do not stay around as ghosts (*bhūta*) but move on.
12 See Bhardwaj (1973) for a geographical study of these. See also Sircar (1971).
13 Max Müller (1878) developed this use of the term.
14 See Salomon (1979, 1985) for an analysis of a textual attempt of this pilgrimage mathematics.

2 Salvific space, narratives and space as divinity

1 Similar statements are found about many places. This quotation is from *Vāmanapurāṇa* 36.25 and describes the site Iḍāspada, a sub-*tīrtha* of Kurukṣetra. Likewise about Jyeṣṭāśrama: *taṃ tu dṛṣṭā naro muktiṃ saṃprayāti* (*Vāmanapurāṇa* 37.69).

2 For the Amarnāth helicopter *yātrā*, see http://www.amarnathhelicopteryatra.com/, downloaded 17 September 2011. Helicopter *yātrā*s are also organized to Kedārnāth (http://www.chardham-pilgrimage-tour.com/kedarnath-yatra-by-helicopter.html, downloaded 17 September 2011) and to Śrī Mātā Vaiṣṇo Devī in Jammu and Kashmir (https://www.maavaishnodevi.org/helecopter_detail.aspx, downloaded 17 September 2011). What these pilgrimage places have in common is that they are not yet accessible by road. Helicopter pilgrimage can also be done to the four *dhāms* Yamunotrī, Gaṅgotrī, Kedārnāth and Badrīnāth (http://www.chardhamtoursindia.com/chardham-yatra-by-helicopter.php). The web page argues that helicopter pilgrimage both saves time and is easy: "The *Char Dham* can be carried out in many ways but considering modern lifestyle and hectic schedule, you must consider *Char Dham Yatra by helicopter* that will save time plus it is the easiest way to explore its extreme scenic beauty and religious significance." Kailās is also reachable by helicopter *yātrā* (http://www.kailashmanasyatra.com/helicopter-yatra.html).

3 For instructions on how Hindu online *pūjā* works, see http://www.saranam.com/cms/1/How-it-works.htm, downloaded 19 September 2011.

4 See Kane (1973) and Saraswati (1985) for some of the various meanings.

5 See Justice (1997) for a study of this institution in contemporary Vārāṇasī.

6 The verse is found in the *Kurukṣetramāhātmya* as printed in the *Nāradapurāṇa* (2.64).

7 *Mahābhārata* (*Vanaparvan*) 3.83.82.

8 In the *Mahābhārata*, Yama is described as a god of *dharma*. Later, he is associated mostly with death, and the fear of him and his messenger Citragupta, who keeps a record of every person's good and bad deeds, is particularly associated with hell.

9 *Parama gati* usually refers to *mokṣa*, which is probably the reference here.

10 *pṛthivyāṃ yāni tīrthāni antarikṣacarāṇi ca,*
nadyo nadās taḍāgāś ca sarvaprasravaṇāni ca.
udapānāś ca vaprāś ca puṇyāny āyatanāni ca,
māsi māsi samāyānti saṃnihityāṃ na saṃśayaḥ.
(*Mahābhārata* 3.81.168–169)

11 *Nāradapurāṇa*, *Uttarabhāga* 48.36, translation by G. V. Tagare.

3 The origin of the Hindu traditions of salvific space

1 See Sikand (2003) for a discussion of this transformation of a number of pilgrimage places in recent years.

2 Some, however, have claimed that the "*Viṣṇusmṛti* is the earliest brāhmaṇical text to refer to places of pilgrimage" (Nandi 1986: 52). Chapter 85 in the *Viṣṇusmṛti* deals with *tīrtha*s that are appropriate for the performance of the *śrāddha* ritual. This text, however, has previously been wrongly dated. Olivelle has demonstrated that the text was composed in Kashmir around the seventh century (Olivelle 2007).

3 Pilgrimage priests still have a low status in Indian society and are associated with greed and deceit (Fuller 1984).

4 Falk writes:

> These huge figures must have been a serious treat, competing in attractiveness with the picture walls of the Buddhists. Attractions made from stone in the compound of one religious group soon led to a demand for something similar in the compound of any other. Vedic religion does not lend itself to being cut into stone. The local cults, however, are more flexible. Popular cults often centred on a simple stone in its natural setting. It is certainly not by chance that the *yakṣa*s are the first pieces of Hindu plastic arts. They are too low in status to offend a stout Vedic brahmin, and they are regarded as so useful for the adorant that they can keep major parts of the population from giving all their donations at the Buddhist sites
> (2006: 159)

5 The role of Jainism on the development of pilgrimage is not well known, but pilgrimage and the idea of salvific space plays a major role in Jainism as a living tradition. Worship of images was part of early Jainism (Cort 2002) and, since in early India the origin of pilgrimage and the origin of the statues – that is, of the permanent presence of divine figures – seem to be closely related, early Jainism was probably also part of the early development of pilgrimage traditions. More research is needed on this topic.
6 *Saṃnyāsin* was first an optional way of life, then later institutionalized as the fourth stage of life (Olivelle 1993).
7 The *Manvartha-Muktāvalī* commentary by Kullūka Bhaṭṭa explains *devalaka* as *pratimāparicārakaḥ*, and claims that they serve the shrine not for the sake of *dharma* but for their own profit (*vartanārthatvenaitat karma kurbato 'yaṃ niṣedho na tu dharmārtham*). The Hindi commentary *Maṇiprabhā* explains *devalaka* as *mandir kā pujārī*.

4 The growth and omnipresence of the Hindu traditions of salvific space

1 *tato macakrukaṃ rājan dvārapālaṃ mahābalam,*
yakṣaṃ samabhivādyaiva gosahasraphalaṃ labhet
2 One of the big changes in pilgrimage culture in recent years is that pilgrims are no longer entirely dependent on the services of the priests.
3 The *Vāyupurāṇa* is considered one of the oldest *Purāṇa*s and the fifth or fourth century CE has generally been proposed as the date of the text (Rocher 1986: 245). The dating of the *Matsyapurāṇa* is difficult because it is a composite text. Parts of the text have been suggested as dating from around the same time as the *Vāyupurāṇa* (see Rocher 1986: 199 for various opinions).
4 Arya thinks that Vārāṇasī became a *tīrtha* in the third century CE. The pre-third century literature refers to Vārāṇasī only as a trade center and a kingdom (Arya 2004: 73).
5 The *Varāhapurāṇa* is dated to around the twelfth century (Rocher 1986: 242).
6 Translation by S. Venkitasubramonia Iyer.
7 Dates proposed for the text varies between 600 and 1000 CE (Rocher 1986: 252).
8 Nandi notes that *Matsyapurāṇa* has 144 verses (Chapter 144), *Vāyupurāṇa* has 126 verses (Chapter 58) and *Viṣṇupurāṇa* has 101 verses (Chapter 122, Part 6) on the *kali*-age. He deems these to be early *Purāṇa*s, while in some of those he considers middle *Purāṇa*s, such as *Liṅgapurāṇa*, *Bhāgavatapurāṇa* and *Bṛhannāradīya*, he claims that the description of the four *yuga*s are missing and, in others that refer to the *yuga*s, the social conditions of the *kali*-age are hardly mentioned (Nandi 1979/1980: 71).
9 Vidyarthi *et al.* (1979: 91–125) discusses the following ritual specialists associated with pilgrimage in their study of Vārāṇasī: Pujārīs (temple priests), Karmakaṇḍis (ritual performers), Ghāṭiyās (persons who perform rituals and accept *dāna* on the *ghāṭ*s), Paṇḍās (priests with *jajmānī* relationship to pilgrims), Bhaddars and Yātrāvāls (pilgrimage hunters), Gumasthās (persons employed to look after the pilgrims), Kathāvācaks (reciters), Tīrthapurohitas (priests who perform rituals at a *tīrtha*; the Tīrthapurohitas of Vārāṇasī claim descent from Vasiṣṭha), Kīrtaniyās (professional singers of devotional songs), Anuṣṭhānīs (a Brahman specialized in the performance of a ritual for a *jajmān* for their welfare or for getting a desire fulfilled), Mahāpātras (some persons specialized in conducting death rituals) and other ritual associates (florists, barbers, boatmen, musicians and the custodians of the cremation fire [Doms of Kāśī]).
10 http://kumbhmela.co.in/kumbhmela1.html, downloaded 18 January2012.

5 Narratives and doctrines of salvific space: the example of sage Kapila

1 For a monographic study of the sage Kapila, see Jacobsen (2008a).
2 Śrīsthala is mentioned in *Skandapurāṇa*. The first historical reference to the place was made by Al-Biruni in his diary. The name Sidhpur is usually explained with

reference to Jayasiṃha Sidhrāj (d. 1143), who completed the great temple of the town, Rudramahālāya. The name Sidhpur was given in his honor.

3 One cannot fail to notice the feminist flavor of this pilgrimage place: men come to pay homage and perform the rituals to their mothers. To describe it as a "site of resistance" to a dominant patriarchal ideology might be an overstatement. The site might nevertheless give room for that kind of interpretation, and perhaps even gain political significance some time in the future as a place of feminist resistance. However that may be, one should not forget that this is a Brahman town, a place in which many Brahman boys are educated in Sanskrit recitation and ritual performance in boarding schools, all the priests are males and it is the sons as well as the daughters, who come to perform the *śrāddha* (a great number of the visitors belong to the middle class), and in that sense it cannot be said to be a place of opposition to Brahmanical culture.

4 These episodes in the life of Kapila are told in the Kapilagītā of the *Bhāgavatapurāṇa* (3.21–33). In this text, the place identified as the *āśrama* is called Bindusaras and lies on the bank of the river Sarasvatī. It is described as a beautiful place with all kinds of trees, birds, wild animals and renunciants. The place where the mother attained *mokṣa* or *brahmanirvāṇa* is, according to the text, called Siddhapada (3.33.31).

5 *Siddhapura (Siddhapada) Māhātmya*. This text consists of 38 printed pages with 114 verses in Sanskrit, and with a Gujarati translation in *devanāgarī* script. The text is composed as a conversation between Devahūti and Kapila. Much of the text is a description of the sacred complex of Sidhpur and the pilgrimage area Mount Ābū (Arbuda).

6 *Mātṛgayāśraddham*, p. 112–113.

7 *Gujarat State Gazetteers: Mehsana District* (Ahmedabad: Government of Gujarat, 1975, p. 830). Pandit S. M. Nateśa Śāstrī, "Mātṛgayā at Siddhapurī," *The Indian Antiquary*, vol. 13, 1884, p. 282–285.

8 It is possible that the ritual has changed over the last 100 years, with a greater emphasis on Kapila and less emphasis on Paraśurāma.

9 Interviews with visitors, November 2000.

10 On the identity and differences of these two Kapilas, see Jacobsen (2008b).

11 For a study of this order, see van der Veer (1988).

12 H. H. Wilson, *Essays on the Religion of the Hindus* (1862), vol. 2, quoted in O'Malley (1914: 256).

13 A storyteller (*kathāvācaka)* called Śaṅkar Puṣkarṇā has recorded his performance during the Kārttik Pūrṇimā festival. The title of the cassette is Śrī Kapila Mahimā Śrī Kolayātjī and it claims to contain the complete Kapil Muni Kī Mahimā. The picture on the front of the cassette shows Kapila in meditation, with beautiful natural surroundings on one side and the Kapil Mandir on the other. Wild animals seem to seek his presence. The woman meditating next to him is perhaps his mother, Devahūti. The cassette is for sale in Kolāyat.

14 The same verse is repeated in *Matsyapurāṇa* 190.10, but instead of *gosahasraphalaṃ labhet* it says *kapilādānam āpnuyāt*, "gets the reward [equal to] giving away one *kapilā* cow."

15 *Kapilapurāṇam*, ed. Śrīkṛṣṇamāṇi Tripāṭhī (Varanasi: Chaukhamba Surbharati Prakashan, 1981). The published edition also contains a summary in Hindi.

16 Interviews with visitors, October 2001.

17 Interviews with visitors, October 2001.

18 The story of Kapilātīrtha told in the *Skandapurāṇa* 7.3.29 is about a cow named Kapilā.

19 *Kāśīkhāṇḍa, Pūrvārdha*, Chapter 33. The connection is perhaps because the Hindi word *kapi* means monkey.

20 Interview with monks at Kapiladhārā, November 2000.

21 *Kalyāṇ Tīrthāṅk* (Gorakhpur: Gīta Press, 1957), p. 439.

22 Ibid., p. 431.

23 Hanumān Bābā, Mahānirvāṇī Akhāṛā, Kankhal, personal communication, 2001.

6 The structure of Hindu salvific space: a pluralistic pilgrimage tradition or why there is no Mecca of Hinduism

1 *Tīrthavivecanakāṇḍa*, p. 213.
2 Quoted from *Pṛtūdaka Māhātmya*, p. 43, in Handa (2004): 6.
3 Quoted from *Pṛtūdaka Māhātmya*, p. 62–63, in Handa (2004): 6.
4 "All *tīrthas*" (*tīrthāni*) is a name of Prayāg.
5 Al-Biruni writes:

> The Hindus have some places, which are venerated for reasons connected with their law and religion, *e.g.* Benares (Bārānasi). For their anchorites wander to it and stay there forever, as the dwellers of the Ka'ba stay forever in Mekka. They want to live there to the end of their lives. That their reward after death should be the better for it. They say that a murderer is held responsible for his crime and punished with a punishment due to his guilt, except in the case he enters the city of Benares, where he obtains pardon.
> (Alberuni's India, vol. II, p. 146).

Al-Biruni then refers to the famous story of Śiva becoming free from the guilt of cutting off one of Brahmā's heads when he entered the city of Vārāṇasī. In addition to Vārāṇasī, Al-Biruni especially notes the sacred ponds and notices that Hindus construct them at every holy place, and he includes descriptions of a number of ponds around Mount Meru and Mount Kailāsa, and among the major pilgrimage places he mentions are Puṣkara, Tānesar (Kurukṣetra) and Mathurā. He also mentions that Hindus visit Kashmir and used to visit Mūltān before the temple there was destroyed.
6 *The Matsyamahāpurāṇam*. Text in Devanagari, translation and notes in English. Two parts. Reprint: Delhi: Nag Publishers, 1983. The *Vārāṇasī Māhātyma* is found in Part 2, on pages 849–881.
7 The Sanskrit text is found in *Kāśīkhaṇḍa*, four vols (Vārāṇasī: Sampurnanand Sanskrit University, 1992); English translation is found in *Skandapurāṇa*, Part X and XI (Delhi: Motilal Banarsidass, 1996–1997).
8 *Kūrmapurāṇa*, Part I, Chapters 31–35. English translation: *The Kūrmapurāṇa*, Part 1 (Delhi: Motilal Banarsidass, 1981), pages 243–265; *Liṅgapurāṇa*, Chapter 92, English translation *The Liṅgapurāṇa* (Delhi: Motilal Banarsidass, 1974), pages 486–502. The date for the *Kūrmapurāṇa* is suggested to be the eighth century CE (Rocher 1986: 186), for *Liṅgapurāṇa* it varies from the fifth to the eleventh century (ibid.: 187–188).
9 The Indian sociologist Dipankar Gupta has noted that, during his lifetime, Vārāṇasī has changed from a city associated with dirt and death in the 1950s to a current-day romantic tourist destination for Indian as well as international tourists (Gupta 2009).
10 However, the claim that Prayāg "is the most vibrant politically and spiritually conscious and spiritually awakened city of India" is made on the information webpage http://allahabad.nic.in/history.htm. Here, it is also claimed that "in mediaeval India the city enjoyed the honour of being the religio-cultural centre of India."
11 But in T. Ring, R. M. Salkin and S. La Boda, *International Dictionary of Historic Places: Asia and Oceania* (London: Routledge, 1996), it is argued that Mathurā "has been called the epicentre of Indian culture" (p. 572).
12 For an example that states that "One could call Rajasthan as the cultural capital of India," see (http://www.articlesbase.com/exotic-locations-articles/rajasthanthe-cultural-capital-of-india-971968.html, downloaded 6 December 2011).
13 http://www.pilgrimage-india.com/north-india-pilgrimage/Vārāṇasī.html; http://www.travelmasti.com/domestic/uttarpradesh/Vārāṇasī.htm.
14 http://www.tripraja.com/destinations/india/north/Vārāṇasī -pilgrimage-temple.html.
15 Bhardwaj (1973: 101). Bhardwaj does not explain what he means by Mecca, but presumably it is a place everyone within a religion accepts as its most sacred center.

16 Many of them are available for viewing on YouTube.
17 Numerous videos of this ritual are available for viewing on YouTube.
18 The number of people in India dying annually in traffic accidents alone is around 100,000.

7 Contradictions and challenges

1 *Kurukṣetramāhātmya* as printed in the *Nāradapurāṇa* 2.64–65.
2 See the Sanskrit text in Salomon (1985: 42); for the English translation, see Salomon (1985: 242–243).
3 See *Tristalīsetu* (110–125) and *Tīrthacintāmaṇi* (51–59) for further discussions on this issue of traveling with a vehicle.
4 This is of course the focus of a large body of literature on India's society. The most famous, influential and debated was by Louis Dumont (1986). For a good discussion and overview of the subject of purity and impurity, see Malinar (2010).
5 Translation, G. V. Tagare (modified).
6 Translation, G. V. Tagare.
7 Translation, G. V. Tagare.
8 This was observed by the author during the *kumbhamelā* in Prayāg in 2001.
9 The ritual is described as I experienced it at Brahmagiri in October 2011.
10 However, this did not seem to influence the texts' presentation of the individual pilgrimage sites.
11 See http://rjbm.nic.in/ (downloaded 2 January 2012).
12 Religious tourism is defined as visits to sacred sites motivated partly or wholly by religious motives, while pilgrimage tourism denotes the move from traditional pilgrimages to vacation tourism. Touristic qualities of pilgrimage include changing patterns of visits to sacred destinations, limited engagement in rituals, commercial organizations typical of package tours, novel ways of marketing the destinations and the consumerist behavior of visitors (Jacobsen 2009d; Shinde, 2007).

References

Primary sources

Alberuni's India: An Account of the Religion, Philosophy, Literature, Geography, Chronology, Astronomy, Customs, Laws and Astrology of India about A.D. 1030: An English Edition with Notes and Indices, two vols, English edition by E. C. Sachau, Dryden House, Gerrard Street: Kegan Paul, Trench, Trübner, 1910.

A Record of Buddhist Kingdoms: Being an Account by the Chinese Monk Fa-Hien of His Travels in India and Ceylon (A.D. 399–414) in Search of the Buddhist Kingdoms, trans. J. Legge, Oxford: Clarendon Press, 1886.

Bhāgavatapurāṇa, five vols, English trans. G. V. Tagare, Delhi: Motilal Banarsidass, 1976–1978.

Brahmapurāṇa, four vols, translated and annotated by a board of scholars, Delhi: Motilal Banarsidass, 1985–1986.

Garuḍapurāṇa, three vols, translated by a board of scholars, Delhi: Motilal Banarsidass, 1978–1980.

Kalyāṇ Tīrthāṅk, Gorakhpur: Gita Press, 1957.

Kāmpilyamāhātmya of Durgadatta Sharma, Sanskrit and English, English trans. C. Puchetti, Venice: Venetian Academy of Indian Studies, 1999.

Kapilapurāṇam, Śrīkṛṣṇamāṇi Tripāṭhī (ed.), Varanasi: Chaukhamba Surbharati Prakashan, 1981.

Kāśīkhaṇḍa of Maharṣi Vyāsa with two commentaries, "Rāmānanda" by Ācārya Śrī Rāmānanda and Hindī "Nārāyaṇī" by Śrī Nārāyaṇapati Tripāṭhī, edited by Ācārya Śrī Karuṇāpati Tripāṭhī, Varanasi: Sampurnanand Sanskrit University, 1991.

Kāśīkhaṇḍa, English translation, The Skandapurāṇa part X and XI, trans. G. V. Tagare, Delhi: Motilal Banarsidass, 1996.

Kūrmapurāṇa. The Kūrma-Purāṇa, trans. G. V. Tagare, two vols, Delhi: Motilal Banarsidass, 1981.

Mahābhārata. The Mahābhārata, critically edited by V. S. Sukthankar, Poona: Bhandarkar Oriental Research Institute, 1933–1966.

Mahābhārata. The Mahabharata of Krishna-Dwaipayana Vyasa, English trans. K. M. Ganguli, Delhi: Munshiram Manoharlal, 1990.

Mahaparinibbānasutta. The Dīgha Nikāya, edited by T. W. Rhys Davids and J. E. Carpenter, vol. II, Oxford: Pali Text Society, 1995 (1903), 72–168.

Mahaparinibbānasutta. Dialogues of the Buddha, trans. T. W. and C. A. F. Rhys Davids, fourth ed., Part 11, Oxford: Pali Text Society, 78–191.

Manusmṛti. The Manusmṛti with the Manvartha-Muktāvalī Commentary of Kullūka Bhaṭṭa with the Maniprabha Hindi Commentary by Haragovinda Śāstrī, Varanasi: Chaukhambha Sanskrit Sansthan, 1992.

Nāradapurāṇa. The Nārada-purāṇa, translated and annotated by G.V. Tagare, five vols, Delhi: Motilal Banarsidass, 1980–1982.

Raghuvaṃśa. The Raghuvaṃśa of Kālidāsa: With the Commentary of Mallinātha, edited by G. R. Nandargikar, fifth edition, Delhi: Motilal Banarsidass, 1982 (third edition: 1897).

Śivapurāṇa, English translation by a board of scholars, four vols, Delhi: Motilal Banarsidass, 1970.

Si-yu-ki: Buddhist records of the Western world: translated from the Chinese of Hiuen Tsiang (A.D. 629), trans. Samuel Beal, two vols, London: Trubner, 1884.

Skandapurāṇa, Prabhāsa Khaṇḍa, Chapters 121–366. *The Skanda-Purāṇa*, Part XX, trans. G. V. Tagare, Delhi: Motilal Banarsidass, 2003.

Skandapurāṇa, Prabhāsakhaṇḍa, Arbudakhaṇḍa, Skandapurāṇa 7.3, English translation, *The Skanda-purāṇa*, Part XXII, trans. S. Balooni and P. Panda, Delhi: Motilal Banarsidass, 2010.

Skandapurāṇa, Āvyantya-khaṇḍa, Revā-khaṇḍa, Chapters 1–101. *The Skanda-Purāṇa*, Part XIV, trans. G. V. Tagare, Delhi: Motilal Banarsidass, 1999.

Skandapurāṇa, Āvyantya-khaṇḍa, Revā-khaṇḍa, Chapters 101–232. *The Skanda-Purāṇa*, Part XV, trans. G. V. Tagare, Delhi: Motilal Banarsidass, 2001.

Śrī Kapila Māhātmya Kolāyatjī, Bikaner: Nadlāl Modī Book Sellers, 1999 (in Hindi).

Tīrthacintāmaṇi of Vācaspatimiśra, ed. Kamalakṛṣṇa Smṛtitīrtha, Calcutta: Asiatic Society, 1912.

Tīrthacintāmaṇi of Vācaspatimiśra: A Critical Edition and Translation of the Sāmānya, Prayāga, and Puruṣottama Sections, by David P. Gold, Dissertation, University of Pennsylvania, 2002.

Tīrthaprakāśa of Mitramiśra. Vol. 10 of *Vīramitrodaya*, edited by Paṇḍit Viṣṇu Prasād, Chowkhambā Sanskrit Series, no. 239. Benares: Chowkhambhā Sanskrit Series Office, 1917.

Tīrthavivecanakāṇḍa. Kṛtyakalpataru of Bhaṭṭa Lakṣmīdhara, Part 8, edited by K. V. R. Aiyangar, Part Baroda: Oriental Institute, 1942.

Vāmanapurāṇa. The Vāmana Purāṇa, Critical Edition, edited by A. S. Gupta, Varanasi: All India Kashiraj Trust, 1967.

Varāhapurāṇa. The Varāha Purāṇa, two vols, translated and annotated by S. Venkitasubramonia Iyer, Delhi: Motilal Banarsidass, 1985.

Literature

Acharya, S. (1997) *Pilgrimage in Indian Civilization*, Delhi: Manak.

Agrawala, V. S. (1963) *Matsya Purāṇa: A Study*, Varanasi: All-India Kashiraj Trust.

Alley, K. D. (2000) "Separate Domains: Hinduism, Politics, and Environmental Pollution," in C. K. Chapple and M. E. Tucker (eds) *Hinduism and Ecology: The Intersection of Earth, Sky, and Water*, Cambridge, Massachusetts: Harvard University Press, 355–388.

Alley, K. D. (2002) *On the Banks of the Ganga: When Wastewater Meets a Sacred River*, Ann Arbor, Michigan: The University of Michigan Press.

Angot, M. (2009) "Land and Location: Errant Gods, Erring Asuras and the Land of Men: Place and Space in Vedic Literature," in D. Berta and G. Tarabout (eds) *Territory, Soil and Society in South Asia*, New Delhi: Manohar, 41–97.

Arya, S. N. (2004) *History of Pilgrimage AD 300–1200*, New Delhi, Munshiram Manoharlal.

Bakker, H. (1982) "The Rise of Ayodhyā as a Place of Pilgrimage," *Indo-Iranian Journal* 24: 103–126.

Bakker, H. (1986) *Ayodhyā*, Groningen: Egbert Forsten.

Bakker, H. (1996) "Construction and Reconstruction of Sacred Space in Vārāṇasī," *Numen* 43: 32–55.

Bakker, H. (2004) "The Structure of the Vārāṇasīmāhātmya in Skandapurāṇa 26–31," in H. Bakker (ed.) *Origin and Growth of the Purāṇic Text Corpus, With Special Reference to the Skandapurāṇa*, Delhi: Motilal Banarsidass, 1–16.

Banerjee-Dube, I. (2001) *Divine Affairs: Religion, Pilgrimage, and the State in Colonial and Postcolonial India*, Shimla: Indian Institute of Advanced Study.

Bayly, C. A. (1983) *Rulers, Townsmen and Bazaars: North Indian Society in the Age of British Expansion 1770–1870*, Delhi: Oxford University Press.

Bharati, A. (1963) "Pilgrimage in the Indian Tradition," *History of Religions* 3 (1): 135–167.

Bharati, A. (1970) "Pilgrimage Sites and Indian Civilization," in J. W. Elder (ed.) *Chapters in Indian Civilization*, Dubuque, IA: Kendall/Hunt, 85–126.

Bhardwaj, S. M. (1973) *Hindu Places of Pilgrimage in India*, Berkeley: University of California Press.

Bhardwaj, S. M. (1990) "Hindu Deities and Pilgrimage in the United States," in G. Rinschede and S. M. Bhardwaj (eds) *Pilgrimage in United States*, Geographia Religionum, Interdisziplinäre Schriftenreihe zur Religionsgeographie, Band 5, Berlin: Dietrich Reimer Verlag, 211–228.

Bhardwaj, S. M. (1991) "Hindu Pilgrimage in America," in M. Jha (ed.) *Social Anthropology of Pilgrimage*, New Delhi: Inter-India Publications, 81–97.

Bhardwaj, S. M. and J. G. Lochtefeld (2004) "Tīrtha," in S. Mittal and G. Thursby (eds) *The Hindu World*, London: Routledge.

Bhaṭṭācārya, T. (1986) *Gaṅgāsāgar Melā (Yatrī Sahacar)*, second edition, Kolkata: Pharmā KLM (in Hindi).

Bigger, A. (2001) "Wege und Umwege Zum Himmel. Die Pilgerfahrten im Mahābhārata," *Journal Asiatique* 289 (1): 147–188.

Case, M. H. (2000) *Seeing Krishna: The Religious World of a Brahman Family in Vrindavan*, New York: Oxford Press.

Chakrabarti, P. (1984) *Social Profile of Tarakeswar: Study of a Pilgrim Town in West Bengal*, Calcutta: Firma KLM.

Chandramouli, K. (1996) *Kashi – The City Luminous*, Calcutta: Rupa.

Chapple, C. K. and M. E. Tucker (eds) (2000) *Hinduism and Ecology: The Intersection of Earth, Sky, and Water*, Cambridge, Massachusetts: Harvard University Press.

Chattopadhyaya, B. D. (1994) *The Making of Early Medieval India*, New Delhi: Oxford University Press.

Chaudhary, M. (1998) "Tourists' Mental Disposition and Choice of Destination – A Study of Kurukshetra as a Religious Destination," in D. S. Bhardwaj, O. P. Kandari, M. Chaudhary and K. K. Kamra (eds) *Domestic Tourism in India*, New Delhi: Indus Publishing Company, 257–267.

Chauduri, B. (1981) *The Bakreshwar Temple: a Study on Continuity and Change*, Delhi: Inter-India.

Colas, G (2010) "Iconography and Images: Ancient Concepts," in K. A. Jacobsen (ed.) *Brill's Encyclopedia of Hinduism, Volume Two: Sacred Texts and Languages, Ritual Traditions, Arts, Concepts*, Leiden: Brill, 529–536.

Cort, J. E. (2002) "'Bhakti in the Early Jain Tradition: Understanding Devotional Religion in South Asia," *History of Religions* 42: 59–96.

Daniel, V.E. (1984) *Fluid Signs: Being a Person the Tamil Way*, Berkeley: University of California Press.

Davis, R. H. (2005) "The Iconography of Rama's Chariot," in D. Ludden (ed.) *Making India Hindu: Religion, Community and the Politics of Democracy in India*, second edition, Delhi: Oxford University Press, 27–54.

Deleury, G. A. (1960) *The Cult of Viṭhobā*, Poona: Deccan College.

Desai, M. (2012) "Urban Space and Narratives in Banaras," in M. S. Dodson (ed.) *Banaras: Urban Forms and Cultural Histories*, New Delhi: Routledge, 17–41.

Dodson, M. S. (ed.) (2012) *Banaras: Urban Forms and Cultural Histories*, New Delhi: Routledge.

Dubey, D. P. (2001a) *Prayaga: The Site of Kumbha Mela: In Temporal And Traditional Space*, New Delhi: Aryan Books International.

Dubey, D. P. (ed.) (2001b) *Kumbha Mela: Pilgrimage to the Greatest Cosmic Fair*, Allahabad: Society of Pilgrimage Studies.

Dumont, L. (1986) *Homo Hierarchicus; the Caste System and Its Implications*, complete revised English edition, Chicago: University of Chicago Press.

Eck, D. L. (1981) "India's Tīrthas: 'Crossings' in Sacred Geography," *History of Religions* 20 (4): 323–344.

Eck, D. L. (1982) *Benares: City of Light*, Princeton: Princeton University Press.

Eck, D. L. (1998) "The Imagined Landscape: Patterns in the Construction of Hindu Sacred Geography," *Contributions to Indian Sociology* 32 (1): 165–188.

Einoo, S. (2001) "Is the Sārasvatasattra the Vedic pilgrimage?" in K. Kimura, F. Sueki, A. Saito and H. Marui (eds) *Kū to jitzusai: Ejima Yasunori hakushi tsuitō ronshū* (Emptiness and Reality: Volume in Memory of Professor Ejima Yasunori), Tokyo: Shunjūsha, 607–622.

Eliade, M. (1961) *The Sacred and the Profane: the Nature of Religion*, New York: Harper and Row.

Eliot, S. C. (1921, repr. 1957) *Hinduism and Buddhism: an Historical Sketch*, three vols, London: Routledge and Kegan Paul.

Ensink, J. (1974) "Problems of the Study of Pilgrimage in India," *Indologica Taurinensia* 2: 57–79.

Entwistle, A. (1987) *Braj: Center of Krishna Pilgrimage*, Groningen: Egbert Forsten.

Eschmann, A., H. Kulke and G. C. Tripathi (eds) (1978) *The Cult of Jagannath and the Regional Tradition*, New Delhi: Manohar.

Falk, H. (2006) "The Tidal Waves of Indian History: Between the Empires and Beyond," in P. Olivelle (ed.) *Between the Empires: Society in India 300 BCE to 400 CE*, New York: Oxford University Press, 145–166.

Feldhaus, A. (1995) *Water and Womanhood: Religious Meaning of Rivers in Maharashtra*, New York: Oxford University Press.

Feldhaus, A. (2003) *Connected Places: Religion, Pilgrimage, and Geographical Imagination in India*, New York: Palgrave Macmillan.

Filippi, G. G. and B. Marcolongo (1999) *Kāmpilya: Quest for a Mahābhārata City*, Venice: Venetian Academy of Indian Studies.

Fuller, C. J. (1984) *Servants of the Goddess: the Priests of a South Indian Temple*, Cambridge: Cambridge University Press.

Gaenszle M. and J. Gengnagel (eds) (2008) *Visualizing Space in Banaras: Images, Maps, and the Practice of Representation*, New Delhi: Oxford University Press.

Gold, A. G. (1988) *Fruitful Journeys: the Ways of Rajasthani Pilgrims*, Berkeley: University of California Press.

Goldman, R. P. (1986) "A City of the Heart: Epic Mathurā and the Indian Imagination," *Journal of the American Oriental Society* 106 (3): 471–483.

Gopal, L. and D. P. Dubey (eds) (1990) *Pilgrimage Studies: Texts and Context: Śrī Phalāhārī Bābā Commemoration Volume*, Allahabad: The Society of Pilgrimage Studies.

Government of Gujarat (1975) *Gujarat State Gazetteers: Mehsana District*, Ahmedabad: Government of Gujarat.

Granoff, P. (1992) "When Miracles Become Too Many: Stories of the Destruction of Holy Sites in the Tāpī Khaṇḍa of the Skanda Purāṇa," *Annals of the Bhandarkar Oriental Research Institute* 72–73: 549–571.

Granoff, P. (2003) "Pilgrimage as Revelation: Śankaradeva's Journey to Jagannātha Purī," in P. Granoff and K. Shinohara (eds) *Pilgrims, Patrons and Place: Localizing Sanctity in Asian Religions*, Vancouver: UBC Press, 181–202.

Gupta, D. (2009) *The Caged Phoenix: Can India Fly?* New Delhi: Penguin Books India.

Gutschow, N. (2006) *Benares: the Sacred Landscape of Varanasi*, Stuttgart: Edition Axel Menges.

Gutschow, N. and A. Michaels (1993) *Benares: Tempel und religiöses Leben in der heiligen Stadt der Hindus*, Köln: DuMont.

Haberman, D. L. (1994) *Journey through the Twelve Forests: an Encounter with Krishna*, New York: Oxford University Press.

Haberman, D. L. (2000) "River of Love in an Age of Pollution," in C. K. Chapple and M.E. Tucker (eds) *Hinduism and Ecology: The Intersection of Earth, Sky, and Water*, Cambridge, Massachusetts: Harvard University Press, 339–354.

Haberman, D. L. (2006) *River of Love in the Age of Pollution: the Yamuna River in North India*, Berkeley: University of California Press.

Handa, D. (2004) *An Epic Pilgrimage: History and Antiquity of Pehowa: Ancient Pṛithūdaka (a Mahābhārata Site on the Sarasvatī)*, New Delhi: Aryan Books.

Hawley, J. S. (1981) *At Play with Krishna*, Princeton: Princeton University Press.

Hazra, R. C. (1940) *Studies in Purāṇic Records on Hindu Rites and Customs*, Dacca: University of Dacca.

Hazra, R. C. (1979, 1st ed. 1963) *Studies in the Upapurāṇas. Vol. II (Śākta and Non-Secterian Upapurāṇas)*, Calcutta: The Principal Sanskrit College.

Hertel, B. R. and C. A. Humes (eds) (1993) *Living Benaras: Religion in Cultural Context*, Albany: State University of New York Press.

Hüsken, U. (2009) *Viṣnu's Children: Prenatal Life-cycle Rituals in South India*, translated from German by Will Sweetman, Wiesbaden: Harrassowitz.

Jacobsen, K. A. (2004) "Establishing Ritual Space in the Hindu Diaspora in Norway," in K.A. Jacobsen and P.P. Kumar (eds) *South Asians in the Diaspora: Histories and Religious Traditions*, Leiden: Brill, 134–148.

Jacobsen, K. A. (2008a) *Kapila: Founder of Sāṃkhya and Avatāra of Viṣṇu*, New Delhi: Munshiram Manoharlal.

Jacobsen, K. A. (ed.) (2008b) *South Asian Religions on Display: Religious Processions in South Asia and the Diaspora*, London: Routledge.

Jacobsen, K. A. (2009a) "Introduction," in K. A. Jacobsen (ed.) *Brill's Encyclopedia of Hinduism, Volume One: Regions, Pilgrimage, Deities*, Leiden: Brill, xxxiii–xlviii.

Jacobsen, K. A. (2009b) "Processions," in K. A. Jacobsen (ed.) *Brill's Encyclopedia of Hinduism, Volume One: Regions, Pilgrimage, Deities*, Leiden: Brill, 445–455.

Jacobsen, K. A. (2009c) "Three Functions of Hell in the Hindu Traditions," *Numen* 56 (2–3): 385–400.

Jacobsen, K. A. (2009d) "*Tīrtha* and *Tīrthayātrā*: Salvific Space and Pilgrimage," in K. A. Jacobsen (ed.) *Brill's Encyclopedia of Hinduism, Volume One: Regions, Pilgrimage, Deities*, Leiden: Brill, 381–410.

Jacobsen, K. A. (2009e) "Uttar Pradesh," in K. A. Jacobsen (ed.) *Brill's Encyclopedia of Hinduism, Volume One: Regions, Pilgrimage, Deities,* Leiden: Brill, 171–186.

Jacobsen, K. A. (2010) "Sevā," in K. A. Jacobsen (ed.) *Brill's Encyclopedia of Hinduism, Volume Two: Sacred Texts and Languages, Ritual Traditions, Arts, Concepts*, Leiden: Brill, 861–865.

Jacobsen, K.A. and N. Smart (2006) "Is Hinduism an Offshoot of Buddhism?" in A. King (ed.) *Indian Religions: Renaissance and Renewal: the Spalding Papers in Indic Studies*, London: Equinox, 41–53.

Jha, M. (1971) *The Sacred Complex of Janakpur*, Allahabad: United Publishers.

Jha, M. (ed.) (1991) *Social Anthropology of Pilgrimage*, New Delhi: Inter-India Publications.

Jindel, R. (1976) *Culture of a Sacred Town: a Sociological Study of Nathdwara*, Bombay: Popular Prakashan.

Justice, C. (1997) *Dying the Good Death: the Pilgrimage to Die in India's Holy City*, Albany: State University of New York Press.

Kane, P. V. (1973) *History of Dharmaśāstra*, vol. IV, second edition, Poona: Bhandarkar Oriental Research Institute.

Karve, I. (1962) "On the Road: a Maharashtrian Pilgrimage," *Journal of Asian Studies* 22: 13–30.

Kerr, I. J. (2001) "Reworking a Popular Religious Practice: the Effects of Railways on Pilgrimage in 19th and 20th Century South Asia," in I. J. Kerr (ed.) *Railways in Modern India*, New Delhi: Oxford University Press, 304–327.

Kessler, A. (2009) "Yakṣas and Yakṣiṇīs," in K. A. Jacobsen (ed.), *Brill's Encyclopedia of Hinduism, Volume One: Regions, Pilgrimage, Deitie*s, Leiden: Brill, 801–806.

Kudaisya, G. (2006) *Region, Nation, "Heartland": Uttar Pradesh in India's Body Politic*, Delhi: Sage.

Kulke, H. (1970) *Cidambaramāhātmya*, Wiesbaden: Otto Harrassowitz.

Kulke, H. (1978) "Royal Temple Policy and the Structure of Medieval Hindu Kingdoms," in A. Eschmann, H. Kulke and G. C. Tripathi (eds) *The Cult of Jagannāth and the Regional Tradition*, New Delhi: Manohar, 125–138.

Kumar, D. (1991) *The Sacred Complex of Badrinath*, Varanasi: Kishor Vidya Niketan.

Lannoy, R. (1999) *Benares Seen from Within*, Seattle: University of Washington Press.

Legge, J. (1886) *A Record of Buddhist Kingdoms: Being an Account by the Chinese Monk Fa-Hien of his Travels in India and Ceylon* (A.D. 399–414) *in Search of the Buddhist Kingdoms*, Oxford: Clarendon Press.

Lipner, J. (2004) "On Hinduism and Hinduisms: the Way of the Banyan," in S. Mittal and G. Thursby (eds) *The Hindu World*, New York: Routledge, 9–34.

Lipner, J. (2006) "The Rise of 'Hinduism'; or How to Invent a World Religion with Only Moderate Success," *International Journal of Hindu Studies* 10 (1): 91–104.

Lochtefeld, J. G. (2010) *God's Gateway: Identity and Meaning in a Hindu Pilgrimage Place*, New York: Oxford University Press.

Lorenzen, D. N. (1999) "Who Invented Hinduism?" *Comparative Studies in Society and History*, 41 (4): 630–659.

Ludvik, C. (2007) *Sarasvatī: Riverine Goddess of Knowledge: From the Manuscript-Carrying Vīṇā-player to the Weapon-Wielding Defender of the Dharma*, Leiden: Brill.

McCormick, T. (1997) "The Jain Ascetic as Manifestation of the Sacred," in R. H. Stoddard and A. Morinis (eds) *Sacred Places, Sacred Spaces: the Geography of Pilgrimage*, Geoscience and Man, vol. 34, Baton Rouge, Louisiana: Geoscience Publications.

McLean, K. (2008) *Pilgrimage and Power: Kumbha Mela in Allahabad*, New York: Oxford University Press.

Malik, A. (1993) *Das Puṣkara-Māhātmya: Ein religionswissenschaftlicher Beitrag zum Wallfahrtsbegriff in Indien: Erörterung, Text, Übersetzung*, Beiträge zur Südasienforschung/Südasien-Institut, Universität Heidelberg, Stuttgart: Steiner.

Malinar, A. (2010) "Purity and Impurity," in K. A. Jacobsen (ed.) *Brill's Encyclopedia of Hinduism, Volume Two: Sacred Texts and Languages, Ritual Traditions, Arts, Concepts*, Leiden: Brill, 435–449.

Mathur, P. R. G. (2009) *Sacred Complex of Guruvayur Temple*, New Delhi: Indira Gandhi National Centre for the Arts.

Medhasananda, S. (2002) *Vārāṇasī at a Crossroad*, Kolkata: The Ramakrishna Mission Institute of Culture.

Michaels, A. (2004) *Hinduism: Past and Present*, Princeton, NJ: Princeton University Press.

Michell, G. (ed.) (1993) *Temple Towns of Tamil Nadu*, Delhi: Marg Foundation.

Mokashi, D. B. (1990) *Palki: a Pilgrimage to Pandharpur*, translated from Marathi by P. G. Engblom, Delhi: Orient Longman.

Monier-Williams, M. (1899, reprint 2002) *A Sanskrit–English Dictionary*, Delhi: Motilal Banarsidass.

Morinis, A. (1984) *Pilgrimage in the Hindu Tradition: a Case Study of West Bengal*, Delhi: Oxford University Press.

Müller, M. (1878) *Lectures on the Origin and Growth of Religion: as Illustrated by the Religions of India,* London: Longmans, Green and Co.

Nandi, R. N. (1979/1980) "Client, Ritual and Conflict in Early Brāhmaṇical Order," *Indian Historical Review* 6: 64–118.

Nandi, R.N. (1986) *Social Roots of Religion in Ancient India*, Calcutta: University of Calcutta.

Narayan, S. (1983) *Sacred Complexes of Deoghar and Rajgir*, New Delhi: Concept Publishing.

Nath, V. (1987) *Dāna: Gift System in Ancient India (c. 600 BC–c. AD 300): a Socio-economic Perspective*, New Delhi: Munshiram Manoharlal.

Nath, V. (2001) *Purāṇas and Acculturation: a Historico-anthropological Perspective*, New Delhi: Munshiram Manoharlal.

Nath, V. (2007) "Purāṇic Tīrthas: A Study of Their Indigenous Origins and the Transformation (Based Mainly on the Skanda Purāṇa)," *Indian Historical Review* 34: 1–46.

Nath, V. (2009) *The Purāṇic World: Environment, Gender, Ritual and Myth*, New Delhi: Manohar.

Nelson, E. (ed.) (1998) *Purifying the Earthly Body of God: Religion and Ecology in Hindu India*, Albany: State University of New York Press.

Oberlies, T. (1995) "Arjunas Himmelreise und die Tīrthayātrā der Pāṇḍavas. Zur Struktur des Tīrthayātrāparvan des Mahābhārata," *Acta Orientalia* 56: 106–124.

Oddie, G. A (2006) *Imagined Hinduism: British Protestant Missionary Constructions of Hinduism, 1793–1900*, New Delhi: Sage.

Olivelle, P. (1993) *The Āśrama System: the History and Hermeneutics of a Religious Institution*, New York: Oxford University Press.

Olivelle, P. (2005) *Language, Texts, and Society: Explorations of Ancient Indian Culture and Religion*, Florence: Firenze University Press.

Olivelle. P. (2007) "The Date and Provenance of the Viṣṇu Smṛti," *Indologica Taurinensia* 33: 149–163.

Olivelle, P. (2010) "The Temple in Sanskrit Legal Literature," in H. P. Ray (ed.) *Archeology and Text: the Temple in South Asia*, New Delhi: Oxford University Press, 191–204.

O'Malley, L. S. S. (ed.) (1914) *Bengal District Gazetteer: 24 Parganas*, Calcutta: The Bengal Secretariat Book Depot.

Pandit, S.M. Nateśa Śāstrī (1884) "Mātṛgayā at Siddhapurī," *The Indian Antiquary*, 13: 282–285.

Panikkar, K. M. (1959) *Geographical Factors in Indian History*, Bombay: Bharatiya Vidya Bhavan.

Parpola, A. (2003) "Sacred Bathing Place and Transcendence: Dravidian *(Kaṭa(vul)* as the Source of Indo-Aryan *Ghāṭ*, *Tīrthaṅkara* and *(Tri)vikrama*," in O. Qvarnström (ed.) *Jainism and Early Buddhism: Essays in Honour of Padmanabh S. Jain*, Freemont, California: Asian Humanities Press, 523–574.

Parry, J. (1994) *Death in Banares*, Cambridge: Cambridge University Press.

Parui, S. S. (1976) *Kurukṣetra in the Vāmana Purāṇa*, Calcutta: Punthi Pustak.

Patil, N. B. (1983) *The Folklore in the Mahābhārata*, Delhi: Ajanta Publications.

Patnaik, N. (2006) *Sacred Geography of Puri: Structure and Organization and Cultural Role of a Pilgrimage Centre*, Delhi: Kalpaz.

Ramesan, N. (1999) *The Tirumala Temple*, Tirupati: Tirumala Tirupati Devasthanams.

Rao, S. C. A. (1952) *A History of the Holy Shrine of Sri Venkatesa in Tirupati*, Tirupati: Tirumala Tirupati Devasthanams.

Ray, H. P. (2004) "The Archaeology of Sacred Space: Introduction," in H. P. Ray, and C. M. Sinopoli (eds) *Archaeology as History in Early South Asia*, New Delhi: Indian Council of Historical Research and Aryan Books International, 350–375.

Ray, H. P. (2009) "The Shrine in Early Hinduism: the Changing Sacred Landscape," *The Journal of Hindu Studies* 2: 76–96.

Ring, T., R. M. Salkin and S. La Boda (1996) *International Dictionary of Historic Places: Asia and Oceania*, London: Routledge.

Rocher, L. (1986) *The Purāṇas, A History of Indian Literature*, vol. 2, fasc. 3, Wiesbaden: Otto Harrassowitz.

Roy, K. (1993) "In Which Part of South Asia Did the Early Brahmanical Tradition (1st Millennum B.C.) Take Its Form?" *Studies in History* 9 (1):1–32.

Sachau, E. C. (1910) *Alberuni's India: An Account of the Religion, Philosophy, Literature, Geography, Chronology, Astronomy, Customs, Laws and Astrology of India about* A.D. *1030: An English Edition with Notes and Indices*, two vols, Dryden House, Gerrard Street: Kegan Paul, Trench, Trübner.

Salomon, R. (1979) "*Tīrtha-pratyāmnāyāḥ*: Ranking of Hindu Pilgrimage Sites in Classical Sanskrit Texts," *Zeitschrift der Deutschen Morgenländischen Gesellschaft* 129: 102–128.

Salomon, R. (1985) *The Bridge to the Three Holy Cities: The Sāmānya-praghaṭṭaka of Nārāyaṇa Bhaṭṭa's Tristhalīsetu*, Delhi: Motilal Banarsidass.

Samanta, D. K. (1997) *Sacred Complex of Ujjain*, New Delhi: D.K. Printworld.

Saraswati, B. (1985) *Traditions of Tirthas in India: the Anthropology of Hindu Pilgrimage*, Varanasi: N. K. Bose Memorial Foundation.

Sax, W.S. (1991) *Mountain Goddess: Gender and Politics in a Himalayan Pilgrimage*, New York, Oxford University Press.

Schilder, R. and W. M. Callewaert (2000) *Banaras: Visions of a Living Ancient Tradition*, New Delhi: Hemkunt.

Schopen, G. (1994) "*Stūpa* and *Tīrtha*: Tibetan Mortuary Practices and an Unrecognized Form of Burial Ad Sanctos at Buddhist Sites in India," in T. Skorupski and U. Pagel (eds) *The Buddhist Forum*, vol. III, 1991–1993, London: School of Oriental and African Studies, University of London, 273–293.

Schopen, G. (1997) *Bones, Stones, and Buddhist Monks: Collected Papers on the Archeology, Epigraphy, and Texts of Monastic Buddhism in India*, Honolulu: University of Hawai'i Press.

Sehgal, K. K. (ed.) (1972) *Rajasthan District Gazetteers: Bikaner*, Jaipur: Government of Rajasthan.

Sekar, R. (1992) *The Sabarimalai Pilgrimage and Ayyappan Cultus*, Delhi: Motilal Banarsidass.

Sharma, R. S. (1965) *Indian Feudalism c.* A.D. *300–1200*, Calcutta: University of Calcutta.

Sharma, R.S. (1982) "The Kali Age: A Period of Social Crisis," in S.N. Mukherjee (ed.) *India: History and Thought (Essays in Honour of A.L. Basham)*, Calcutta: Subarnarekha, 186–203.

Sharma, R.S. (1987) *Urban Decay in India (c. 300–c. 1000)*, Delhi: Munshiram Manoharlal.

Sharma, R. S. (2001) *Early Medieval Indian Society: a Study in Feudalization*, Calcutta: Orient Langman.

Shinde, K. A. (2007) "Visiting Sacred Sites in India: Religious Tourism or Pilgrimage?" in R. Raj and N.D. Morpeth (eds) *Religious Tourism and Pilgrimage Festivals Management: an International Perspective*, Cambridge: CAB International.

Shulman, D.D. (1980) *Tamil Temple Myths: Sacrifice and Divine Marriage in the South Indian Śaiva Tradition*, Princeton: Princeton University Press.

Sikand, Y. (2003) *Sacred Spaces: Exploring Traditions of Shared Faith in India*, Delhi: Penguin.

Singh, R. P. B. (ed.) (1993) *Varanasi: Cosmic Order, Sacred City and Hindu Traditions*, Varanasi: Tara Book Agency.

Singh, R. P. B. and P. S. Rana (2002) *Banares Region: a Spiritual and Cultural Guide*, Varanasi: Indica Books.

Sinha, S and B. Saraswati (1978) *Ascetics of Kashi: An Anthropological Exploration*, Varanasi: N. K. Bose Memorial Foundation.

Sircar, D. C. (1971) *Studies in the Geography of Ancient and Medieval India*, second edition, rev. and enl., Delhi: Motilal Banarsidass.

Sircar, D. C.(1973) *The Śākta Pīṭhas*, second revised edition, Delhi: Motilal Banarsidass.

Spencer, G. W. (1970) "The Sacred Geography of the Tamil Shaivite Hymns," *Numen* 17 (3): 232–244.

Stein, B. (1982) "Towns and Cities: The Far South," in T. Raychauhuri and I. Habib (eds) *The Cambridge Economic History of India*, vol. I, Cambridge: Cambridge University Press, 453–457.

Stietencron, H. v. (1977) "Orthodox Attitudes Towards Temple Services and Image Worship in Ancient India," *Central Asian Journal* 21 (2): 126–138.

Stietencron, H. v. (2010) *Gaṅgā and Yamunā: River Goddesses and Their Symbolism in Indian Temples*, translated from the German by M. Cohen, Ranikhet: Permanent Black.

Sukul, K. N. (1974) *Varanasi Down the Ages*, Benares: Bhargava Bhushan Press.

Sutherland, G. H. (1991) *The Disguises of the Demon: the Development of the Yakṣa in Hinduism and Buddhism*, Albany: State University of New York Press.

Thakur, U. (1979) *The Geographical Information in the Skanda-Purāṇa (Based on the Tīrtha-Yātrā Portions)*, Maheshnagar, Darbhanga: Mithila Institute.

Thapar, R. (2003) *The Penguin History of Early India: From the Origins to AD 1300*, New Delhi: Penguin.

Upasak, C. S. (1990) "Dhammayātrā: the Pilgrimage of the Buddhists," in L. Gopal and D. P. Dubey (eds) *Pilgrimage Studies: Text and Context*, Allahabad: Society for Pilgrimage Studies, 55–59.

Vassilkov, Y. (2002) "Indian Practice of Pilgrimage and the Growth of the *Mahābhārata* in the Light of New Epigraphical Sources," in M. Brockington (ed.) *Stages and Transitions: Temporal and Historical Frameworks in Epic and Purāṇic Literature*, Zagreb: Croatian Academy of Sciences and Arts, 133–156.

Veer, P.v.d. (1988) *Gods on Earth: the Management of Religious Experience and Identity in a North Indian Pilgrimage Centre*, London: Athlone.

Verardi, G. (1996) "Religions, Rituals, and the Heaviness of Indian History," *Annali* (Istituto Universitario Orientale, Napoli) 56: 215–253.

Vidyarthi, L. P. (1961) *The Sacred Complex of Hindu Gaya*, Bombay: Asia Publishing House.

Vidyarthi, L. P., M. Jha and B. Saraswati (1979) *The Sacred Complex of Kashi: a Microcosm of Indian Civilization*, Delhi: Concept.

Willis, M. (2009) "The Formation of Temple Rituals in the Gupta Period: *pūjā* and *pañcamahāyajña*," in G. J. R. Mevissen and A. Banerji (eds) *Prajñādhara: Essays on Asian Art, History, Epigraphy and Culture in Honour of Gouriswar Bhattacharya*, two vols, New Delhi: Kaveri Books, 66–88.

Xuan, Z. and S. Beal (1884) *Si-yu-ki: Buddhist Records of the Western World, Translated from the Chinese of Hiuen Tsiang* (A.D. 629), trans.Samuel Beal, two vols, London: Trubner.

Yang, A.A. (1998) *Bazaar India: Markets, Society, and the Colonial State in Bihar*, Berkeley: University of California Press.

Index

Ādibadarī 141
Ādiparvan 14, 50, 51, 57
agnihotra 55, 58
agniṣṭoma 55
agrarian expansion 74, 75, 78–79, 84
Ahilyabai Holkar 144
Aiyangar, K. V. Rangaswami 127
Alaknandā 142
Al-Biruni 77, 129, 153
Āḻvārs 15, 142
Allāhābad, see Prayāg
Alley, K. D. 163, 164
alms 5
Amarkaṇṭak 29, 45, 99, 117
Amarnāth 4, 21, 127, 147, 172n2
Amarāvatī 81
Ambā 58
Angot, Michel 44
Anuśāsanaparvan 14, 51
Apsarases 54, 58, 168, 169
Āraṇyakaparvan, see Vanaparvan
āratī 144–145
Arbuda 37–38, 122, 174n5
Arjuna 24, 25, 50, 51, 57, 58
Arthaśāstra 67
Aruṇācalam 39, 50, 92, 145
Arya, S. N. 78, 79, 80, 81
asceticism 55, 66, 99, 102, 104, 158, 159
ascetics 5, 8, 17, 21, 25, 27, 43, 46, 48, 49, 53, 58, 66–67, 96, 99, 102, 107, 109, 117, 150–152
aśvamedha 55, 124, 146, 149
atonement for the sin of killing a cow 154–155
atonement for the sin of murder 153, 154, 155
attitude of pilgrims 18, 20–21, 126, 156, 160–161
avabhṛta 43, 48
Avantikā, *see* Ujjain
avatāra 5, 9, 102, 151, 152
Avimukta 10, 38, 44, 131, 134, 154, 168
Ayappan 139, 166
Ayodhyā 17, 28, 32, 36, 38, 39, 42, 76, 77, 79, 80, 93, 108, 109, 123, 128, 139, 140, 141, 163, 165–166, 167

Babri Masjid 166
Badarīnārāyaṇa 141
Badrīnāth 17, 126, 127, 134, 140, 141, 142, 172n2
Bakker, Hans 80
Bakranāth 93
Bakreśvar, Bakreshwar 17, 93–94
Baladeva 45, 46, 52
Baladevatīrthayātrāparvan 45, 46
Balarāma 50
bards 51, 58, 89
Baudhāyanadharmaśāstra 146
Beas 42
Bhagavadgītā 24–25, 30, 155
Bhāgavatapurāṇa 18, 90, 102, 104, 173n8
Bhāgīrathī Gaṅgā 125, 141, 142
Bhairava 132, 136
bhakti 15, 39, 72, 83, 86, 90, 93
Bhanvargaḍh 117, 119
Bharati, Agehananda 9–10, 63, 73
Bhardwaj, Surinder M. 19, 20, 43, 74, 127, 139, 152
Bhaṭṭa, Nārāyaṇa 149
Bhaviṣyabadarī 141
Bhīmarathī 35
Bhīmaśaṅkar 141
Bhīṣma 53, 54, 58
Bhṛgukṣetra 141
bhūtaliṅga (element *liṅga*) 141
Bhuvaneśvar 91

Bigger, Andreas 46
Bindusarovar 102, 103, 104, 105, 142
Bodhgayā 61, 122
Brahmā 30, 31, 37, 55, 114, 153, 168, 175n5
brahmadeya 73
Brahmagiri 154–155
brahman 7, 25, 104, 113, 152
Brahmapurāṇa 14, 35, 42, 43, 89, 90, 125
Brahmasarovara 25
Brahmasūtrabhāṣya 135
Brahmāvarta 37
Braj 14, 17, 36–37, 128, 140, 147, 165
Buddha 49, 59–65, 70, 71
  presence of at sacred places 61
Buddhism 13, 49, 59–65, 71, 72, 76, 78, 80, 83, 88, 103
Buddhist image worship 60
Buddhist influence on Hindu traditions of salvific space 11, 31, 87
Buddhist pilgrimage 36, 49, 59–65
  as model for development of Hindu pilgrimage traditions 61–65, 71
Buddhist sacred sites 41, 59–65, 87, 122
  as model for Hindu *tīrtha*s 61–65, 87
bus pilgrimage tours 20, 129

Caitanya 152
cārdhām 141
cāturmāsa 119
celibacy 58, 148, 157
Chattopadhyaya, Brajadulal 91
Chaudhuri, Buddhadeb 93–94
Christian Catholic pilgrimage 36
Cidambaram 91, 128, 141
circumambulation 14, 45, 53, 82, 112, 140, 147
Citragupta 112, 132, 172n8
Citrakūṭ, Citrakūṭa 28, 50, 80, 128, 147, 148
competition for pilgrim donations 13, 54, 63, 64, 65, 68–70, 71, 81, 84, 86, 87, 134, 167
composite culture 166–167
conflict 13, 42, 65, 66, 67, 68, 86, 146, 165–167
confluence 31–32, 34, 47, 56, 72, 125, 132, 134, 140, 142, *see* also *saṅgama*
cremation 39, 104
cremation *ghāṭ*s 131
cremation ground 131–132
cremation priests 17

daivya tīrthas 42
Dakṣīnakāśī 141
dāna 17, 28, 54, 63, 64, 65, 70, 71, 72, 73, 77, 79, 83, 84, 85, 86, 87, 88, 114, 157, 169, 173n9, *see* also donation
dargāh 11, 167
darśan, darśana (seeing) 18, 19, 50, 57, 60, 61, 72, 87, 99, 104, 108, 110, 152, 160
darśana (philosophical school) 15, 20
death 20, 23, 25, 63, 93, 96, 97, 104, 105, 106, 107, 114, 131–133, 134, 142, 150, 152, 161, 167, 172n8
decentric polycentrism 142, 145
Deoghar 17, 141
description texts 51
devagṛha/*devatāgṛha* 66
Devahūti 98, 102–104, 174n5
devalaka (temple priest) 66, 68–70, 86, 173n7
devaloka 112
Deva Prayāg 142
devāyatana/*devatāyatana* 66
Devī 11, 12 *see* also Mahādevī
dhām (sacred place) 21, 37, 136, 140, 141, 172n2
dharma 13, 15, 16, 24, 31, 73, 78, 144, 146, 152–161
dharmakṣetra 24
Dharmanibandha 11, 12, 13, 15, 16, 20, 31, 73, 127, 148, 150, 152, 153, 155, 156, 158, 159
Dharmaśāstra 12, 15, 16, 17, 66, 67, 68, 97, 146, 153, 156, 159
Dhauli Gaṅgā 142
dirt 158, 163
diversity 122, 123, 126
donation 17, 47, 54, 58, 63, 64, 68–70, 71, 73, 79, 81, 84–87 *see* also gifts and *dāna*
Draupadī 58
Dṛmi 56
Dṛṣadvati 31
dvāparayuga 26, 42, 116
Dvārkā, Dvārakā 38, 80, 141

Eck, Diana 49–50, 125
Ekāmraka 80
Ellora 65
environmental degradation 161–165
environmentalism 18
expansion of traditions of salvific space 2, 7, 12, 14, 28, 42, 49, 61, 65, 71–95, 123, 166, 167, 169

Falk, Harry 64
Faxian 17, 79
Feldhaus, Anne 125
festivals 4, 5, 6, 17, 20, 68, 70, 86, 89, 98, 107, 117, 119, 129, 140, 143, 152
feudal kingdoms 90
feudalization 74, 75, 76–77, 83
five confluences of Gaṅgā, *see* five Prayāgs
five element *liṅga*s 141
five Kāśīs 141
five Kedāras 141
five Prayāgs 142
five sacred ponds 142
five types of people who do not share the results of *tīrtha* 156
five *vidyāpīṭha*s 141, 142
food 5, 8, 37, 52, 56, 75, 79, 85, 86, 94, 114, 131, 148
four *dhām*s 21
four shrines in the Himālayas 142, see also *cārdhām* and four *dhām*s

*gaṇa*s 49
gandagī, see dirt
Gandharva 54, 131, 168, 169
Gaṇeśa 148
Gaṅgā 9, 20, 26, 29, 31–32, 35, 37, 39, 42, 45, 53, 87, 98, 106–107, 124, 131, 132, 134, 135, 140, 141, 159, 163–164, 167, 168
  salvific power of 9, 26, 98, 107, 108, 120, 124
Gaṅgā Sāgar, Gaṅgā Sāgara, Gaṅgāsāgara 20, 35, 98, 99, 100, 101, 106–109, 116, 118, 119, 151
Gaṅgotrī 127, 141, 142
Garuḍapurāṇa 38, 90
*gauṇatīrtha*s 156, 158, see secondary *tīrtha*s
Gautamī 35, 39, 125, 154
Gayā 16, 17, 25, 28, 35, 43, 50, 79, 87, 88, 91, 93, 98, 101, 105, 125, 138, 141, 142, 146, 147, 149
gayāśrāddha 101, 102, 105
geographical expansion 2, 12, 73, 74, 85, 88–89, 123
ghāṭ 33, 48, 93, 125, 132, 135, 137, 143, 144, 145
Ghṛṣneśvar 141
gifts, gift giving 2, 28, 46, 48, 49, 53, 54, 55, 56, 65, 68, 70, 73, 77, 78, 79, 84, 85, 86, 87, 94, 109, 113, 114, 116, 131, 134, 153, 157, 168, *see* also donation, *dāna*
Girnār 122
Godāvarī 43, 89, 141, 154, 161
Goloka 168
Gold, Ann 160
Gopratara 36
Gorakhpur 142
Gotīrtha 35
Govardhana 50, 128, 148
Granoff, Phyllis 92, 150–151
gṛhya rituals 86
guardians of pilgrimage places 49, 118, 132, 150
Gupta empire/period 78, 80
Guptakāśī 141
Guruvāyūr 17

Haberman, D. L. 163, 164
Hānuman 33, 108, 129
Hardvār 17, 22, 38, 126, 127, 130, 140, 141, 142
Hariharkṣetra 141
Harīścandra 132
Hātakeśvara 89
heartland 88, 137–138, 139
helicopter *yātrā* 21, 172n2
henotheism 15, 126
Himālaya shrines 4, 141, 142, 147
Himālayas 127, 131, 151
hiring someone as a resident of a *tīrtha* 80

impurity 7, 12, 19, 20, 22, 23, 25, 27, 30, 31, 34, 35, 36, 55, 56, 82–83, 85, 87, 89, 96, 97, 104, 105, 106, 107, 115, 119, 120, 122, 123, 133, 140, 153, 154, 162, 163, 164, *see* moral impurity, *pāpa*
increase in the number of pilgrims 4, 86, 93, 94
India's sacred geographies 11, 122, 128
Indra 27, 28, 29, 30, 32, 33, 37, 44, 169

Jagannāth 6, 14, 29, 44, 91, 127, 128, 139, 146
Jainism 13, 48–49, 63, 71, 72, 78, 80, 122, 173n5
jajmānī 75, 85, 86, 94, 173n9
Jambukeśvara 141
Janakpur 17, 118, 128
jyotirliṅga 39, 128, 140, 141, 142
Jyotisar 24

Kailās, Kailāsa 21, 131, 141, 147
Kālahastī 141
Kālidāsa 76
Kālindī 141
Kaliṅga 146

kaliyuga 26, 32, 33, 34, 37, 38, 42, 76, 83, 84, 85, 92, 109, 111, 116
Kalpeśvar 141
Kāmākhyā 128, 137, 138
Kāmarūpa 39
Kāmpil 118
Kāñcīpuram, Kāñcī 38, 39, 91, 140, 141
Kane, P. V. 12, 141
Kānyakubja 80
Kapil *guphā* (Kapila's cave) 117
Kapila 2, 9, 43, 96–121
  salvific power of 97, 98, 99, 101, 103, 105, 106, 109, 110, 112, 113, 119, 121
kapilā cow 55, 79, 99, 100, 113–117
Kapilā river 99–100
kapilādāna (gift of a *kapilā* cow) 114
Kapiladhārā 99, 116, 117, 118, 119
Kapilāhrada 80
Kapilapurāṇa 115
Kapilatīrtha 115
Kapileśvara 109
kārttika pūrṇimā, Kārttik Pūrṇimā 55, 110, 117, 118, 119
Kāśī 10, 16, 23, 33, 34, 38, 39, 42, 124, 125, 133, 136, 141, 146, 153, *see* also Vārāṇasī
Kāśī Viśvanāth 6, 44, 132, 139
Kāśīkhaṇḍa 14, 23, 38, 80, 130, 133, 134, 146, 148, 156, 159, 161, 167
Kāverī 141
Kedārnāth, Kedāranātha 4, 37, 80, 127, 134, 141, 142
Khajuraho 91
Kokāmukha 124
Kolāyat 32, 34, 99, 100, 109–113
Kolāyat Māhātmya 32
Kolyād 117, 118
Koṇārk 91
Kośambi 80
Kṛṣṇa 6, 14, 24, 30, 36–37, 39, 43, 50, 52, 56, 58, 93, 102, 128, 140, 152, 164, 165
kṛtayuga 26, 42, 103, 116
Kṛtyakalpataru 15, 156
kṣatriya 59, *see* also warrior
kṣetra 4, 22, 27, 92, 109, 124, 128, 130, 133, 140, 141, 147, 148, 158
kṣetrapāla 118
Kucch 142
Kulke, Herman 90–91
Kumbhakoṇam 91, 127
kumbhamelā 4, 17, 20, 93, 95, 128, 132, 140, 154
kuṇḍa 49
Kūrmapurāṇa 23, 130, 132
Kuru 27, 28
Kurukṣetra 17, 24–31, 32, 37, 38, 56, 72, 80, 118, 123, 124, 125, 127, 130, 134, 141, 147, 148, 155, 156
Kuṣāna 78
Kusinārā 61

Lakṣmī 6
Lakṣmīdhara, Bhaṭṭa 15, 28, 127, 156, 157, 158
liṅga 28, 39, 92, 115, 127, 128, 133, 141
Liṅgapurāṇa 130
living in presence of the divine 9, 96
local patriotism 25
Lochtefeld, James G. 20
Ludvik, Catherine 46
Lumbinī 60, 61

Macakruka 49, 72, 118
Madhyameśvar 141
Madurai 39, 91, 128
Māgh, month of 34, 35–36, 123, 134
Mahābhārata 10, 13, 14, 15, 16, 22, 23, 24–31, 36, 45, 49, 50–59, 68, 71, 79, 84, 87, 98, 100, 114, 118, 121, 124, 152, 153, 155, 156
Mahādevī 6
Mahākāla 141
Mahāparinibbānasutta 61–63
Maharishi Mahesh Yogi 132
Māhātmya 10, 13, 15, 22, 23, 42, 53, 89, 120, 123, 124, 126, 130, 134, 142, 147, 156
Mahāvīra 71
Maheśvar 144
Mahiṣmatī 80
Makara Saṃkrānti 106
Mallikārjuna 141
Mānasarovara, Mānsarovar 142
Mandakinī 142
Maṇikārṇikā 125, 132
Ma<u>nn</u>arkuṭi 39
Manusmṛti 13, 48, 66, 68
Mārkaṇḍeyapurāṇa 90
Mathurā 22, 37, 38, 39, 79–80, 82, 87, 88, 135, 140, 141
Mātṛgayā 103, 105
*mātṛkā*s 49
Mātṛṣodaśī 104–105
Matsyapurāṇa 14, 23, 35, 80, 85, 87, 124, 158
Mecca 129, 130, 139, 140, 145
*melā*s 93, 117, 119, 129, 154
mental *tīrtha*s 156, 157, 158

merit 7, 16, 19, 20, 22, 25, 43, 47, 49, 53, 55, 61, 63, 67, 69, 71, 72, 96, 103, 105, 114, 115, 120, 126, 133, 140, 146, 149, see also *puṇya*
  calculation of 16, 159–160
  compared to the rewards of sacrifice 13, 16, 27, 52, 54, 55, 56, 63, 68, 124, 146, 149, 168
  tension between easy access and restrictions 31, 152–161
Michaels, Axel 68
Michell, George 91
Miśrik, Misrikh 56, 57, 124, 127
mokṣa 9, 19, 20, 23, 24, 26, 27, 30, 32, 33, 38, 50, 67, 78, 95, 96, 97, 98, 99, 101, 102, 103, 104, 105, 106, 107, 108, 109, 111, 112, 119, 120, 130, 131, 132, 133, 141, 154, 158, 159, *see* also salvific liberation
monasteries 5, 65, 75, 77, 96, 141
moral impurity 7, 19, 20, 22, 23, 25, 27, 30, 31, 34, 35, 36, 55, 56, 82, 83, 87, 96, 97, 104, 105, 106, 107, 115, 119, 120, 123, 131, 140, 153, 162, 163, 164, *see* also *pāpa*
Morinis, E. Alan 22
Mount Ābū 122
muktibhavan 23, 132
Muktināth 147
multiple sacred geographies 11, 122, 128
mūrti 8, 31, 36, 40, 107, 111, 116
Murukaṉ 142
Muslim sacred space 11, 122, 166, 167
Muttūrkūṟṟam 32
Mysore 142

nāga 47–50, 72, 131, 168, 169
nāgarāja (king of snakes) 58
Nāgeśvar 142
Naimiṣa, Naimiṣāraṇya 23, 30, 35, 56, 124, 126, 127, 130, 141, 156, see also Nimsār
Nanda Prayāg 142
Nandakinī 142
Nandi, R. N. 83, 84, 85
Nārada 33, 53
Nāradapurāṇa 14, 86, 89, 153
Nārāyaṇasarovara 142
Narmadā 14, 28–29, 35, 42, 45, 89, 90, 99, 100, 109, 117, 124, 141, 161, 162
Nāsik 81, 140, 161
Naṭarāja 128
Nāth Sampradāy 142
Nath, Vijay 83, 88, 89
Nāthdvāra 17
Nāyaṉārs 15
Nayar 142
Navadvīp 142
New Age 18
nibandhas on *tīrthas* 12, 16, 127, 150, 152, 156, 158, 159
Nimsār 23, 124, 126, 127, 147, 156, *see* also Naimiṣāraṇya
nine temples of the planets in Tamil Nadu 142
Nirukta 41
nomads 8, 10, 44
Nṛsiṃhabadarī 141

Olivelle, Patrick 13, 66, 82
Oṃkāreśvar 141, 147, 161, 162
orthopraxis 161

Padmapurāṇa 14, 164
Pampāsarovara 142
paṇḍā 18, 22, 93, 123, 124, 152, 160
Pāṇḍavas 40, 58, 88
Paṇḍharpūr 15, 137
pāpa 7, 19, 22, 23, 25, 30, 34, 55, 82, 85, 87, 103, 105, 124, 131, *see* also moral impurity
pāpahara 87
Paraśurāma 101, 105, 154
parikrama 3, 29, 45, 147, 148
Parpola, Asko 48–49, 63
Pārvatī 4, 6, 45, 115, 130, 131
phala (awards, benefits) of pilgrimage 15, 22, 28, 52, 53, 54, 55, 80, 113, 146, 156, 159
pilgrim tax 93
pilgrimage
  and economic change 73–78
  and sacrifice 55–56, 65
  as kingly procession 51–52
  as the poor man's ritual 51–52
  as way to salvation 7, 20
  critique of 18
  definition of 22
  in hagiographies 152
pilgrimage priest 5, 13 18, 22, see also *paṇḍā*
pilgrimage sites
  as competitors to the gods 27, 32, 33
  as divinities 31–40
  as superior to other sites 34–40
  as the centre of the world 124
  as the sacred center of the world 130

pilgrimage sites (*cont.*):
as the ultimate power 30, 32, 33, 56
challenges to the traditions of 161–167
competition between 34–38
containing all sacred rivers 128
contradictions in the traditions of 146–161
divinities permanently present at 8, 9, 65–70
dust particles of 10
each treated as the foremost 126
four divisions of 42–43
gods protecting themselves from the salvific power of 33
gods jealous of 111
going on pilgrimage to other sites 34–38, 136
hidden treasures of 49–50
hiding of 9, 32–34, 92, 109, 111
hierarchies of 123–129
located in the divine world 39
monasteries at 96
natural beauty of 130
permanent divine presence at 41, 66–70, 72–73
personified as divinities 6–7, 32–40, 140
power of purification inherent at 163–164
ranking of 126–128
reduplication of 125, 133, 135, 136
staying permanently at 23, 132–133, 136
systems of classification of 140–142
travel to other *tīrtha*s 34–39
piṇḍa 87, 104, 120
piṇḍadāna 23, 104
Pinder Gaṅgā 142
pīṭha 43, 93, 128, 138, 140, 141, 142
placelessness 45, 50, 57, 60, 66, 70
Plakṣa Prāsravaṇa 45
pollution 161–165
polycentrism 142, 145
Prabhāsa 37, 42, 58
Prabhāsakṣetra 141
pradakṣiṇā 45, 147, 148
prakṛti 7
Prayāg, Prayāga 4, 16, 17, 23, 31–32, 34, 35, 36, 37, 50, 56, 80, 87, 93, 95, 124, 126, 132, 134, 135, 137, 139, 140, 141, 149, 150, 154, 163
Prayāgamāhātmya 35
procession 4, 6, 8, 45, 46, 50, 52, 53, 58, 147, 166
promotion texts 51, 53, 54, 57, 113, 123, 168
Pṛthūdaka 56, 124
pūjā 21, 39, 49, 59, 72, 99, 105, 128, 150
Pulastya 53, 54, 88
puṇya 7, 19, 20, 22, 26, 52, 54, 56, 57, 67, 71, 84–85, 87, 96, 103, 105, 112, 125, 159, 161, *see* also merit
Purāṇa 5, 10, 12, 13, 14, 15, 16, 17, 22, 25, 39, 42, 44, 53, 59, 64, 68, 69, 76, 79, 80, 81–89, 98, 113, 123, 126, 147, 152, 155
Purī 4, 6, 14, 17, 22, 29, 44, 50, 91, 126, 127, 128, 141, 142, 146, 152, 168
purification 19, 20, 51, 82, 85, 97, 120, 153, 154, 161, 163, 169
purity 12, 19, 20, 26, 31, 82, 83, 87, 89, 104, 120, 146, 148, 152, 153, 158, 159, 160, 163, 164
purity and impurity 12, 153
Puruṣottama, see Purī
Puruṣottamakṣetra 141
Puṣkar, Puṣkara 26, 30, 35, 38, 39, 42, 54–55, 56, 79, 80, 124, 130, 142
Puṣkarasarovara 142
Puṣpagiri 32–33

railway 5, 21
Rādhā 43
Rājgir 17
Rākṣasa 46, 131
Rāma 36, 39, 67, 93, 105, 128, 165–166
Rāmāyaṇa 79, 98, 100, 121
Rāmēśvaram 128, 141, 154
rāthyātrā 6
Ray, Himanshu Prabha 65
regional center 90, 126, 136–139
regional groups of *tīrtha*s 142
regional kingdoms 90–91
regional traditions 15, 39, 135, 145
relics 59–65
religious geographies 10–11, 122, 128
religious history and secular identity 42
religious merit, *see* merit, *puṇya*
Reṇukā 105, 154
Reṇukākṣetra 141
reverence of nature 44
rewards *see* merit, *puṇya*
Ṛgveda 43
ritual bathing 20, 25, 26, 32, 34, 35, 36, 43, 47, 48, 50, 55, 56, 57, 58, 72, 82, 83, 87, 99, 104, 107, 108, 109, 110, 111, 113, 114, 115, 116, 119, 120, 123, 124, 130, 134, 135, 140, 144, 148, 153, 157, 158, 159, 160, 162, 163, 164, 165, 167
ritual clients 12, 55, 73, 75, 81, 83, 86, 87, 134

rivers 7, 17, 22, 23, 26, 28, 30, 32, 34, 35, 36, 39, 43, 45, 46, 47, 48, 56, 58, 59, 72, 87, 91, 99, 100, 104, 120, 123, 124, 126, 128, 131, 135, 140, 142, 161–165, *see* also names of individual rivers
ṛṣi 56, 88
Rudrakoṭi 57
Rudranāth 141
Rudra Prayāg 142
Rūpa Goswamī 43

Śabarimala 17, 122, 137, 147, 166
sacrifice 13, 16, 27, 44
  Śramaṇa critique of 63, 65, 69, 71, 83
sādhu 18, 94, 118, 150–152
Sagara/Sagar, King 107
saint 150–152
śaktipīṭha 93, 128, 141
salvific cities 38, 39, 78, 123, 140
salvific liberation 7, 9, 10, 19, 20, 25, 32, 34, 38, 67, 78, 87, 96, 97, 98, 99, 103, 104, 105, 106, 109, 117, 133, 134, 154, see *mokṣa*
salvific power of sites 1, 6, 7, 9, 10, 11, 20, 26, 27, 43, 44, 47, 54, 99, 168–169
  and pollution 161–165
  and travel 146–150
  as the supreme powers 30
  celebrated in festivals 117, 119
  competing hierarchies of 123, 125, 126, 136
  considered a threat to the power of gods 9, 113
  created by the presence of sages 96, 99, 106, 119, 120
  definition of 19
  equaling with sacrifices 13, 54
  events that endow sites with 99
  focuses on rewards of visiting 97
  gods depending on 37
  gods trying to make unavailable for humans 33
  inclusiveness of 10
  key element in the promotion of 109
  meaning being present at places to experience closeness to the divine 93
  modeled on Buddhist sites 61
  movable 38–39, 133
  opposed to the idea of salvation as a gradual attainment of purity 152–161
  origin of 22, 41–70
  permanent presence of 59
  personification of 123
  promoted in texts 89
  residing in the dust of places 10
  sādhus representing the power of 150
  stories illustrating the idea of 9, 25–40, 104, 105, 111–113
  structure of 122–145
  tension between personal gods and 27, 32, 33
  to give *mokṣa* to all 25, 95
  to give *mokṣa* to animals 111, 130, 133
  transportability of 29
salvific rewards, see merit, *puṇya*
Śalyaparvan 14, 27, 30, 51, 52, 53, 54, 57
samādhisthān, samādhisthāna 5, 132, 150
saṃkalpa 168–169
Sāṃkhya 96, 97, 98, 99, 102, 103, 106, 107, 109, 119, 120
saṃnyāsin 96, 112, 120
sampradāya 108, 128, 129, 142
  pilgrimage geography of 142
saṃsāra 23
Sāndīpani 128
saṅgam, saṅgama 31, 34, 72, 132, 139
Śani 129
Śaṅkara 135, 140, 141, 151, 152
Śaṅkarācāryas 142, 146, 164
Śaṅkaradigvijaya 151
Śaṅkaradeva 151
Sarasvatī 31, 35, 37, 42, 45, 56, 57, 104, 124, 141
sarasvatīsattra 45, 72
Saraswati, B. 92
Sarayū 36, 76, 163
Sārnāth 61, 62
Sātavāhana 78
satyayuga 34, see also *kṛtyuga*
Schopen, Gregory 60, 64
sculpture 63
secondary *tīrthas* 156–159
sevā 164
seven Badarīs 141
seven Gaṅgās 141
seven Himālaya rivers 142
seven *kṣetras* 141
seven salvific cities 38, 123, 136, 140, 141
seven salvific rivers 141
Sharma, R. S. 74, 76, 77
siddhas 168, 169
Siddhapura Māhātmya 102–103, 105
Sidhpur 98, 99, 100, 101–106, 119, 142, 154
Sikand, Y. 167
Sindhu 141

Sindhusāgara 35
Singh, Rana P. B. 136
Śirḍī 167
Śirḍī Sāī Bābā 167
Śiva 4, 6, 10, 11, 12, 30, 32, 33, 34, 37, 38, 39, 44, 45, 57, 67, 93, 94, 109, 115, 116, 129, 130, 132, 153
Śivakāśī 141
Śivapurāṇa 39
six abodes of Murukan̲ 142
Skanda 32, 67, 111, 130, 131
Skandapurāṇa 14, 23, 37, 38, 100, 116, 130
snana, *see* ritual bathing
Somnāth 141
śrāddha 16, 23, 25, 38, 69, 72, 82, 86, 87, 97, 101–106, 107, 116, 119, 120, 142, 149, 171n11
śrāddha for mothers 98, 101–106, 154
Śrāddhamāhātmya 87
Śramaṇa 2, 63, 98, 71, 72, 83
Śravastī 80
Śrī Kapila Māhātmya Kolāyatjī 109, 111
Śrīmādhva Sampradāy 142
Śrīraṅgam 128
Śrīśailam 141
Śṛṅgerī 141
Sthalapurāṇa 13, 15, 23, 89
Stein, Burton 91
Stietencron, Heinrich von 67, 68
stūpa 59–65, 71
  as permanently demarcated sacred place 60
Subhadrā 50
śūdra 86
Sūkrakṣetra 141
Sumeru 131
svayambhūliṅga 116, 117

Taittirīya Saṃhitā 43
Tamil temple narrative 32, 39
Tañjaur 91
tapas 5, 32, 55, 98, 99, 102, 105, 107, 109, 111, 118, 120, 121, 154
Tarakeśvar 116
temple 4, 5, 8, 14, 18, 21, 22, 31, 32, 33, 36, 39, 41, 47, 54, 56–70, 72–75, 77, 83, 86, 87, 88, 90, 91, 92, 93, 94, 99, 102, 105, 107, 108, 110, 111, 115, 117, 118, 119, 120, 128, 129, 132, 133, 134, 135, 140, 142, 144, 150, 162, 166, 167, 170
Teṅkāsī 39
Thapar, Romila 60
tīrtha, see pilgrimage sites
Tīrthacintāmaṇi 16, 127, 158, 168–169
Tīrthakamalākara 16
Tīrthaprakāśa 16
tīrtharāja 36, 140
Tīrthavivecanakāṇḍa 15, 28, 73, 124, 127, 133, 156, 158
tīrthayātrā 4, 7, 10, 11, 13, 14, 17, 22 85, 152, *see* pilgrimage
  not a requirement 23
Tīrthayātrāparvan 13, 14, 36, 50, 51, 52, 53–55, 71, 84, 153, 156
Tīrthenduśekhara 16
Tirukkūṭalaiyār̲r̲ur 39
Tirumala 6, 91, 99, 115, 128, 134, 135, 137
Tirupati 6, 14, 29, 44, 99, 115, 126
Tiruvaiyār̲u 39
Tiruvaṇṇamalai 91, 128, 141, 145, 147
Tiruvārūr 33
titthakara 48
tonsure 16
tourism 18, 21, 128, 144, 176n12
tretāyuga 26, 42, 116
Tristhalīsetu 16, 127, 146, 148, 149, 158
Tristhalīsetusārasaṃgraha 16
Tryambakeśvara 39, 141, 154–155
Tuṅganāth 141

Udayapur 91
Udyogaparvan 51, 57, 58
Ujjain 17, 38, 128, 140, 141, 145, 147
Ulūpī 58
urban decay 74–78, 83
urbanization 76, 91
Uttar Pradesh 4
Uttarkāśī, Uttarakāśī 125, 141
Uttarakhand 4

Vaidyanāth 141
Vaikuṇṭha 111
Vaiṣṇodevī 127, 135, 147
Vallabhācārya 164
Vanaparvan 14, 30, 40, 51–55, 124
Varāhapurāṇa 14, 37, 39, 80, 82, 140
Vārāṇasī 4, 6, 10, 11, 15, 16, 17, 20, 22, 23, 24, 28, 29, 33, 37, 38, 39, 44, 45, 67, 80, 85–86, 88, 93, 99, 109, 116, 117, 123, 124, 127, 129–140, 141, 142, 143–145, 147, 153–154
Vārāṇasī Māhātmya 130–131
Vārkārī pilgrimage 4
Vassilkov, Yaroslav 46, 47
Vāsudeva 39, 67, 104
Vedic gods

did not become the main gods of Hinduism 44, 67
mobility of 36
placelessness of 44, 50, 66, 70
Vedic religious tradition 8, 10, 12, 13, 30, 39, 41, 43–47
Veṅkaṭeśvara 14, 29, 44, 99, 115, 139
Vetāraṉiyam 39
Vidiśā 80
vidyāpīṭha 140, 141
Vikramaditya 36
Viṣṇu 6, 7, 11, 12, 30, 56, 100, 104, 111, 116, 165, 169
Viṣṇu Divyadeśam temples 142
Viṣṇu Prayāg 142
Viṣṇusmṛti 13, 172n2
Viśveśvara 142, see also Viśvanāth
Viṭṭhal 4, 139
vrat, vrata 96
Vṛddhabadarī 141
Vṛddhagaṅgā 141
Vṛndāvan 14, 28, 43, 93, 128, 139, 141, 142
Vyāsa 85, 131

wandering of ascetics 5, 21, 49, 66, 67
warrior ascetics 108, 150
warriors 27, 30
water 19, 23, 26, 32, 47, 50, 82, 95, 102, 110, 115, 120, 124, 161–165, *see* ritual bathing, river

Xuanzang 17

Yājñavalkyasmṛti 13
yakṣa 49–50, 58, 63, 64, 71, 100, 118–119, 131, 148
yakṣī/yakṣinī 49–50, 63
Yama 28, 112, 132, 172n8
Yamunā 31–32, 35, 37, 42, 45, 87, 124, 132, 134, 140, 141, 163–165
Yamunotrī 127, 141, 142, 147
yoga 57, 109, 120, 130, 135
yoga powers 130
Yogabadarī 141
yogapīṭha 43
Yudhiṣṭhira 58
yuga 37, 42